Combat Uniforms
OF THE
Civil War

Combat Uniforms
OF THE
Civil War

Mark Lloyd

Illustrated by Michael Codd

MALLARD
PRESS

First published in the United States of America
in 1990 by the Mallard Press
An imprint of BDD Promotional Book Company, Inc.
666 Fifth Avenue
New York, N.Y. 10103

ISBN 0 792 45075 2

Printed in Spain

Title page: Ex-General Twiggs,
formerly of the United States
Army, surrenders to Texan troops
in the Gran Plaza, San Antonio,
Texas, on 16 February 1861.

CONTENTS

INTRODUCTION

The conflict between the American states introduced the world to the awful realities of total warfare. In four years of bitter fighting over 160,000 soldiers died in action – an estimated 90,000 of their wounds, 60,000 in prison camps and perhaps 10,000 in accidents. In many instances, details of Confederate casualties simply do not exist.

The Civil War had little to do with slavery. By 1861 the United States was one of only three nations within the American continent to tolerate the institution and all but the most reactionary conceded that its days were numbered.

During the 1850s the North and South had grown steadily apart until, by the end of that decade, a national identity had virtually ceased to exist. Huge numbers of European immigrants had flooded into the north-eastern seaboard in seach of a new life. A few had prospered but most, having found the harsh realities of crowded urban life not to their liking, had either moved west in search of space or had formed introverted ghettos. Eager to exploit the wealth of new labor, and spurred on by the advent of the industrial revolution, the inhabitants of cities such as New York, Boston and Philadelphia had transformed them into vast industrial complexes.

In complete contrast, life in the South had remained largely unchanged. Almost totally dependent on the growth and export of cotton, still feudal in its social outlook and uncompromisingly conservative, it had come to regard itself as the poor relation of the North from which it felt itself increasingly alienated. By 1861, in social and economic reality if not in political theory, the United States existed as two totally independent entities.

In hindsight, the election of Abraham Lincoln as President made war inevitable. Nevertheless when open hostilities actually began, neither side was in any way prepared for the rigors ahead. The North had made no real attempt to mobilize while the South, despite its military ancestry, had no standing army.

Patriotic men in both camps rallied to the colors only to find their national administrations sadly wanting. Frustrated, they turned to their states, to their counties, even to their townships, indeed to any viable organization attempting to form bodies of men for the war. Independent companies and battalions were formed, clothed and armed by local dignitaries rich and influential enough to do so.

Dress regulations, where they existed, were largely ignored. Volunteer units of both sides frequently dressed themselves in elaborate and quite impractical costumes more suited to the European parade ground than to war. Gradually the armies became more unkept and dishevelled as the realities of modern combat became apparent. Gaudily clad *chasseurs* and Zouaves abandoned their bright crimsons and blues in favor of the anonymity of blue or gray. Cumbersome and heavy equipment was modified for comfort and surplus issue simply discarded without a thought to the future. Issue greatcoats were abandoned in the hot summer of 1861 by raw recruits who had no concept of the pri-

vations of a winter campaign.

Of the regulation equipment, only the haversack remained universally popular. Items which would not fit into the haversack were carried rolled in a blanket over one shoulder. Few troops carried spare clothing or washing equipment. Basic sanitation was ignored, with the result that disease became rampant. Even weapons were not spared. Whole battalions, particularly within the Confederacy, abandoned their heavy and awkward bayonets to their obvious disadvantage in subsequent close quarter battle.

As the war progressed soldiers relied heavily upon their families for resupply, with the result that uniforms became increasingly civilianized. Long overcoats, colored waistcoats and all manner of individual headgear became popular. Certain general staff officers at times achieved an almost comical appearance, although there is no evidence to suggest that their attire ever detracted from their (usually) excellent military judgment. Other generals, particularly George Custer – whose ego was later destined to prove his downfall – appeared in ornate uniforms made ludicrous by quantities of gold braid and ornament.

As the Northern blockade began to bite, Confederate resupply became critical. In flagrant breach of the rules of war, clothing was looted from prisoners, many of whom subsequently died of exposure, and corpses were robbed of anything serviceable. Troops began to appear in a mishmash of issue gray and looted blue which inevitably led to confusion and a Federal threat to shoot as spies all prisoners thus clad.

To compound the problem most uniforms were made of "shoddy," an inferior substance compris-

ing reclaimed wool and scraps, prone to disintegration under heavy treatment or in bad weather. Dyes were rarely if ever universal, particularly in the South where issue uniform varied in hue from Confederate gray to light brown. As the war progressed, "butternut," a buff dye made from boiled nutshells and iron oxide filings, predominated.

Shoes and boots were scarce from the outset and by the end of the war hardly merited such a description. Most infantrymen's shoes consisted of green untreated leather crudely nailed to a wooden sole and rarely lasted a campaign. Thereafter the unfortunate soldier was expected to make do and mend. Often this consisted of his obtaining raw hide from the regimental slaughterman, wrapping his feet in old rags and sewing the hide around them.

Extraordinarily, despite the many privations, morale remained high in many units even during the final stages of the war when soldiers traditionally look to the future and are therefore less likely to take risks.

The Civil War produced insurmountable administrative problems. It also produced some of the finest generals in American military history. Without men of the caliber of Lee, Jackson and Stuart, the South would not have survived its first winter. On the other hand, were it not for commanders of the worth of Grant, Sherman and McClellan the North could not have hoped to have fielded and controlled the massive armies which eventually overwhelmed the Confederacy and restored the Union.

It must never be forgotten that the Civil War was

For the South, independence was more a matter of theory rather than fact. Within months of the secession the Confederate States had formed a union as rigid and uncompromising as that which they had left.

fought over vast areas on a previously unknown scale. If the uniforms of 1861 seem ridiculous and the administration lacking, this is surely understandable. It was not, after all, until the First Battle of Bull Run (Manassas) that either adversary had any clear idea of the consequences of modern war. The soldiers who faced each other at Appomattox had little if anything in common with the idealists who had rushed to the enlistment offices only four short years earlier.

Bands were formed by many battalions to play their men into battle. In reality, by early 1862 most bands had been scrapped, the musicians having been transferred to less glamorous duties as medical orderlies and stretcher bearers.

THE FEDERAL ARMY

The American Civil War was the last romantic war. During the previous 50 years, Federal troops had fought first the British, then the Indians and finally the Mexicans in a series of successful, if limited, engagements. Losses had been light, the civilian population had suffered minimal inconvenience, and commerce had positively gained. Consequently, as the North/South divide grew and with it the possibility of secession and war, no one thought that the resulting hostilities would last for more than a few weeks. Absolute war was simply beyond the comprehension of all but the greatest pessimist.

The first violent act – the bombardment of Fort Sumter – had a dramatic effect on the population of the North. In the northeastern seaboard states, tens of thousands of newly arrived immigrants saw military service as a way of establishing their right to equality of treatment in a postwar society. Although many of them had lived in the United States for only a few months and were not even citizens, they demanded the right to fight for the Union. When an unprepared Federal government failed to provide them with uniforms and equipment, they turned to the states and when state resources proved inadequate, they simply formed their own companies. Many volunteered for just 90 days in the belief that the war would be fought and won in that time; only later did the states call for two-year volunteers. Units which formed locally naturally looked to their own society for leadership. Officers were elected by their own men on the basis of their social standing without reference to their military potential. Colonels with little or no formal training led their fledgling regiments into battle, and, on occasion, into wholesale destruction.

Ethnic minorities which had been forced by religious and/or social differences to live in overcrowded, unsanitary ghettos formed regiments from within their own communities. For example, the Irish Brigade was formed exclusively from New York, Boston and Philadelphia immigrants by Thomas Francis Meagher, an influential first-generation American who had been banished by the British to Tasmania for sedition and treasonous activity, only to escape to the United States in 1852.

The 79th New York (Highlanders) were formed from Scottish immigrants, many of whom had seen service with the British army during the Crimean War. Dour, hardy and deeply religious, they encompassed completely the traditions and discipline of a European regular army. Even when they were expanded to ten companies with the introduction of Irish and English expatriates, they refused to compromise their heritage, continuing to parade in the full dress uniform of the 79th (Cameron Highlanders) from whom they took their traditions.

Where traditions did not exist, they were often invented. Troops who had little idea where North Africa was eagerly donned the gaudy uniform of the French colonial Zouave regiments. Others wore less dramatic but, as history was to prove, far more realistic gray or blue.

The 1st Battle of Manassas (Bull Run) brought home to the North the full realities and horror of war. On 16 July 1861 the Union army moved south from Washington to march against the Confederates. No formal battle plan existed nor were the troops provisioned adequately for the hot days ahead. The 30-mile march to Manassas Junction took two full days, during which good order and military discipline largely disintegrated. The troops were further impeded by the presence of a large number of civilians who had driven out from Washington to watch their heroes annihilate the enemy. In terms of ground captured, the battle itself was indecisive. The Confederates held the field, forcing the green Union troops to retreat in total disorder toward the safety of Washington, but they failed completely to consolidate their victory. The losses were, however, staggering: of the 35,000 Union troops committed to battle (many of whom were held in reserve and actually saw no action), 460 were killed, 1,124 wounded and 1,312 captured or reported missing. At once the harsh realities of war became apparent. Wholly inappropriate European-orientated dress uniforms were abandoned in favor of plain serge. Gray uniforms were dyed blue lest the wearers be mistaken for the enemy, as had happened at Manassas. Two-year volunteers replaced 90-day men, and ultimately conscription was introduced. By 1863 the Union felt confident enough to take the initiative and introduced a policy of total war never before seen on the American continent.

As the conflict grew in momentum and ferocity, supply outstripped demand, forcing the Union to purchase arms and equipment from every source available. Gradually the rifled musket, mostly imported from Europe, began to replace the smoothbore until, by 1865, the latter was a rarity. Early artillery, much of which had seen action in the Mexican wars, was replaced by far superior Napoleons and occasionally by rifled muzzle-loaders with their greater range and accuracy. Massed Union artillery reasserted itself as the true "God of War." Specialist units – medics, engineers, signalers, supply and ordnance, each with their own distinctive uniforms and insignia – began to play an important part in the order of battle.

By 1865, the Union army was a hardened, thoroughly professional force. Its commanders, once sadly lacking in expertise, were now second to none. In keeping with an army trained to live off the (enemy) land, its troops had learned to travel light whenever possible to facilitate speed and maneuverability and were capable of covering considerable distances without additional support. Federal cavalry, once the Cinderella of the battlefield, had learned from its mistakes and, at Brandy Station, had actually checked the seemingly invincible Confederates. Few armies in history have grown as fast and as positively as the Union forces between 1861 and 1865.

ULYSSES S. GRANT

Few military leaders have ever shown less early promise than Ulysses S. Grant. Born the son of an Ohio tanner on 27 April 1822, Grant was originally named Hiram Ulysses but decided to reverse his names when enrolling for West Point in 1839. Inexplicably the registration was erroneously made in the name of "Ulysses S. Grant," a name which he eventually accepted, maintaining to the end that the "S" did not stand for anything. Never a natural soldier, there is evidence to suggest that Grant agreed to attend West Point simply as a means of continuing his education and that he had no intention whatsoever of making a formal career of the army. Graduating 21st in a class of 39, Grant distinguished himself in horsemanship and showed considerable promise in mathematics, neither of which he was able to exploit fully in his first few years with the colors. Assigned as brevet second lieutenant to the 4th U.S. Infantry upon graduation in 1843, he was posted to St. Louis, Missouri where he met and, in 1848, married Julia Boggs Dent, by whom he eventually had four children.

The young soldier's first taste of battle came with the Mexican War of 1846–48 during which he received two citations for gallantry and one for meritorious conduct while serving under General Zachary Taylor. Promoted to the rank of brevet captain in recognition of his bravery, he however remained a substantive first lieutenant reverting to that rank after the war until his formal promotion in August 1853.

On 5 July 1852, when the 4th Infantry sailed from

New York to undertake a tour of duty at Fort Vancouver in Oregon Territory on the west coast, Grant left his family behind rather than submit them to the dangers of the Isthmus of Panama. Impoverished, lonely for his family, and increasingly unable to bear the futility and monotony of postwar military service, Grant began drinking heavily and neglecting his duty. Determined to be reunited with his family, he entered into a number of unsuccessful business ventures in an attempt to raise capital, but only compounded his misfortune. Promoted to captain and posted to Fort Humboldt, California in 1853, Grant's lifestyle immediately brought him into conflict with an unsympathetic commanding officer, as a result of which he chose voluntary resignation the following year rather than face the possibility of court martial, which could well have gone against him.

During the next few years, Grant became increasingly destitute as he failed at a number of undertakings. Attempts to eke out an existence by farming 80 acres given to his wife Julia by her father proved less than successful, as did a speculative partnership in the volatile world of realty.

On the outbreak of the Civil War, a thankful and by now thoroughly frustrated Grant offered his services unreservedly to the Union. He helped recruit, equip, and drill troops in the Galena area of northwest Illinois before accompanying them to the state capital at Springfield, where Governor Richard Yates appointed him an aide and assigned him to the state adjutant general's office. Promoted

General Ulysses S. Grant in typical pose, photographed at City Point, Virginia, in August 1864.

colonel by the governor in June 1861 and given command of the 21st Illinois Volunteers, a somewhat unruly unit then in formation, Grant was almost immediately elevated to brigadier general at the instigation of Congressman Elihu Washburne, and was given control of the District of Southeast Missouri based on Cairo at the southernmost tip of Illinois, where the Ohio and Mississippi rivers meet.

Frustrated by the inactivity that marked the first few months of the war in the West, Grant allowed his impatience to get the better of him when he was ordered to make a limited demonstration of power along the banks of the Mississippi. Acting on his own, and in the mistaken belief that a sizeable Confederate raiding party was about to move into Missouri, Grant led a mixed force of 3,114 infantry and cavalry supported by a battery of six guns in a formal assault against the Confederate position at Belmont. Although the attack was successful, Grant was nearly cut off from his own lines and forced to retire amid some confusion. The Federals lost a total of 607 men compared with Southern casualties of 642, and Grant learned a valuable lesson about overcommitment.

In 1862, Grant at last received permission to go onto the offensive and, on 16 February, won the Union its first major victory when, in Tennessee, he forced the surrender of Fort Donelson with its garrison of 15,000 troops. Promotion to major general followed, as did national acclaim. However, the gratitude of a civilian population toward the military has always been notoriously fickle, and veneration turned to hostility in April of that year when Grant's troops sustained 1,754 killed while driving off an unexpected Confederate attack at Shiloh Church. Grant was relieved of command, which reverted to General Halleck. When the latter was recalled to Washington as general-in-chief of the army in July 1862, Grant was restored to his command – a position which, in hindsight, he should never have lost.

In the latter part of 1862, Grant began his advance toward Vicksburg, the last major Confederate stronghold on the Mississippi and one of the strongest natural defensive positions in the country. Grant's natural drive, aggressiveness, and perception of tactics did much to accelerate the fall of the city, which surrendered, aptly enough, on 4 July 1863. When Port Hudson, Louisiana fell a few days later, the entire Mississippi passed under Federal control, effectively bisecting the Confederacy.

After his subsequent victory at Chattanooga, Grant was promoted to lieutenant general (9 March 1864) and, three days later, was appointed "General-in-Chief of the Armies of the United States." He at once took over the strategic direction of the war and set about the economic and military destruction of the South. Utilizing fully the numerically vastly superior forces at his disposal, he ordered General Meade with the Army of the Potomac to continue its relentless war of attrition against Robert E. Lee's Army of Northern Virginia, while General Sherman cut a swathe of destruction through Georgia.

Grant's strongest points at this time – his drive, his versatility, and his receptiveness to innovation – were also, ironically, often his greatest enemies. Never a man to court fools nor to waste time on the niceties of etiquette, he would frequently pass direct orders to regiments in action, ignoring completely the usual chain of command. On more than one occasion, the long-suffering General Meade found his orders countermanded or his troops committed to a course of action of which he knew nothing. Had it not been for the extreme professionalism of his staff, it is more than likely that Grant's well-meaning but precipitant actions would have led to chaos.

In late 1865, within a few months of engineering its defeat, Grant toured the South at the request of President Andrew Johnson and was given so friendly a reception that he submitted a report advocating leniency. In 1866, he was appointed to the newly created rank of "General of the Armies" and a year later accepted the appointment of Secretary of War. His appointment was, however, blatantly political, and when Congress demanded the reinstatement of his predecessor Edwin Stanton, he resigned to the considerable chagrin of Johnson who felt that Grant had let him down.

Grant was nominated as Republican candidate for the presidency in 1868 and, on 4 March 1869, entered the White House. Politically inexperienced and, at the age of 46, the youngest President thus far, Grant was honest and well meaning but too reliant on his advisers to be a success. Although returned for a second term of office, the final years of his tenure were marked by a series of scandals. The Secretary of War, William Belknap, was impeached for taking bribes, but although a majority of Senators voted to convict him, there was not the necessary two-thirds. Those who voted to acquit him did not believe in his innocence; they simply considered that they no longer had jurisdiction over Belknap because he had resigned his office.

In 1884, the still commercially naive Grant entered into a financial venture with the unscrupulous Ferdinand Ward, as a result of which he lost his entire life savings. Fortunately, however, he had signed a contract for the publication of his memoirs, which were eventually a great success with over 300,000 copies sold. In agony from cancer of the throat and scarcely able to eat, he labored on with his memoirs, determined to finish them before he died. In July 1885, a few weeks after completing his much acclaimed book, he died peacefully and now lies buried in Riverside Park, New York City.

Before his own untimely death, Lincoln described his great friend in two simple, succinct words: "He fights." Colonel Theodore Lyman of Meade's staff was more forthright, if no more accurate, when he described Grant as "rather under middle height, of a spare strong build; light-brown hair, and short, light-brown beard . . . eyes of a clear blue; forehead high; nose aquiline; jaw squarely set, but not sensual. His face has three expressions: deep thought; extreme determination; and great simplicity and calmness."

Ulysses S. Grant was never a smart soldier, preferring to dress for comfort rather than dignity. His uniform coat and waistcoat were invariably unbuttoned, his black felt slouch hat often missing. Frequently he discarded his sword, spurs and sash and might easily have been mistaken for a somewhat disheveled civilian had it not been for the three gold bars of a lieutenant-general which he wore on his shoulder straps.

5TH NEW YORK VOLUNTEERS (DURYEE ZOUAVES)

Many volunteer regiments of the Union and Confederate armies modeled themselves on the dashing Zouaves of the French colonial service. The original Zouaves (pronounced zoo-aves) were Algerian light infantry troops famous for their marksmanship (particularly their ability to fire and reload from the prone position), for the precision of their drill, and, above all, for their dress. Although regiments varied, all wore bright gaudy colors, baggy trousers, short open jackets with gaiters and either a turban or fez.

Despite the relatively small influence of French culture on the pre-war North, Zouave uniforms became very popular with the many militia units formed in the late 1850's and early 1860's in response to the growing threat of political unrest in the South. Many volunteer regiments were raised by general consensus and public subscription. Others were mustered by wealthy individuals, often but by no means always with previous military experience, who then assumed the mantle of command. Abram Duryee, a highly successful New York City merchant, had been active in the state militia prior to the outbreak of the Civil War, twice sustaining wounds during the 1849 Astor Place riots. On the outbreak of hostilities, therefore, he was ideally placed to raise his own unit and, on 25 April 1861, was gazetted the first colonel of the 5th New York Volunteers (Duryee Zouaves).

The 5th New York became one of the most illustrious of all volunteer regiments, earning the esteem of the regular troops with whom it operated and the approbation of General George Sykes, the commander of V Corps, Army of the Potomac, under whom it served throughout the bloodiest stages of the war.

Initially, many inexperienced volunteer officers regarded drill, regulation dress, and such overt acts of discipline as saluting as a wasteful distraction from the fighting. However, Duryee, the one-time

colonel-in-chief of the 7th New York State Militia, realized the need for strict discipline and demanded from the outset consistently high standards from his subordinates. As a direct result, the regiment gained an enviable reputation for unsurpassed smartness on parade, a factor which later manifested itself on the battlefield at Gaines's Mill (27 June 1862) when, under withering volley fire, it gained the respect of friend and foe alike by halting, "counting off," and realigning its ranks before continuing its assault.

Due to its proficiency, the regiment was given the honor of serving as part of "Sykes Regulars," a division within V Corps otherwise comprising professional soldiers. Commanded at various times by Duryee, G.K. Warren, Hiram Duryea, and Cleveland Winslow, its members fought at the battles of Big Bethel, Gaine's Mill, Manassas, Shepherdstown Ford, Fredericksburg, and Chancellorsville and at the Yorktown siege. During the final stages of the 2nd Battle of Manassas (29–30 August 1862) – also known as the 2nd Battle of Bull Run – the 5th New York Zouaves sustained 117 killed out of 490 in action, the highest losses of any infantry regiment in the war and a rate of attrition from which it never fully recovered.

Manassas began ominously for the North. Despite their vast superiority in numbers and equipment, the Union armies had failed totally to halt, let alone destroy, the superbly motivated and far more versatile Confederate forces. Command of the newly formed Army of Virginia had been delegated to John Pope, a relatively junior major general whose sole recent field experience had been gained with the Army of the Mississippi in the West. From the outset, Pope made himself unpopular with officers and men alike, compounding the problem by delivering an ill-timed and ill-conceived introductory address in which he made ample reference to the virtues of his old command to the detriment of his new. Even the enigmatic General Robert E. Lee expressed disgust at the severity of several of the marshal law edicts introduced by Pope into the occupied areas of Virginia.

Immediately upon assuming his new command, Pope used his geographical proximity to Washington advantageously, tirelessly lobbying Lincoln and General Henry Halleck, the newly appointed general-in-chief of the U.S. land forces, until both agreed to allow his army to attempt an overland assault on Richmond from the north. McClellan's Army of the Potomac, currently bogged down in the Peninsula campaign, would assume a subordinate role.

Impatient for victory, Pope moved his forces on the Confederacy on 12 July. Fully aware of the impossibility of fighting on two fronts, Lee rightly guessed that Pope and not McClellan now posed the immediate threat, and so he ordered Major General "Stonewall" Jackson with 11,000 men north to hinder his advance. Gradually Lee sent Jackson more reinforcements until, by early August, he had a corps of 24,000 under his command. On 3 August,

Fighting as part of Sykes Regular Corps, the 5th New York sustained 117 fatalities during the Second Battle of Bull Run

Headdress: Unusually, the officers dressed less ostentatiously than their men. While the latter paraded in a white turban and wore a blue-tasselled cap in the field, the officers contented themselves with a red and blue kepi.

Uniform: Whereas the rank and file were issued with a conventional Zouave-pattern jacket, shirt and pantaloons, again the officers restricted themselves to a variant of the regulation frock coat, adorned with Confederate-style cuff-braid and sash, and red trousers.

McClellan was ordered to disengage in the Peninsula and to join Pope in a concerted attack. Lee at once moved north with the 28,000 men of Longstreet's Corps, many of them Texans, in a desperate attempt to link up with Jackson and defeat Pope before the latter could be reinforced by McClellan. Everything would depend on luck and perfect timing.

Pope's advance was halted on 9 August when his leading units met elements of Jackson's Corps on Cedar Mountain. The Union forces withdrew behind the Rappahannock River to await reinforcements; the stage was set for confrontation. In an attempt to maneuver Pope from his strong position, Lee ordered Jackson to execute a left flanking movement behind the Federal lines. With his rail link thus cut and his supply lines to Washington and to Alexandria across the Potomac from the capital denied him, Lee reasoned that Pope would have to chase Jackson, allowing Lee and Longstreet to bring up the residue of the Confederate army across the Rappahannock. Pope initially dismissed Jackson's move as nothing more than a diversionary raid into the Shenandoah Valley, and it was not until elements of Confederate cavalry led by J.E.B. Stuart appeared at Manassas Junction on 26 August that he fully realized the extent of the threat to his rear.

Pope immediately ordered his army to abandon its position on the Rappahannock and to proceed to Manassas Junction, just southwest of the small river known as Bull Run. Simultaneously Jackson moved his small force north and took up a defensive position behind the banks of an unfinished railroad. Fearful that Jackson might escape him, and heedless of the whereabouts of Longstreet's Corps, which in the interim had moved fast to attempt to link up with Jackson's exhausted and hard-pressed forces, Pope ordered a full frontal assault without first establishing the exact size and disposition of the enemy. Throughout Saturday, 29 August, Jackson's troops parried attack after attack, sustaining

Colonel Abram Duryee, an experienced soldier, administrator and first commander of the 5th New York.

terrible casualties until nightfall brought a brief respite. So confident of victory was Pope that he again discounted the whereabouts of Longstreet's as yet uncommitted troops.

On Sunday, 30 August, Pope ordered a final assault on the depleted Confederate lines. The 5th New York Zouaves were deployed on the extreme left flank, the weakest part of the attack. Unknown to Pope, Longstreet's fresh corps had joined Jackson during the night and was now deployed on the Confederate right, directly opposite the hapless and unsuspecting New Yorkers. In the early afternoon, 18 Confederate guns were suddenly brought into action, tearing great swathes in the already thin lines of Federal attackers. Still the Union troops pressed forward until by 4:00 p.m. their lines

were broken. Seizing his opportunity, Lee ordered Longstreet's infantry to counter-attack. The Union left flank held briefly but eventually succumbed to the Texan onslaught. Pope was driven from the field and, but for the heroic actions of a few units, would have stood no chance of regrouping. As has already been stated, the 5th New York lost heavily during the counter-attack and indeed never fully recovered. However, had it not been for the bravery which it demonstrated during that fateful Sunday afternoon, the subsequent rout might have turned into annihilation.

Unusually for a two-year regiment, "Duryee's Zouaves" contained a number of three-year enlistees. When the Regiment's enlistment expired, therefore, many of its volunteers were transferred

into the 146th New York. Colonel Winslow subsequently reorganized the 5th New York, and sustained fatal injuries as its commander in the Battle of Bethesda Church, ten miles from Richmond, Virginia, but the new unit contained none of the panache of the old.

The 5th New York were generally considered the smartest of all the Zouave regiments in the Union army. Officers' uniforms were somewhat less ostentatious than those of their men which closely resembled the French original. For full dress, the enlisted men wore a white turban round the fez, russet leather and white canvas gaiters bound with black leather straps, voluminous red trousers and a blue *chasseur*'s jacket. In the field, the fez was replaced by a red stocking cap.

Had it not been for the bravery exhibited by the already decimated 5th New York, the retreat from Bull Run would have turned into a rout with disastrous consequences for the North.

9TH NEW YORK VOLUNTEERS (HAWKINS' ZOUAVES)

Despite months of forewarning, the Union was far from ready for war when the Confederacy eventually seceded in the spring of 1861. The majority of the 16,000 strong regular army was scattered in 79 frontier posts west of the Mississippi; 90 percent of the navy was thousands of miles away in foreign waters; and the military reserve remained firmly under jealously guarded state control. Early Federal attempts to raise 75,000 "90-day volunteers" from among the militia met with ridicule when it was realized that the war would most certainly last for more than three months and would inevitably require far more than 75,000 men to bring about victory. On 3 May 1861, Lincoln authorized the induction of a further 42,000 three-year volunteers, but by then, many of the states had seized the initiative and had enrolled their own two-year volunteers.

Frustrated by what they regarded as the lack of purpose at Federal Government level, state governors, city councils, and, occasionally, philanthropic individuals raised independent units, clothing, feeding, and where possible training the troops until Washington was able to absorb them into the Union army. Governors sent purchasing agents to Europe where they competed with each other and with their Confederate rivals for the acquisition of surplus uniforms and ammunition. New York State, for instance, acquired thousands of Zouave uniforms regardless of their impracticality and despite the fact that the majority of its citizens were Anglo-Saxon rather than French.

Volunteer regiments retained close ties with their states and municipalities. Enlisted men elected many of their officers from within the community and the governors appointed the rest. Companies and even whole regiments often consisted of men from a single township, city, or county. Although, initially, this did much to enhance morale both among the men and their relatives waiting at home, as the war progressed the effects of a single bloody battle in which losses of 50 percent were not unusual were calamitous.

Once formed, a regiment did not receive reinforcements to replace the dead and injured. Instead it simply diminished in size and effectiveness until,

A wounded Zouave of the Federal Army is guarded by a Confederate.

Headdress: Although a scarlet fez was retained for formal wear, most troops favored a soft dark red woolen cap in the field.

Jacket: A sky-blue overcoat was worn over a dark blue jacket and *chasseur*-pattern dark blue trousers. Despite the total lack of camouflage, the uniform was retained until the regiment's disbandment in 1863.

Gaiters: White gaiters, originally made of russet but later constructed of pigskin or canvas, were worn over conventional black boots.

at the end of its contractual recruitment period, it was disbanded.

The 9th New York Volunteers exemplify perfectly the early two-year state-organized regiment. Its members were primarily drawn from Albany, Brooklyn, Hyde Park, Mount Vernon, Staten Island, and parts of Connecticut and New Jersey, supplemented by a few friends and relatives from as far afield as Canada. The majority of the officers were American born, and a few possessed considerable previous military experience. The lieutenant colonel, George F. Belts, although a lawyer by profession, had been a militia field officer. Major Edgar Kimball had been breveted for gallantry at Chirubusco and Contreras as a captain while serving with the 9th U.S. Infantry in 1847/48 during the Mexican War, and the regimental surgeon had seen active service with both the British and the French.

If the regiment was conventional, its commander was most definitely not. Born in 1831, Rush Christopher Hawkins served as a junior officer in the Mexican War while still a minor. Anticipating secession with all its ramifications, Hawkins formed a military club in 1860 with himself as president, and a year later, on 4 May 1861, he transformed it into a fighting unit. He then offered it, with himself at its head, to the state of New York.

Hawkins subsequently married Annmary Brown, the daughter of the founder of Brown University, Rhode Island, and after making a fortune from real estate and investments, he dedicated the last years of his life to the collection of rare 15th-century books. At the time of his death in 1920, Hawkins was reputed to have had a collection second only to that of the British Museum.

The Regiment – which inevitably became known as "Hawkins' Zouaves" after its charismatic leader and mode of dress – fought as part of the Army of the Potomac in the Maryland campaign, on South Mountain, at Antietam (Sharpsburg), and in eastern Virginia, before being mustered out on 20 May 1863, having lost 358 officers and men on active service.

The Union armies of 1862 were poorly led, and after the 1st Battle of Manassas/Bull Run (in which the 9th New York played no part), they were demoralized. When Lee crossed the Potomac on 5 September 1862, entered Maryland, and invaded the North, McClellan, commanding the Army of the Potomac, failed to take decisive action. Instead he allowed the Confederates to divide their forces and advance simultaneously on Harpers Ferry and Sharpsburg. Despite ample evidence of Lee's intentions, set out fully in a captured copy of his field

Recruiting for Hawkins' New York Zouaves. The recruiting drive attracted a large body of men to its ranks, nearly all of them under 30 years of age.

orders, McClellan insisted in pursuing the enemy to Sharpsburg, leaving Harpers Ferry, with its massive arms foundry, to its unenviable fate. The Federals, with the 9th New York in the forefront, fought their way methodically over South Mountain, carefully deploying to Lee's front.

On 17 September, the armies of Lee and McClellan joined battle south of Antietam Creek. Despite his massive numerical advantage (Union soldiers outnumbered the Confederates by nearly two to one), McClellan refused to commit his troops in a single concerted attack and thus probably denied them total victory. After the battle, in which the North lost an estimated 2,100 dead, 9,550 injured, and 750 captured against Confederate losses of 1,510 dead, 7,800 wounded, and 1,850 captured, Lee was forced to retire south rather than risk his lines of communication. Yet despite optimistic proclamations in Washington, Antietam was far from a Union victory, and a few days later McClellan was relieved of command.

In July 1862, the 9th New York Volunteers were belatedly issued with the .58 caliber Springfield rifle-musket in lieu of their outdated smoothbores. In all, over 700,000 "1861 Springfields" were manufactured before mass production ceased in 1863; a quarter of a million of these were made in the Springfield armory itself, the rest by outside contractors. Equipped with a simple hammer-and-nipple firing mechanism the new percussion Springfield with its maximum range of 1,000 yards (915m) revolutionized the battlefield.

The 9th New York was one of the few Zouave units to wear their uniforms throughout their period of enlistment. Officers were issued with formal Zouave dress uniform including a dark blue shako adorned with a bushy white plume, but they tended to wear more conventional dress in the field. In line with most "Americanized" units, the enlisted men's uniform was principally of the Zouave pattern but with dark blue *chasseur* trousers. A regulation sky blue overcoat was worn over a dark blue jacket and undershirt, the whole relieved by a magenta trim, magenta or light blue rank chevrons, and a turquoise or blue sash. A scarlet fez with a blue tassel was issued but invariably replaced by a soft, dark red, woolen cap. The *chasseur* trousers were of the same cloth as the jacket. Cut full at the pleated waist, they tapered to cuffs below the knee and were closed with buckles or buttons. Twelve-inch (30cm) white gaiters, originally made of russet leather but later often constructed from pigskin or even canvas, were worn over the conventional black boots.

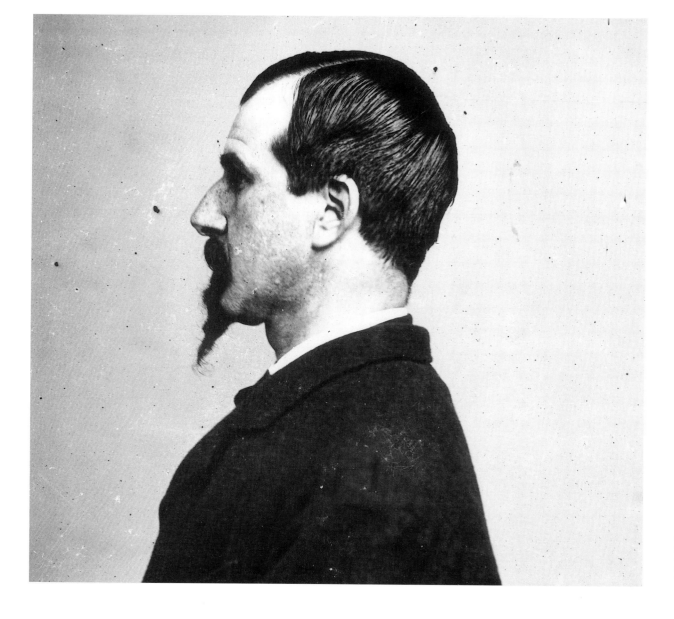

Rush Christopher Hawkins, commander of the 9th New York Volunteers.

39TH NEW YORK VOLUNTEER INFANTRY REGIMENT (GARIBALDI GUARD)

By 1861, Italy had scarcely resolved the question of its own unification and was in no position to influence the destiny of a faraway country with which it had few ties. Giuseppe Garibaldi had just declared Victor Emmanuel King of Italy, but Rome remained apart and aloof, its independence assured by the presence of powerful elements of the French army. Few Italians looked beyond the Mediterranean for inspiration and even fewer emigrated. Those who did rarely exported their political ideals, preferring to work hard and merge themselves into their new society. Consequently Italian settlers in the United States suffered little of the bigotry felt so keenly by the more volatile Irish and southern Germans crammed into the slums of the northeastern seaboard cities. Instead the community spread southward and westward, integrating well wherever it attempted to lay down new roots.

Not surprisingly, therefore, many Italians who volunteered their services to the Union at the outbreak of war happily followed their neighbors into local militias rather than attempting to form expatriate units. Such Italian regiments as were formed were often only superficially authentic. The 39th New York Volunteer Infantry Regiment – the Garibaldi Guard – was typical. Although dressed in uniforms virtually identical to those worn by the crack riflemen and sharpshooters of the Bersaglieri Light Infantry, the regiment in fact consisted of three companies of Germans, three of Hungarians, one each of Swiss, Italians, and Frenchmen and a composite company of Spanish and Portuguese immigrants.

Raised by the Union Defense Committee of the Citizens of New York simultaneously with the 40th, 41st, and 42nd New York Volunteers in response to an urgent Presidential call for more troops, the regiment was formed on conventional pre-war lines.

It was commanded by a colonel with a lieutenant colonel as second-in-command. Headquarters consisted of a major, two lieutenants acting as adjutant and quartermaster, a surgeon, his assistant, a commissary sergeant, a hospital steward, two principal musicians, and 24 bandsmen. (Soon after its formation, the Garibaldi Guard gained considerable unwelcome notoriety when its first colonel-in-chief, Frederick George D'Utassey, was convicted of fraud, cashiered and sent to Sing Sing prison.)

In bivouac, the band, which contained few accomplished musicians and whose playing was more often described as spirited than tuneful, acted as a general support, providing guards or music as the need arose. In battle, however, its members took on the far more crucial and dangerous role of stretcher bearers, transporting the wounded from the battlefield to the comparative safety of the regimental dressing station. Although few bandsmen were decorated for bravery, many earned the uncompromising respect of men whose lives they had saved.

President Lincoln and General Scott review the Garibaldi Guards prior to their leaving for the front line.

20

Hat: The black brimmed hat, adorned with the letters "GG" in gold and a flowing plume, bore witness to the regiment's Bersaglieri traditions.

Tunic: The *chasseur*-style tunics with their pleated flared skirts and red piping were largely replaced in 1863 by standard New York-issue blue.

Weapons: Most troops were armed with the 1841 "Mississippi" rifle capable of accuracy at great range.

A stirring recruiting poster which helped to swell the ranks of the Garibaldi Guard.

Each of the ten companies was commanded by a captain supported by a lieutenant and second lieutenant. Theoretically it contained 98 enlisted men: a first sergeant, four sergeants, eight corporals, two musicians, a wagoner and 82 privates. However, within a year, due to the inexplicable Union habit of not drafting battle replacements into existing regiments but instead utilizing them to form new units, many of the companies were below half strength.

Two of the ten companies were designated flank companies. They were given additional light infantry training to enable them to operate forward of the main body prior to close contact with the enemy, at which time they would fall back to their designated flank. Most regiments chose their best and fittest marksmen for this role, but the sheer problems of language in so cosmopolitan an outfit as the 39th would have made this impossible. Furthermore, rifled muskets with which the regular flank companies were supposed to be armed were in such short supply in the early stages of the war that they would not have been available to the majority of line volunteer regiments. Flank troops therefore would have carried conventional smoothbore muskets no better than those equipping the massed ranks of the enemy facing them; denied the advantage of greater range and accuracy, they must have found their task suicidal.

Unusually the 39th was armed almost exclusively with the Model 1841 United States rifle. Known affectionately as the "Mississippi," in memory of Jefferson Davis's 1st Mississippi Regiment which used it to such good effect in 1847, or more commonly as the "Jäger" after the German huntsmen and light infantry units which pioneered its design, the rifle was considered one of the finest of its day. Manufactured originally as a .54 caliber percussion cap weapon, it was $48\frac{3}{4}$ inches (124cm) in total length and weighed about $9\frac{3}{4}$ lb (4.4kg). The seven-grooved barrel was fitted with a brass blade foresight and fixed rearsight then considered adequate for all purposes. Originally designed to accept a paper cartridge and spherical lead ball, most rifles were modified to .58 caliber to accept the hollow-based and far more accurate Minié bullet after its introduction in 1850.

Uniquely for a general-purpose weapon, there was no provision on the original models for a bayonet. However, the weapons were altered and equipped with a somewhat basic though effective rearsight and various mounts for a fiercesome $22\frac{1}{2}$ inch (145cm) saber bayonet. Despite the obvious potential of the weapon in hand-to-hand combat, however, the bayonet remained unpopular with the infantry of both sides, who preferred to use the rifle as a club rather than as a pike in close-quarter fighting. It is quite possible therefore that many members of the 39th would have conveniently "lost" their unusually heavy and inconvenient saber bayonets on the first available occasion.

As part of the 3rd Brigade, 3rd Division, II Corps, Army of the Potomac, the regiment was surrendered at Harpers Ferry on 15 September 1862 but was later exchanged in time to serve at Gettysburg, in the Wilderness campaign, and at Spotsylvania and Petersburg before being mustered out at the beginning of July 1865.

Although the surrender of Harpers Ferry was ignominious for the North, it should not be seen as a reflection of the fighting potential of the 39th Regiment nor indeed of any of the approximately 12,000 men comprising the garrison. Situated at the junction of the Shenandoah and Potomac rivers and dominated on three sides by high ground, the town's very position frustrated its effective defense. Besieged as a prelude to the Battle of Antietam (Sharpsburg), the outpost was surrounded by 27,000 battle-hardened Southern troops under the command of the redoubtable "Stonewall" Jackson. Confederate artillery was immediately placed on all the vantage points overlooking the Union camp and annihilation offered as the only alternative to surrender. Not realizing that Lee's Army of Northern Virginia was outnumbered and dangerously split, that McClellan was in possession of a detailed copy of the Confederate plan of campaign (found by a Union soldier wrapped around three cigars and passed immediately to army Headquarters), and that Jackson's men were required urgently elsewhere, the garrison commander felt that he had no option but to surrender his post, which was in the event of no strategic importance to the North. Neither he nor any of his subordinates were subsequently admonished for this decision.

The original uniform of the Garibaldi Guard was distinctly nationalistic. Whereas the enlisted men were issued with relatively plain *chasseur*-style jackets adorned with a pleated flared "skirt" and red piping, many officers wore ornate gold frogging across their chests and relieved the drabness of their blue jackets with heavily braided cuffs and collars. Until the introduction of standard blue uniforms for all New York militia regiments in May 1863, all enlisted men and most officers in the 39th wore plain red wool flannel shirts above blue trousers tucked into black leather gaiters when operating in the field. A striking black brimmed hat, adorned with the letters "GG" in gold and complemented by a flowing green plume attached to the left of the chin strap button, completed the outfit.

Colonel Frederick d'Utassey, the first commander of the Garibaldi Guard, dressed in formal uniform.

79TH NEW YORK (HIGHLANDERS)

The 79th New York (Highland) Volunteer Regiment was unique in many respects. On the face of it a conventional militia unit, it in fact owed its structure and many of its traditions to the British army in which a number of its officers and men had seen previous service. Spurred on by hunger and economic deprivation, many Scots had emigrated to the New World in the 1850's. Unlike their Irish counterparts, they had not brought with them a deep-seated hatred of Britain but instead had continued the maintainance of close and friendly links with the homeland. Dour, religious, and, above all, industrious, many had become lynchpins of local society.

By the mid-19th century, Scots' prowess on the battlefield was universally respected. Against Napoleon, a lone piper had rallied the wavering lines of Redcoats at Quatre Bras, turning potential defeat into assured victory, and a few hours later at Waterloo, the Highland brigade had swept all

French resistance before it. In the Crimea, oblivious to their own losses Highlanders had stormed the heights of Alma and had subsequently held the famous "thin red line" against overwhelming odds. It is not surprising therefore that, when New York State began to increase the size of its militia, the introduction of a Scots unit was heavily mooted, and when Captain Roderick of the British Consulate in New York City suggested on 9 October 1859 that a unit be formed based on an existing Highland regiment, the idea was readily adopted. The British regiment chosen for the honor was the 79th (the Cameron Highlanders), today amalgamated into the Queen's Own Highlanders (Seaforth and Camerons) but then a fiercely independent regiment with an uncompromising reputation and an enviable array of battle honors.

Initially, the Union 79th was formed into four exclusively expatriate companies. However, when it was called into Federal service on 18 May 1861, its

Lt-Colonel Morrison of the 79th New York Highlanders on the parapet of the Tower Battery, James Island, South Carolina.

Headdress: Initially all ranks wore the traditional Glengarry of the Cameron Highlanders, but as the war progressed this was increasingly replaced by the conventional Union blue cap.

Kilt: A few diehards continued to wear the Cameron of Erracht kilt throughout the war. Most however succumbed to practicality, relegating it to formal wear only.

Dirk: Worn sheathed in the right sock, the dirk, a short vicious fighting knife, proved devastating in close quarter action. Officers, N.C.O.s and bandsmen were armed with a long straight sword, other ranks with the bayonet.

strength was increased to the conventional ten companies and 1,000 officers and men by the introduction of Scottish, Irish, and English New Yorkers along with a few of other nationalities. Despite this, great care was taken not to compromise the Scottish identity of the regiment. A pipe and drum band – an integral part of any Scottish regiment – was formed and proved so proficient that, within weeks of the outbreak of war, it was seconded to the White House for Presidential duties. Despite the obvious honor this bestowed upon the regiment, it did have its disadvantages, not least because it deprived the unit of stretcher bearers, which was the duty of bandsmen in battle. It was a perennial complaint of company commanders that their best men were frequently taken away from front-line service to undertake regimental and other duties, and in this instance, the place of the bandsmen would have had to be taken by much needed infanteers.

Initially, as befitted a Scottish regiment, the 79th wore a most distinctive uniform. In full dress, soldiers wore a traditional Highland doublet adorned with red shoulder straps bearing the numbers "79" engraved in brass. Red cuff-patches with light blue piping and a collar which was usually red edged with light blue but occasionally light blue with a red and white patch provided contrast without gaudiness. The whole was completed by rear tails carrying embroidered twin yellow exploding grenades. A blue Glengarry cap with a red bobble and red-and-blue tartan hat strap was worn with the dress uniform, but this was replaced in the field by a conventional Union-issue blue cap. Originally a large brass regimental badge was worn on the Glengarry, but as the conflict progressed, tradition succumbed to financial expediency and a simpler replica of the New York State seal was substituted.

The kilt, the very epitome of the British Highland regiment, was issued and usually worn as part of the formal dress, although occasionally it was replaced by trews, a form of heavily decorated plaid trousers more usually associated with the Scottish Lowlands. The kilt was made of cloth woven into the Cameron of Erracht tartan, similar to that of the sister British regiment. A heavy white-hair sporran with twin black horsehair tails and a white metal thistle badge secured by a thin black leather strap were worn to the front. Red-and-white checkered, knee-length, woolen socks with red gaiters, black leather shoes, silver shoe buckles, and a fiercesome curved knife, worn sheathed in the right sock and known as a "dirk," completed the formidable uniform.

N.C.O.s wore red sashes, yellow epaulettes, and light blue chevrons. The long, straight, traditionally Scottish sword issued to all officers, N.C.O.s, and bandsmen was secured in a black scabbard attached to a leather belt with a gilt, 2-inch (5cm) wide rectangular buckle embossed with a silver wreath of laurel and palm encircling the Old English letters "SNY." Bayonets, which varied in design according to the weapon carried, but which on average were $38\frac{1}{2}$ inches (98cm) long, were issued to the private soldiers who, unlike so many of their Union compatriots, proved on more than one occasion that they were not afraid to use them.

Traditionally, the 79th elected its officers. Colonel James Cameron, the brilliant and charismatic brother of the self- seeking and far less worthy Secretary of War, was chosen to lead the regiment into its baptism of fire at the 1st Battle of Manassas (Bull Run), during which tragically he and 197 of his troops were killed. When Isaac Ingalls Stevens was appointed in his place without the regiment's prior approval, a minor bloodless mutiny occurred as a result of which the 79th was stripped of its colors.

Stevens, who eventually became extremely popular with his men, was an experienced military engineer, politician, and explorer. An expert on Indian affairs, he had been severely criticized in the past for his placatory attitude toward the Plains Indians whom many of his colleagues regarded as their natural enemy. He was a member of the House of Representatives from 1857 until he assumed command of the 79th on 30 July 1861. Promoted brigadier general the following September and major general on 4 July 1862, he was given command of 1st Division, IX Corps (which included the Highlanders) and was killed at Chantilly, Virginia during the 2nd Battle of Manassas, with the recently restored regimental colors in his hands, having rescued them from the sixth standard bearer to have fallen. A short and rather stout man with a massive head, Stevens was described as dignified and humorless. Yet he was an officer of great potential and, at the

time of his death, was being considered as the next commander of the Army of the Potomac.

In all, the 79th served with distinction in 59 engagements before it was mustered out on 13 May 1864 (after which men with unexpired terms formed two companies of the New Cameron Highlanders). It lost 110 officers and men from a total of 474 engaged at the Battle of James Island and 105 at 2nd Manassas, after which its colors were restored in recognition of its valiant conduct.

At no time did the 79th demonstrate the true tenacity of the Highlander more than at the 1st Battle of Manassas. Arguably the most obscene destroyer of American idealism of all time, this battle – called Bull Run by the North and Manassas by the Confederacy – should never have been fought. Green troops, often dressed in gaudy uniforms more befitting the ballroom than the battlefield and armed with rifles and muskets few of them could handle, clashed in a bloody battle demanded by the politicians and dreaded by the generals. The battle itself was neither big nor decisive. The Union fielded an army of 35,000 and the Confederacy 32,500, yet such was the rawness of the battalion officers and the ineptitude of the staff that only 18,572 Northerners met 18,053 Southerners in actual combat. Light by later standards, the casualty lists nevertheless seemed dreadful at the time: the Union sustained 2,896 casualties includ-

ing 460 dead, and the Confederacy 1,982 casualties of whom 387 were fatalities. Initially all went well for McDowell's Northerners as they relentlessly pushed the (at that stage) heavily outnumbered Southern troops back from the sluggish waters of Bull Run itself up onto Henry House Hill. However, the Confederate General Beauregard, anticipating the central axis of the Federal attack, brought up reserves and began to turn the Union tide. Stagnation in the latter's advance turned to indecision and quickly to fear as many of the "90-day" troops comprising the bulk of the Washington army, their three-month term almost up, fell back. As inexperienced officers lost control and men became separated from their friends, fear turned to panic and a withdrawal to a rout until the greater part of the army was retreating to the protective defenses of Washington.

As the majority of Federal troops discarded their guns, packs, and anything else which might impede their escape, a few units maintained their discipline, slowing and disorganizing the Confederate pursuit. Many of these units were regulars but others were volunteers, mainly from Sherman's brigade. Of these, few fought more bravely than the 79th New Yorkers, proving to the world that their tenacity and fighting ability as well as their uniforms were a match for their venerated Highland ancestors.

General Kearney leads the charge at the Battle of Chantilly.

27

U.S. COLORED INFANTRY

No event has so affected black people in the United States as did the Civil War. Contrary to popular opinion, however, slavery was a catalyst and never a cause of the war. Lincoln realized early that precipitate action against slavery would compromise the neutrality of the border states, would undermine his position in the North where anti-Negro feelings were running high and would make virtually impossible his overriding aim to save the Union. As late as August 1862, Lincoln confided in the influential anti-slavery editor Horace Greeley that "If I could save the Union without freeing any slave, I would do it; and if I could save it by freeing all the slaves, I would do it; and if I could save it by freeing some and leaving others alone, I would do that."

Surprisingly perhaps, by mid-1862 Lincoln had already decided privately to issue a proclamation of emancipation and was only awaiting a suitable time for its publication. The war was going badly for the North. The Confederacy had been able to release the bulk of its fit young men for front-line combat, relying on its 3.5 million slaves for the production of food, raw materials and ammunition without which it would have found it impossible to survive the first winter. Its armies had seized the initiative early on, winning a series of swift vic-

tories which threw the North into a crisis of self-doubt and recrimination. Ominously the British government, if not its people, were showing signs of a distinct bias toward the South.

Abolitionists advised strongly that, were Lincoln to introduce emancipation, he would elevate the war to the level of a social crusade. Emancipation would be followed by a groundswell of unrest among the Southern slaves, possibly leading to sporadic insurrection. Furthermore, Britain would certainly be deterred from direct intervention on the side of slavery against freedom.

Union army generals remained ambivalent toward the question of slavery. Some relied on the provisions of the Fugitive Slave Law of 1850 to return escapees to their masters, ignoring completely the fact that the society from which they had fled was now at war with the North. Others, notably General Benjamin Butler commanding troops on the Virginia coast, deemed all slaves "contraband of war" and put them to work for the Federal cause. In August 1861, Congress passed the Confiscation Act, empowering the authorities to seize all property employed "in aid of the rebellion," including "contrabands," as a result of which thousands of ex-slaves found themselves working for the downfall of their former masters. None,

54th Massachusetts (Colored) Regiment storming Fort Wagner, 3 July 1863.

Kepi: Many Colored Infantry wore black waterproofs over their otherwise conventional blue kepis.

Frock coats: Many units formed later in the war were issued with excellently tailored dress uniforms including the traditional frock coat which most wore with the collar down.

Units retained for garrison duty might be expected to parade in their full packs as depicted here. "Fighting" troops would usually contrive to lose much of the unnecessary kit.

29

however, was allowed to join the ranks of the Union army itself.

During 1862, a series of enactments forbade the return of fugitive slaves, abolished slavery within the District of Columbia, prohibited its practice in Federal territories and ultimately freed all slaves in the Confederacy. Lincoln delayed the formal Proclamation of Emancipation until September 1862 by which time the Union army had gained a crushing victory at Antietam (Sharpsburg). In so doing, he carefully obviated any suggestion that the law was being changed simply to provide cannon fodder.

Whereas the Proclamation made little immediate difference to the slaves still under Confederate sovereignty, it did offer them great hope for the future. News of the Proclamation spread by word of mouth among the slaves who at last realized the potential of a Union victory.

The inevitable migration to the Northern industrial cities of thousands of freed and escaped slaves brought serious social unrest which occasionally manifested itself in openly racist rioting. Attempts

Although this photograph is obviously posed, it demonstrates clearly the high standard of uniform issued to black troops during the latter stages of the war.

by Lincoln to mitigate the problem through the medium of black emigration failed in the face of mushrooming black patriotism. Increasingly, black Americans were demanding the right to fight for their new country.

The United States navy, which had traditionally accepted men of all races, recruited an estimated 20,000 blacks during the Civil War. Although the majority were confined to the anonymity of the lower decks, a few obtained fame and promotion, none more so than Captain Robert Smalls of the *Planter* who daringly sailed his ship under the guns of the Charleston shore batteries to join the blockading Union fleet.

By the winter of 1862, the Federal government had committed itself to emancipation. Despite the bravery of their brothers in the navy and the increasing eloquence of men such as Frederick Douglass, himself an escaped slave and now an influential lecturer and author, Lincoln continued to doubt the potential military value of ex-slaves. Not only did he fear that the loyal border states would be affronted at the sight of ex-slaves bearing arms against their "natural" masters, but he also doubted that blacks, particularly ex-plantation workers, would have the confidence to face in close-quarter battle those whom for generations they had been taught to fear and defer to.

By September 1862, however, the Northern situation was critical. Few of the 300,000 volunteers called for in July had materialized and the army was now far below strength. Against his better judgment, Lincoln at last agreed to the necessity for black regiments. Ben Butler raised the Corps d'Afrique (Louisiana Native Guards), and on 27 September 1862, his 1st Louisiana National Guard became the first black regiment to be mustered into Federal service. The 2nd Louisiana National Guard was formed a month later, and the 3rd and 4th in November. At about that time, General David Hunter, a veteran of the Indian and Mexican wars, sanctioned the formation of the 1st South Carolina Volunteers from freed slaves in the areas of the Carolinas and Georgia then under Union control. Inspired by their enlightened commander, the Massachusetts abolitionist Thomas Wentworth Higginson, the South Carolinas distinguished themselves in a number of early skirmishes with Confederate platoons, encouraging their leader to report, that "no officer in this regiment now doubts that the key to the successful prosecution of this war lies in the unlimited employment of black troops." Convinced, Lincoln immediately ordered the implementation of full-scale black enlistment. The President's initial demand for four black regiments was soon overtaken by events, and by August 1863, 14 black regiments – 14,000 troops in all – were in the field or ready for deployment, with another 24 in the process of forming.

On 27 May 1863, two Louisiana regiments became the first black troops to participate in a general engagement when they led the assault on the Confederate stronghold at Port Hudson, Louisiana, on the Mississippi. Although unsuccessful, such was the nature of their bravery that all but the most stalwart of conservatives were forced to concede that the commitment of such troops was now beyond doubt. On 7 June 1863, the raw and untried black garrison at Milliken's Bend, Louisiana held its position in hand-to-hand combat against the veterans of General Walker's division. On 18 July, the 54th Massachusetts, the first black regiment to be recruited in the North, led an attack on Battery Wagner overlooking Charleston harbor. Out of a total of 650 engaged, the regiment lost 272 wounded and killed, (including its commanding officer), but although unsuccessful, it at once won itself the universal respect of Union and Confederate leadership alike. Prominent politicians who had once sneered at the idea of black soldiers were forced to admit their worth, and Lincoln at once accelerated their enlistment.

As Union forces advanced deeper into Southern territory, they gathered more able-bodied blacks into their ranks until, by 1865, there were a total of 166 regiments – 145 infantry, 7 cavalry, 12 heavy artillery, 1 field artillery and 1 engineer – of which approximately 60 had experienced combat. Thirty-eight regiments participated in the invasion of Virginia while others led the advance into Charleston and Richmond – a final humiliation for the defenders. Few black troops fought in more than one major battle. Nevertheless, of the 178,895 who enlisted and were deployed in the 449 engagements in which black troops were involved, over 3,700 lost their lives. This is a massive number when it is remembered that black troops fought only in the latter half of the war.

Seventeen black soldiers and four sailors were awarded the Congressional Medal of Honor, the highest accolade of a grateful government.

Black troops did not receive special uniforms, although their smartness on parade was commented on by more than one senior officer. However, whether this was due to the fact that many were employed on garrison duties where standards were easier to maintain or whether it was due to a higher level of regimental *élan* remains a moot point. Many of the regiments that formed late in the war were equipped with uniforms made of high-quality cloth rather than the conventional serge which was in short supply at the time, a factor which greatly enhanced their appearance.

Negro soldiers, among the most devout in the Federal army, attend an impromptu religious service.

OFFICER: U.S. CORPS OF ENGINEERS

At the outbreak of war, the United States army boasted two highly efficient but independent establishments: the Corps of Engineers, responsible for the planning, supervision, construction, and maintenance of the network of railroads, roads, canals, and bridges mushrooming throughout the country; and the Corps of Topographical Engineers, responsible for the provision and updating of maps. In 1863, in recognition of their complementary nature, the two corps were amalgamated into a single Corps of Engineers consisting of 105 officers and 752 enlisted men.

Battlefield surveys, although often far from accurate, were vital to the planning of the war, particularly as many engagements took place in areas which had never been properly mapped. There were problems reproducing these in sufficient quantities. Initial attempts at photographing maps at the front met with limited success due to the distortion caused by the varying focal lengths of the primitive lenses employed. High-quality maps could be produced by lithography, but this was demanding of men and materials and had therefore to be carried out well behind the front line. For quick repro-

duction, maps were drawn on thin sheets of cloth, stretched over a silver nitrate-sensitized sheet and held up to the sunlight. The lower sheet was then "fixed," resulting in a map comprising white lines on a black background. Although such primitive reproductions soon faded, they usually proved adequate for the task required and had the benefit of being easily replaceable.

The Topographic Engineers also reconnoitered routes, from the point of view of potential enemy movement as well as that of friendly forces, taking particular account of the strength and location of bridges, the nature of the railroads, and the adequacy of food and water supplies. In this respect, they were among the first true "intelligence" troops.

The Union army was well endowed with officers competent in engineering and therefore found no difficulty in expanding the Corps as circumstances demanded. Knowledge at the time was comparatively primitive, lacking the exactitude which marks present undertakings. Sophisticated equipment simply did not exist, the majority of works being undertaken with the traditional pick and

U.S. Engineers constructing a landing stage at Belle Plain, Virginia in May 1864. Note the informal inscription in the foreground.

Headdress: Officers wore a standard black dress hat with a brass cap badge denoting a castle with a sally port in front and turrets on either side. Even after their amalgamation in 1863, many Topographical Engineers continued to wear their traditional cap badge denoting a gold shield within a wreath.

Tunic: Branch of service was denoted by black shoulder tabs and gold trouser cords. Once again Topographical Engineers tended to wear buttons denoting a shield above the old English letters "TE."

shovel. Never was the maxim "Soldier first and specialist second" more true than with the engineers, whose front-line involvement often brought them into direct contact with the enemy to the extent that the Corps actually fought as infantry at the Battle of Malvern Hill in Virginia (1 July 1862).

A number of states raised their own independent troops. New York raised the 1st Engineer Regiment (Serrell's Engineers) which operated along the South Carolina coast. It eventually participated in the siege of Petersburg, together with the 15th and 50th Engineer Regiments, both formerly infantry units, which, together with the 1st U.S. Engineer Battalion, provided brigade support for the Army of the Potomac. Missouri raised Bissell's Engineer Regiment, which amalgamated in 1864 with the 25th Missouri Infantry to form the 1st Missouri Engineer Regiment, while Michigan raised a further regiment and Kentucky and Pennsylvania independent companies.

The primary role of the Corps of Engineers in wartime – the construction of defenses and fortifications – grew considerably in importance as each side obtained bigger and heavier artillery and mastered the art of mounting huge siege mortars on floating rafts. Traditionally, fire trenches and gun emplacements were designed by engineers but constructed by the infantry destined to occupy them. However, as the war progressed units of pioneers were introduced to take over the actual construction work to allow the hard-pressed infantry a modicum of rest between actions.

Pre-war coastal forts, designed on classical European principles, tended to be large, masonry affairs invariably pentagonal in shape and occasionally with protruding bastions. Many had two or three floors of guns. Although presenting an enormous target, the forts relied on their overwhelming firepower to annihilate an enemy fleet before the latter could sail close enough to return effective fire. Ships, it was argued, were not steady firing platforms and accurate targeting was virtually impossible. Fortresses, on the other hand, with their stability and protection, could concentrate fire onto a single target with devastating effect. Land approaches were protected by traditional water-filled ditches and outworks.

The Civil War heralded the advent of powerful new artillery pieces which obviated the need for the traditional coastal assault. Forts once considered impregnable now found themselves at the mercy of long-range rifled ordnance, small and light enough to be moved across land. The death knell for the traditional fortification was convincingly sounded on 11 April 1862 when the 40 casemated guns of Fort Pulaski (outside Savannah, Georgia) were battered into submission by Federal rifled artillery standing off nearly two miles from their target. Where possible, all future fortifications were constructed with sloping earthen ramparts to absorb and, if possible, deflect incoming shells.

Field fortifications, which soon proliferated on the battlefield, varied in dimensions and complexity, from simple shell scrapes dug with nothing more advanced than the standard infantry bayonet to vast gun emplacements. Most began life simply and were gradually strengthened as time went on

by the addition of revetments, shelters, and listening and sentry posts. At one point, 68 minor forts interconnected by 20 miles of trenches surrounded Washington D.C.

Responsibility for the strengthening of the major fortifications passed to the Corps of Engineers. Fields of fire were made to interlock; mines consisting of artillery shells or mortar bombs detonated by a basic percussion fuze were strewn; and obstacles in the form of pits, sharpened staves, and felled trees were strategically placed to slow the enemy advance.

Engineers tasked with the storming of enemy fortifications relied largely on the traditional method of "sap and parallel." The attacking forces first laid out their own lines well clear of the defender's artillery in such a way as to deny him reinforcements and replenishment. Zig-zag trenches, or "saps," were then excavated toward the enemy defenses. While still some distance from the enemy lines, the

saps were halted and linked by a consolidating trench or "parallel." Heavy artillery was then brought forward and the position strengthened. New saps were dug toward the positions of greatest vulnerability within the enemy front line and were eventually used as a staging point for a night assault. The carnage resulting from such attacks can only be imagined.

Bridging, both of rivers and of land obstacles, constituted one of the most important duties of the Corps, particularly in the latter stages of the war when the Union found it necessary to move huge armies over hostile territory. In his "march to the sea," General Sherman allotted each of his four corps a detachment of engineers equipped with a pontoon train offering bridging facilities of 900 ft (275m). Two such trains combined, it was argued, would be capable of crossing any river east of the Mississippi. Inevitably, bridging trains, with their vast array of heavy and complex equipment, could not always sustain the rapid rate of advance of unencumbered infantry, with the result that, where possible, the latter would often construct makeshift bridges from available resources rather than run the risk of losing the initiative through delay.

Engineer officers wore the standard officer's dress with black shoulder tabs and gold trouser cords to denote the branch of service. The cap badge – a brass castle with a sally port in front and turrets at each side (still proudly worn by the modern Corps) – was worn on a black dress hat. Prior to the amalgamation, Topographical Engineers wore a cap badge consisting of a gold shield within a wreath and buttons depicting a shield above the Old English letters "TE." After 1863, many Topographical Engineers continued to retain the old insignia, and indeed to refer to themselves by their traditional name. Enlisted men wore the plain fatigue uniform, although provision did exist for the issue of white coveralls in the field.

Far left: U.S. Engineers spent much of their time repairing bridges destroyed by the retreating Confederacy. Note the casualness of their uniforms.

Left: An officer of the U.S. Corps of Engineers, painted by H. Charles McBarron.

U.S. SHARPSHOOTERS

To be effective, sharpshooters – or "snipers" as they are known today – must be as skilled in fieldcraft as they are in marksmanship. They must be self-assured yet highly disciplined, and above all, they must be dedicated. Traditionally, the United States has always enjoyed a fine tradition of marksmanship, extending back to the woodsmen of the 18th century whose Kentucky and Pennsylvania long rifles scored such resounding successes against the British redcoats during the War of Independence. It is not surprising, therefore, that when Hiram Berdan set about the formation of the Sharpshooters on 30 November 1861, he was immediately inundated with volunteers.

The high minimum standards required – notably the ability to place ten consecutive rounds within the 10-inch (25cm) diameter of a bull's eye at 200 yards (185m) – plus the necessity for excellent references did, however, soon reduce the number of aspirants until, eventually, 1,392 officers and men were accepted into the ranks of the 1st Regiment. A further 1,178 all ranks enlisted into the 2nd Regiment when it was formed under the command of Colonel Henry Post soon after.

Berdan himself was a brilliant if unlovable indi-

vidual. A mechanical engineer practicing in New York City at the outbreak of war, he had been the top rifle shot in the country for a staggering 15 years. Admired and therefore somewhat protected by General Winfield Scott, Berdan was nevertheless regarded as unscrupulous and untrustworthy by the vast majority of his peers. He nevertheless created in the Sharpshooters some of the most versatile and respected soldiers of the war.

Initially, the volunteers brought their own hunting rifles, but when this created acute problems of ammunition resupply, Berdan requested the universal issue of the coincidentally named Sharps rifle. James W. Ripley, the conservative and hot-tempered Chief of Ordnance, joined with Scott in insisting instead that Berdan's troops be issued with muzzle-loading Springfields. In making this decision, Ripley was merely mirroring the views of the majority of traditional military minds. The .52 caliber single-shot breechloading Sharps rifle was revolutionary in design and therefore expensive to produce at a time when financial saving was all-important. More fundamentally, it was feared that the additional ammunition expenditure would lead to insurmountable resupply problems. After per-

The fine tradition of marksmanship in the United States produced many volunteer sharpshooters.

Tunic: All ranks were issued with dark green caps and jackets, the latter with black, non-shine, thermoplastic buttons to offer maximum camouflage.

Weapons: Despite initial objections from the Pentagon, from 1862 the Sharpshooters were issued with the deadly accurate Sharps rifle capable of picking off enemy artillerymen at ranges in excess of 800 yards.

Leggings: Black leather leggings were issued to all ranks but abandoned by most as unnecessarily cumbersome.

sonally witnessing a spectacular exhibition of marksmanship by Berdan, however, Lincoln personally intervened and the coveted Sharps were issued between May and June 1862.

Uniquely among volunteer units, the Sharpshooters constituted Federal rather than state troops, although they were in practice recruited on a local basis. Within the 1st Regiment, Companies "A," "B," "D," and "H" were drawn from New York, Companies "C," "I," and "K" from Michigan, "E" from New Hampshire, "F" from Vermont and "G" from Wisconsin. The smaller 2nd Regiment, which unusually was confined to eight rather than the orthodox ten companies, drew from Minnesota (Company "A"), Michigan (Company "B"), Pennsylvania (Company "C"), Maine (Company "D"), Vermont (Companies "E" and "F"), and New Hampshire (Companies "F" and "G").

Never trained to fight conventionally, the Sharpshooters were invariably deployed as skirmishers, usually in company strength. The 1st Regiment, which lost 546 killed and wounded in four years of fighting, acquitted itself well at the Battle of Mine Run, when it lost its commander Lieutenant Colonel Caspar Trepp who had only recently succeeded Colonel Berdan. It was active throughout the Peninsula campaign, particularly in the battle for Yorktown when its members used their sniping rifles to excellent effect, neutralizing Confederate gun batteries. Although the regiment was granted its wish and issued with the Sharps rifle soon thereafter, there is evidence to suggest that a few picked marksmen retained their original personal weapons.

In 1863, the regiment was transferred to III Corps and in 1864 to II Corps. It distinguished itself amid the bloodletting of Chancellorsville (1–4 May 1863), at which time its skirmishers wreaked havoc among the forward elements of the 23rd Georgia Regiment, and at Gettysburg where it did much to stabilize the confused position facing General Dan Sickles and III Corps in the area of the Emmitsburg Road.

Gettysburg did, however, demonstrate the dangers inherent in relying on a single unit for the provision of an overall picture of a battle. General Sickles, in command of III Corps, unnerved by the lack of immediate intelligence and fearful of a large enemy build-up to his front and left flank, dispatched four companies of Sharpshooters supported by the 3rd Maine Infantry Regiment to establish the exact position. Berdan's men made contact with and drove back the enemy skirmishers but then met stiff resistance in the area of Pitzer's Wood. Withdrawing in good order, Berdan immediately reported the presence of a large number of Confederates. Although the concept of size is notoriously subjective (there were, in fact, only three regiments of Wilcox's Alabama Brigade deployed), Sickles immediately assumed that his earlier premonitions were true and that he was actually facing an entire army thrust. He at once ordered an advance *en masse*, leaving his designated position and his flanks wide open. Only the sheer professionalism of his own troops, aided by the quick reaction of General Sykes when ordered to bring forward V Corps from the reserve by General Meade, averted a catastrophe.

The 2nd Sharpshooters served with the ill-fated McDowell's Corps during the Peninsula campaign but as such were held in reserve. At Antietam (Sharpsburg) (17 September 1862),they were unusually, and wastefully, deployed into line of battle as part of Phelp's Brigade (Hooker's I Corps), losing 66 men in what is generally agreed to have been the bloodiest day's fighting of the war. Thereafter the regiment served successfully with I, III, and II Corps, usually as part of Birney's Division and alongside its sister regiment the 1st Sharpshooters. Its heaviest losses occurred during the Wilderness campaign and at Spotsylvania where it sustained, respectively, 76 and 53 casualties. In all, the regiment lost 462 killed and wounded before its disbandment.

Not all Sharpshooters accepted the Sharps rifle. A few picked marksmen were issued with heavy and meticulously manufactured sniper's rifles, often equipped with telescopic sights. Properly maintained and loaded and in the hands of experts, such weapons were capable of consistent 20-round

12-inch (30cm) groups at ranges in excess of 880 yards (805m). Such weapons were invariably muzzle loading, often with a false muzzle to minimize friction from the ramrod.

As tactics progressed and the musket became obsolete, the infantry's marksmanship improved and the commanders began to find it less necessary to rely on skirmishers to disrupt the enemy front line. More fundamentally, experience was proving that skirmishing lines were simply too flimsy to withstand the sustained attack of massed rows of bayonet-wielding infantry. By 1864, therefore, the role of the Sharpshooter was considered largely over. In the autumn of that year, the 1st Regiment was merged into the 2nd, and in February 1865 the entire unit was disbanded.

Uniforms issued to officers and men alike were among the most unusual and practical of the war. Originally both regiments wore dark green coats and caps (the latter with a black ostrich plume), light blue trousers (soon replaced with more practical green garments), and leather leggings. With comfort at a premium, personal innovations were tolerated with particular regard to the leggings which many volunteers discarded, preferring simply to tuck their trousers into their long woolen socks. A gray felt great coat trimmed with green was issued but abandoned by most after the first winter rains due to its unfortunate habit of stiffening uncomfortably when wet. The regulation U.S. army fatigue uniform was generally worn in the field, often with the addition of a blue flannel jacket. Dark green chevrons and stripes were worn by all N.C.O.s and non-shine, black thermoplast buttons by all ranks. The cap badge consisted of crossed rifles with the letters "US" above and "SS" below.

In close-quarter action, some volunteers abandoned their knapsacks in favor of smaller, more conventional haversacks worn in conjunction with the standard-issue black leather belt with its distinctive "US"-emblazoned buckle. Others found the Prussian-designed, hair-covered calfskin knapsack with its externally slung cooking utensils and additional storage space to be both comfortable and practical.

As the war progressed, formal lines of skirmishers were replaced by single sharpshooters trained to work on their own initiative.

N.C.O.: U.S. CAVALRY

Prior to 1861, the cavalry was considered in the United States to be militarily unimportant. It had produced no great leaders, had none of the social connections of its European counterparts, and totally lacked political patronage. With a few exceptions, it was based in a series of primitive and isolated forts in the far West from which it eked out a lonely, celibate existence far from the public eye. Few among the hordes of European immigrants who swelled the cities of the northeastern seaboard in the 1840's and 1850's felt any affinity for the horse, with the result that those who did enlist in the army tended to join the infantry. Not surprisingly the cavalry became a magnet for uninspiring officers and social misfits.

At the outbreak of war, there were only five regular U.S. cavalry regiments: the 1st and 2nd Dragoons, the Mounted Rifles, and the 1st and 2nd Cavalry, each consisting of five squadrons of two troops. Early in 1861, a sixth regiment, the 3rd Cavalry, was authorized, and a further squadron, again with two troops, was added to each regiment. Soon thereafter the entire force was streamlined. The 1st Dragoons became the 1st Cavalry, the 2nd Dragoons and Mounted Rifles became the 2nd and 3rd Cavalry, while the original 1st, 2nd, and 3rd Cavalry were redesignated the 4th, 5th, and 6th Cavalry – a move sure to have caused resentment

The charge of the 5th Cavalry during the Battle of Gaynes Mill.

among these ranks who were bound to have regarded their new names as a demotion. Troops were increased officially to 100 men, although many remained under strength.

A regiment was commanded by a full colonel assisted by a lieutenant colonel, three majors, an adjutant, a quartermaster, a commissary, and a regimental surgeon and his assistant. Each troop was led by a captain supported by a lieutenant, a second lieutenant, and a so-called supernumerary, or "third" lieutenant. Each regiment contained a sergeant major, a quartermaster sergeant, a commissary sergeant, a saddler sergeant, a blacksmith, and two hospital stewards. Besides its officers, each troop had a first sergeant, a quartermaster sergeant, five sergeants, eight corporals, two teamsters, two blacksmiths, one saddler, a wagoner and two musicians.

In mid-1863, the Union army at last conceded the superiority of the Confederate cavalry and undertook a fundamental reorganization of its own mounted forces. The rank of "supernumerary" was scrapped, troops were increased in size from 82 to 100 men, and squadrons were eliminated in favor of battalions of four troops each. Onerous escort duties and camp pickets, which until then had fallen to the cavalry, were delegated to more suitable troops, while the cavalry itself at last began to

Headddress: Cavalry kepis were molded to individual preference. All however bore the crossed sabers, regimental numbering and squadron lettering which differentiated them from the infantry.

Saddle: The McClellan-pattern saddle was hardy but uncomfortable. A fully-laden trooper was forced to sit bolt upright, allowing him little grip on the flanks of his mount.

Weapons: A pistol was secured to the right of the leather belt, a saber to the left. Regular cavalrymen carried the U.S. Pistol Carbine Model 1855, the volunteers any of a wide variety of carbines.

41

Company J, of 6th Pennsylvania Cavalry, rest during maneuvers. The lances, seen stacked in the foreground, would eventually be abandoned as impractical.

practice the *manoeuvre en masse* which had made its European equivalent such a formidable fighting force. An unnamed Confederate officer confirmed the success of the new training by stating at the end of the war that: "During the last two years, no branch of the Army of the Potomac contributed so much to the overthrow of Lee's army as the cavalry, both that which operated in the Valley of Virginia and that which remained at Petersburg."

Each cavalry regiment carried a regimental standard some 2 ft 5 inches (74cm) long by 2 ft 3 inches (69cm) deep. On its blue background was depicted a spread eagle bearing a red, white, and blue Federal shield upon its breast and holding a branch of laurel and sheaf of arrows in its talons. Above and below the eagle were two scrolls, the upper inscribed "*E Pluribus Unum*" in black lettering, the lower bearing the regimental title. Prior to the restructuring in 1863, after which each troop was issued with a guidon bearing the stars and stripes, a designated troop corporal carried the individual troop guidon. Each swallow-tailed guidon consisted of a red upper half bearing the letters "US" in white and a white lower portion containing the troop identifying letter. They were flown from 9 ft (2.7m) long poles, surmounted by standard brass pike-heads. Whatever effect the sight of the unfurled guidons may have had on the morale of the attacking cavalry, their bearers must have known that all available enemy guns would be turned on

them and it is unlikely therefore that the "honor" of bearing the guidons would have been universally popular.

Cavalry uniform was as practical as possible and relatively comfortable. Although the broad-brimmed slouch hat was occasionally worn, most troops favored the more common fatigue or forage cap, distinguished from the conventional infantry apparel by a brass badge on the crown comprising crossed sabers beneath the regimental number and above the squadron (later battalion) letter. Contemporary photographs show that many variations in the cut of the cap were tolerated as was the growing of facial hair, the latter probably a concession to the need to put water for the horses before personal hygiene. The short shell jacket, which had been in issue since the 1830's and which the cavalry now shared with the light artillery, was originally trimmed in orange for the dragoons, green for the mounted rifles, and yellow for the cavalry. However, after the amalgamation of the six regiments into one, all wore yellow. Trousers, which were sky blue with a thick yellow stripe, were heavily reinforced in the seat and inner leg to prevent chafing during the hours spent in the saddle. Ordinary black shoes were issued but, wherever possible, were replaced by a far more practical pair of black boots worn either hidden under the trousers or thigh high in the manner of the 17th-century English cavalier. The universal black leather belt held a "hog-leg" revolver holster on the right with the butt-cover extending forward, small pouches for percussion caps and pistol ammunition to its front, and a sword scabbard on the left.

The standard saddle throughout the Federal cavalry, both regular and volunteer, was the McClellan pattern first introduced into service in 1858. The saddle tree was made of wood, either beech or poplar, with a leather seat over a black rawhide cover. The stirrups were of wood with leather hoods. The girth, known as a "cinch," contained a ring at either end connected to the pommel and cantle of the saddle. A large leather carbine holster ran diagonally on the right of the saddle. Saddle bags, a blanket roll, and a poncho were all standard and attached to the saddle by means of individual straps. Contemporary sources suggest that the cavalryman was forced to sit bolt upright and consequently could not exert much grip on the flanks of his mount. Surrounded as he was by bags of oats, blankets, coats, and weaponry, he must have looked strange when traveling fully laden.

The traditional cavalry weapon – the saber – came in two types: light and heavy. The light cavalry saber Model 1860 had a 41-inch (104cm) blade, was 1 inch (2.5cm) wide at the hilt and slightly curved. The guard was of brass in half-basket form, the grip was covered in black leather bound in brass wire, and the pommel was in the shape of a Phrygian helmet. The slightly heavier Model 1840 saber had a thicker blade – $1\frac{1}{4}$ inches (3cm) thick at the hilt – but was otherwise similar in design. Both were carried in a plain wrought-iron scabbard with two rings for attachment to the belt. During the war, the Federal government purchased 203,285 light and 189,114 heavy sabers, more than ample to fully equip its cavalry forces.

All troopers and non-commissioned ranks in the cavalry carried carbines. Although in essence a carbine was little more than a lighter and shorter version of the standard rifle-musket, in practice those issued initially to the regular cavalry bore no real resemblance to the latter. The U.S. pistol carbine Model 1855, of which only 8,000 were ever manufactured, was based on the standard Model 1855 single-shot .58 caliber pistol and was used exclusively by the regular cavalry. The weapon, which was carried in a purpose-built saddle holster, consisted of a long-barreled but otherwise conventional pistol and a second shoulder stock. Normally it was fired single handed but when extra accuracy was demanded or the weapon was fired when the rider was dismounted, the shoulder stock was fitted and the whole became an improvised carbine.

Sheridan's Cavalry charge the Confederate lines at Five Forks, Virginia, 1 April 1865.

THE IRISH BRIGADE

Between 1846 and 1854, more than 3 million immigrants, a large number of them Irish Catholics, flooded into the United States. Although a few were educated, most were rural workers attempting to escape the deprivations of a subsistence existence eked out in a land plagued with blight and famine. Not unnaturally, the population already ensconced on American shores, itself no more than 20 million strong and traditionally Protestant, grew fearful for its established ways. The Irish were forced into ghettos in the seaboard cities of New England, New York, Pennsylvania, and Maryland where it was felt that they would be easier to control. Abused by the political parties, they were encouraged to vote but given no control over their destiny. Many became introverted, returning to secret societies and Fenianism for an outlet. Most regarded themselves as anti-British first and Americans second.

Between 1861 and 1863, a further 180,000 Irish emigrated to the United States, and of these, over 100,000 enlisted in the Union army. Others, however, remained impervious to the needs of their new country, regarding the war in general, and the question of slavery in particular, with little sympathy. A crisis occurred in 1863 when the Union introduced conscription. Fueled by the blatantly discriminatory terms of the Enabling Act under which a man might avoid service by paying $300 (more than a year's pay for an unskilled worker) or hiring a substitute, and no doubt egged on by drink, a mob of New York Irish broke into the provost marshal's office, destroying the draft records and setting fire to the building. Looting followed, during which an unfortunate and totally innocent black man was beaten and burned to death. Order was only restored with the help of the militia who arrived four days later.

By no means all Irishmen avoided service, and indeed there is evidence to suggest that large numbers emigrated to the United States specifically to join the Union forces. Their reasons for doing so were, however, often complex. Whereas many joined out of loyalty to their new country, others enlisted simply to gain military experience for the future war against the British. As if to emphasize this fact, on at least one occasion Irishmen from both the Union and Confederate forces met in no man's land to hold a "neutral" Fenian meeting to discuss future tactics. In addition, in 1866, many of the participants captured in the unsuccessful Fenian invasion of Canada were found to be wearing Federal uniforms.

Not surprisingly for a ghetto people wary of outsiders, the Irish preferred to enlist in their own regiments with leaders whom they knew and trusted. Responsibility for raising the Irish Brigade with its massive New York nucleus therefore fell to Thomas Francis Meagher, an influential Irish-American who had been transported to Tasmania for sedition and treasonous activity by the British only to escape to the United States in 1852. No fool, Meagher had at once taken out citizenship papers and had thereafter embarked on a noteworthy career as a lawyer, lecturer, and newspaper editor. Commissioned into the rank of brigadier general in February 1862, he commanded the Irish Brigade which he himself had formed that winter, serving with it in the Peninsula campaign, at the 2nd Battle of Manassas (Bull Run), and at the battles of Antietam (Sharpsburg), Fredericksburg, and Chancellorsville before resigning in May 1863, when the brigade, having been decimated, ceased to function as an effective unit. In December of that year, Meagher was reappointed to his rank and given a series of administrative commands under Sherman. After the war, he was appointed temporary governor of Montana, a position which he held until 1867 when tragically he fell off the deck of a Missouri steamer and drowned.

The Irish Brigade itself, which formed part of the 1st Division, II Corps, was large by Union standards. Originally it consisted of the 63rd to 69th New York Volunteers, the 88th New York Volunteers, the 166th Pennsylvania, and the 29th Massachusetts. This last regiment was replaced by the 28th Massachusetts in late 1862. The 166th Pennsylvania was withdrawn in 1864 and replaced in September of that year by the 7th New York Heavy Artillery, by then "relegated" to an infantry role.

It is impossible in the space available to describe in detail the actions of each individual regiment. Typically the 69th New York fought throughout the war, re-enlisting in September 1864 at the end of its three years' service. It lost eight regimental color bearers at Bloody Lane during the Battle of Antietam, and 16 of its 18 officers and 112 of its 210 men at Fredericksburg. During that battle, a color sergeant was found dead, shot through the heart, with the regimental flag concealed wrapped around his body.

The 28th Massachusetts, formed from the Boston Irish in January 1862, transferred to the Brigade in

Sunday morning Mass was a ritual attended by virtually every officer and man of the Brigade. These particular troops are from the 69th New York Volunteers.

Kepi: Service-issue kepi was adorned with a red clover-leaf badge.

Service coat: Embossed with distinctive green collar and cuffs.

Many troops abandoned the issue knapsack, with its tendency to disintegrate in the wet, in favor of the traditional blanket roll seen here.

the November of that year. Known as the "*Faugh-a-Ballagh*" (Gaelic for "clear the way"), it had by then already seen action as part of Stevens' Division, IX Corps at 2nd Manassas, sustaining 234 casualties, and at Antietam where it lost a further 48 out of its remaining strength of fewer than 200. As part of the Irish Brigade, it was heavily engaged at Fredericksburg, sustaining 158 casualties out of 416 officers and men; during the Wilderness campaign, losing 115 out of 505; and at Spotsylvania, losing 110 men, half in a single attack. When the regiment was mustered out on 13 December 1864, it refused to die, re-enlisting its recruits and men into a consolidated battalion of five companies which served for the duration of the war.

It is indicative of the fighting spirit of the Irish Brigade that three of its five commanders were killed in action, all in Virginia: Colonel Patrick Kelly at Petersburg; Major General Thomas Smyth (while commanding another brigade) at Farmville; and Colonel Richard Byrnes at Cold Harbor.

It is generally considered that the brigade experienced its finest, and one of its bloodiest, hours during the battle for the stone wall at the base of Marye's Heights at Fredericksburg (13 December 1862).

Both in conception and execution, Fredericksburg was a catalogue of Union ineptitude. General Burnside – jovial, trusting but inexperienced in large-scale warfare – had just assumed command of the Army of the Potomac, replacing the popular and, in the opinion of many, badly treated McClellan. Lincoln at once pressed for action, demanding exploitation of the "victory" at Antietam. Burnside hurriedly organized the army into three grand divisions: the left under General Franklin; the center under General Hooker; and the right – containing Major General Darius Couch's II Corps with its Irish Brigade – under General Sumner.

Elements of Sumner's 'Right Grand Division' were ordered to advance south from the army's headquarters in Warrenton toward the largely evacuated city of Fredericksburg, with a view to crossing the Rappahannock River and proceeding south to Richmond. Initially, Lee was slow to realize Burnside's intentions and only belatedly ordered Longstreet to adopt a defensive position on Marye's Heights overlooking the river. Inexplicably, the Federals made no immediate attempt to cross into the virtually defenseless city but instead consolidated along the river's northern banks, allowing Lee ample time to prepare. Subsequent attempts to construct five pontoon bridges across the Rappahannock proved impossible due to the presence of 3,000 Mississippi sharpshooters positioned in buildings and slit trenches along the southern bank. Efforts by Union batteries to support the exposed engineers proved ineffectual, and it was not until Burnside ordered massed artillery fire onto the city, with its resultant confusion and carnage, that Union troops were able to cross in pontoon boats and dislodge the tenacious Confederates. Two days later, the bulk of Burnside's troops were across the river and in a position to assault Lee's by now excellently prepared positions.

After attempts by Franklin to probe the Confederate's right wing met with failure, Sumner was ordered to assault their center-left with its apex on the gently rising Marye's Heights. The Confederate position was formidable. Fresh troops were positioned four to six deep along a sunken road at the base of the hill, which was further protected by a stone wall along its forward edge. Artillery was dug into the rear, making a frontal assault virtually suicidal. Nevertheless Sumner's troops, with the Irish in the vanguard, charged no fewer than 14 times, rarely getting within 100 yards (91m) of the enemy position before being driven back. In all, 900 Union troops died in the futile assault on Marye's Heights, many of them from exposure as they lay wounded and freezing in no man's land. Two days later, dejected and defeated, Burnside withdrew the remnants of his shattered army north across the river. Major General Couch wrote of his friend Burnside that, after the battle, "he [Burnside] wished his body was also lying in front of Marye's Heights." The bodies of an undisclosed number of the Irish Brigade were. Yet unlike units endowed with less spirit, the brigade recovered and fought on throughout another vicious 18 months of war.

The Irish Brigade wore a distinctive uniform consisting of the regulation fatigue coat with the addition of green collar and cuffs, and gray trousers. A red clover-leaf badge adorned the top of the service kepi. To emphasize its national heritage, each regiment carried its own individual flag as well as its conventional state and regimental colors.

Facing page, top: The Irish Brigade experienced its finest hour during the carnage of Fredericksburg, when no fewer than 14 fruitless attempts were made to scale the Confederate stronghold on Marye's Heights.

Facing page, bottom: Few photographs show more clearly the slaughter of Bloody Lane.

Exhausted troops pose for a photograph during a respite in the battle for Bloody Lane.

GUNNER: UNION LIGHT ARTILLERY

Despite the steady growth in the importance of artillery throughout early 19th-century Europe, the pre-war Union army had largely failed to recognize the significance of this arm of service. The scale and establishment of ordnance had been laid down by the Secretary of War but this was largely ignored. Theoretically, one field piece was allotted per 1,000 infantrymen and two per 1,000 cavalry. Of this allocation two-thirds were guns, of which three-quarters were 6–pounders and the residue 12-pounders, and one-third were the less mobile howitzers with 12- and 24-pounders in the same ratio. Light artillery was organized into either horse or field batteries, each with six guns and either six or 12 ammunition wagons depending on the caliber of the weapons. The battery itself was subdivided into sections of two guns and an ammunition wagon, the whole commanded by a lieutenant. Six additional ammunition wagons were held in company reserve, as was a mobile forge and supply wagon. In the horse artillery, the crews of nine were mounted, but the rest were expected to walk or hitch lifts on the support vehicles. Guns were invariably allocated piecemeal along the entire battle front, there being no centralized plan for their concerted use.

After the disaster of the 1st Battle of Manassas/ Bull Run (21 July 1861), immediate steps were taken to reorganize the artillery. Wherever possible, the six guns within each battery were standardized, considerably relieving the problems of resupply; batteries were reallocated on the scale of four per division, at last making it possible to bring down concentrated fire on a single point; and divisional artillery assets were placed under the command of a regular army captain. For added versatility, a mobile reserve of 100 light guns was created and placed in the rear.

It is testament to the organizational ability of Major (later Brigadier General) William Farquhar Barry, tasked with the rebuilding of the artillery,

Headdress: At the outset of hostilities most Union gunners were professional soldiers attached to regular army units with long traditions borrowed from their European ancestors. The wool-covered leather shako with its shiny leather vizor, red plume and ornate badge was soon found to be impractical and was abandoned in favor of the kepi or "Hardee" hat.

Tunic: The dark blue shell jacket with its red adornments and high collar was soon withdrawn from service but nevertheless remained popular "informal" wear among many of the older soldiers.

Weapons: Defense was delegated to specially trained infantry units. Nevertheless, many gunners were issued with long, curved sabers which most soon abandoned as too heavy and impractical.

49

that, although the Army of the Potomac had only nine incomplete batteries with a total of 30 pieces when it was formed, by the time it was ready to take to the field, its artillery had been increased to 92 batteries with 520 pieces and a strength of 12,500 men. Years of experience had taught Barry that artillery was too important to be handled by half-trained amateurs. Accordingly, batteries of regular artillery were withdrawn from the outlying forts and coastal batteries (it having been correctly assessed that the Confederacy did not then have the strength to attack the latter) and transferred to the ranks of the Army of the Potomac as field gunners. By August 1861, over half of the regular gunners in the Union army were stationed under McClellan's command in the Washington area.

As the war progressed, it was realized that Barry's innovations, however good, did not utilize the dreadful potential of artillery to its full extent. After the Battle of Chancellorsville (1–6 May 1863), the four divisional batteries were removed, consolidated into artillery brigades, and allocated direct to the corps commander. Simultaneously, horse artillery, which had become unfashionable after the Mexican War, was returned to favor and attached in increasing numbers to the cavalry.

Field artillery was invariably positioned in the very front lines of the troops that it was supporting, with the result that losses to counter-battery artillery and snipers were inevitably high. During the Spotsylvania campaign (8–20 May 1864), Battery "C", 5th U.S. Artillery found itself in action ahead

of its own front line and immediately attracted enemy fire. The left-flank gun succeeded in discharging nine rounds before it was silenced; another managed 14 rounds. By the end of the action, 22 of the 24 gunners had been wounded, seven of them fatally. Every horse had been killed and the limbers rendered useless by enemy cannon and rifle fire. Such was the nature of close-quarter artillery engagement.

The organization and support provided to the artillery by the individual states within the Union varied tremendously. Regiments, battalions, and even independent batteries were raised on an *ad hoc* basis to fulfill Washington's insatiable desire for specialist units. Delaware produced one battery of light guns, while the far more affluent and secure states of Massachusetts and New York donated 17 and 36 independent batteries respectively. Once raised, individual units might expect to serve in a variety of capacities. Although most horse artillery units comprised regulars, due presumably to their known ability to ride, volunteer field gunners were occasionally seconded to the cavalry with mixed results. In times of greatest need, less fortunate gunners (presumably those who found themselves in the wrong place at the wrong time) were even "relegated" to the infantry.

In the early stages of the war, muzzle-loading, smoothbore cannon – some with ranges little in excess of those of rifle-muskets – dominated the battlefield, but as the conflict progressed, these were gradually replaced by a new generation of

Battery D, 5th U.S. Artillery deploy for action.

more powerful rifled weapons. Breechloaders were experimented with but remained unpopular with the conservatives in overall command in Washington.

The most common gun in service with both armies was the ubiquitous light 6-pounder, a simple smoothbore muzzle-loader mounted on a two-wheeled, wooden "stock trail" carriage pulled by a pair of horses. Less numerous but far more successful and popular was the "Napoleon," a bronze 12-pounder designed by Emperor Napoleon III and first used by the French in the Crimea. Lighter by 530 lb (240kg) and shorter by 12 inches (30cm) than the Model 1841 12-pounder which it replaced, it could nevertheless project a 12 lb (5.5kg) shot (identical to that fired by the Model 1841) 1,620 yards (1,480m), virtually as far as its much larger predecessor.

Local battery defense was delegated to specially trained infantrymen rather than to the gunners themselves who were not issued with muskets. Some, however, were issued with pistols, while others received large, sharply curved, brass-hilted sabers which were generally considered to be more of a hindrance than a help in close quarters.

In accord with the fashion of the day, light artillerymen wore distinctive uniforms which owed much to their European heritage. For dress, a tall, wool-covered leather shako topped, tailed, and vizored with shiny leather was issued. A single red worsted cord, decorated at either end with a tassel, ran from the left to the right side of the shako to prevent the unwieldy headpiece falling off the wearer's head in rough conditions. It was secured to the tunic by a further red cord which passed down the back, under the arm and then attached to the third upper button. Two large, worsted, tassels of circular, interwoven design decorated the front of the cord. A brass crossed-cannon badge with the regimental number below and battery letter above the central point was worn beneath a brass eagle plate, the whole surmounted by a large plume of red horsehair.

A dark blue cloth shell jacket – decorated with a row of 12 small, equidistant buttons and a narrow strip of red lace along the front and around the entire lower edge – formed part of the dress uniform. Officers' shoulder straps, N.C.O.'s chevrons and trouser strips were also of red. Uniquely, the artillery was never issued with dark blue trousers, wearing from the outset the light blue pattern destined to become universal issue.

When hostilities commenced, the full dress uniform was almost immediately replaced by the standard fatigue dress, and it is doubtful if many volunteer units ever received the shakos and shell jackets. Although regular units were quick to replace the unwieldy shako with the more practical "Hardee" hat, the dress jackets, featuring the "Russian" shoulder knot with the silver insignia of rank in the case of the officers, remained popular and continued to be worn in the field by a number of units and individuals despite orders to the contrary.

Light artillery could only operate within range of enemy snipers. Casualties were therefore high and crews frequently supplemented by untrained infantrymen.

U.S. NAVAL OFFICER

At the outbreak of hostilities, the U.S. navy was in no fit state to undertake the blockade of the South demanded of it. Anticipating secession, John B. Floyd, the Secretary of War and a latent Confederate sympathizer, had sent five ships to the East Indies, three to Brazil, seven to the Pacific, three to the Mediterranean, and seven to the coast of Africa. In February 1861, only two steamships – the 25-gun *Brooklyn* and the *Relief* with two guns – remained in domestic waters, the latter under orders to sail with supplies for the Africa squadron. Twenty-eight ships languished in home ports, decommissioned and unfit for immediate service. Funds made available for maintenance and repairs had simply not been spent.

The already critical situation was made worse soon after the attack on Fort Sumter, when the defenders of Norfolk, Virginia overreacted to a Confederate attack and destroyed ten warships and most of the naval supplies rather than let them fall into enemy hands. To compound the problem, they failed in their attempt to destroy large numbers of cannon in storage in the Norfolk navy yard thus presenting the South with 3,000 pieces of ordnance with which to equip its own fledgling fleet.

Gideon Welles, Secretary of the Navy, and Gustavus Fox, his Assistant Secretary, tirelessly and efficiently set about the task of rebuilding the navy. Every seaport in the North was scoured and all suitable ships bought, chartered, or commandeered. Orders were placed with government yards for eight new sloops while private tenders went out for the production of 23 screw gunboats. Shipbuilding continued unabated throughout the war until, by mid-1865, the Federal navy had swelled from its original 23 warships to a staggering 641 ships of all types.

So huge an increase in shipping inevitably led to manning problems. In 1861, the 1,457 officers and 7,600 men of the U.S. navy were demoralized, a situation made no better when 16 captains, 34 commanders, 76 lieutenants and 111 regular and active midshipmen defected to the Confederacy. Nevertheless, as the war progressed, the navy managed to produce officers of sufficient mental flexibility to handle the radically new ships and tactics then being adopted.

The problem was compounded considerably by the introduction in the 1860's of revolutionary new methods of propulsion and armored protection. The standard warships of the day were still of wooden construction with masts and sail providing the main means of propulsion. However, by now the steam engine had become a practical machine with the result that the latest ships were fitted with screws or paddles to provide an alternative method of movement. Although not totally reliable, steam power provided a degree of maneuverability

The Naval Practice Battery, Washington – in the background are a Dahlgren rifled gun and Cochran breech loader.

Badges of rank: After 1863 captains, as depicted here, wore three gold lace rings on each sleeve. Rank was also denoted on the shoulder boards.

Frock coat: Traditionally deck officers wore a dark blue frock coat with high collar and two rows of nine buttons each. Most officers wore the jacket undone to reveal the waistcoat worn underneath. Many abandoned the cumbersome coat completely in favor of more comfortable privately purchased civilian attire.

Weapons: Deck officers carried a Model 1852 sword ideally suited to close quarter fighting. Many also carried a variety of privately purchased knives and pistols.

previously undreamed of, and destined to prove of crucial importance in the river battles ahead.

More fundamentally, warships were taking on a completely new design. In 1858, the French began the construction of *La Gloire*, the world's first sea-going ironclad warship, and a year later the British responded with *Warrior*, not only ironclad but built entirely of iron. Earlier attempts by the French navy to operate floating batteries of heavy guns, protected by iron, had proved successful in the Crimean War, as a result of which many naval authorities, including the Confederates, began toying with the idea of mounting large guns on "unsinkable" platforms. Therefore, not only did the Union have to appoint a large number of new deck officers to swell its depleted ranks but it also had to create from nowhere naval traditions in long-range gunnery and engineering.

Perhaps because of its tendency to operate far from home, the pre-war navy had developed traditions of dress, discipline, and class very different to those of the army. Black sailors served below deck without let or hindrance and, after the outbreak of hostilities, were commissioned. The very best, such as Captain Robert Smalls of the gunship *Planter* actually attained command.

Prior to 1862, only the commissioned ranks of captain, commander, and lieutenant existed. However, to accommodate the rapid expansion of the navy during the war, the ranks of lieutenant commander, commodore, and admiral were reintroduced in 1862 and a new system of rank marking devised in 1863.

Throughout the war, the basic officer's uniform consisted of a dark blue, double-breasted frock coat. Individual appointments were denoted by the pattern of buttons: deck officers besported two rows of nine buttons each; until February 1861, engineers wore only a single row of buttons; secretaries wore a row of eight buttons and clerks six. All wore dark blue wool trousers in winter and white duck or linen in summer. Officers were permitted to wear double-breasted blue wool or white drill jackets when at sea, but with the exception of young graduates straight from the naval academy at Annapolis – for whom the dress presumably gave status – few actually did. The ornate dress uniform of tail coat and standing collar, cocked hat, gold-trimmed trousers and heavy gold epaulettes was abandoned early in the war as too expensive. As demand outstripped supply and the ranks became swelled by those who saw their sole task as the destruction of the enemy, standards of dress and tradition were often compromised in the name of expediency. Officers began to dress for comfort rather than sartorial elegance. "Sack coats," more familiar on the battlefield than at sea, began to replace the more formal and less practical frock coat. As is so often the case, officers who provided their own clothing at their own expense soon began to demand more personalized cuts and embellishments until, by 1862, few officers showed any real signs of uniformity.

Prior to the introduction of the new rank structure, captains wore three gold stripes around each cuff, commanders two, and lieutenants one. Masters wore three buttons parallel to the cuff and

midshipmen none, presumably relying upon the cut of their uniform to denote their somewhat dubious status. Dark blue shoulder straps edged in gold embroidery further denoted rank. A captain wore an eagle over an anchor, a commander two fouled anchors, a lieutenant a single fouled anchor, and a master plain straps with no insignia. A qualified midshipman wore a narrow gold strip on each shoulder. Similar insignia within a gold wreath were worn by the senior commissioned ranks as cap badges, masters and midshipmen wearing a fouled anchor on its side within a wreath. Engineers, pursers, surgeons, and other specialists each wore distinctive insignia denoting their rank and status.

When new ranks were introduced on 16 July 1862, confusion reigned supreme. Rear Admirals wore three wide and three narrow gold cuff stripes, a captain three wide stripes, a commander two wide and one narrow stripe, a lieutenant commander two wide stripes, and a lieutenant a single narrow stripe over a wide one. The full status of the ranks of master and midshipman were now recognized by the awarding of, respectively, a single wide and a single narrow stripe. Cap badges were simplified as were shoulder boards, which now took on a distinctly military air.

Badges of rank were altered yet again, this time fundamentally, in May 1863. All officers wore thin gold stripes on their sleeves to indicate seniority. Ensigns, the most junior rank, wore one stripe while rear admirals, the most senior, wore eight. Line officers were identifiable by a gold star worn centrally above the top stripe. Specialists, whose ostentatious insignia had made them easy prey for snipers, now adopted standard badges of rank save for their cap badges which continued to denote their arm of service.

Officers were armed with the Model 1852 sword with a fishskin grip and brass hilt featuring a design incorporating oak leaves, acorns, and the letters "usn." With its slightly curved blade, the sword was essentially similar to that carried by officers today. Despite the horrendous power of the ships' guns of the day, close-quarter, cross-deck fighting between crews remained a particularly savage aspect of combat. Officers, particularly those in charge of boarding parties or guns, therefore carried not only regulation pistols holstered on the right hip but also, on occasion, a variety of knives and axes including the highly effective Dahlgren knife-bayonet.

Officers of the U.S.S. *Monitor* pose for a photograph during a patrol of the James River.

Facing page: Sailors pose on the deck of the U.S.S. *New Hampshire.* The formal naval uniforms would have been relaxed at sea.

U.S. MARINE CORPS

Despite its long and proud history, the U.S. Marine Corps remained relatively small throughout the Civil War. At no time did it number more than 4,167 officers and men, of whom 148 were killed in action. The Corps was too lightly armed and equipped to take a major part in the land war. It did, however, see action at the 1st Battle of Manassas (Bull Run) on 21 July 1861, and fought with conspicuous gallantry in the successful siege of Fort Fisher (6–15 January 1865). More conventionally, detachments served with all but the smallest ships, frequently giving a good account of themselves in the numerous bloody naval engagements of the war.

The prime task of the Union navy, and therefore of the Marines, was blockade. From the outset, General Winfield Scott, Lincoln's chief military adviser, realizing that the war would not be won within the enlistment period of the first 90-day volunteers, advocated the "Anaconda Plan" or constriction of the South. In essence, the navy would blockade the coast from the Potomac to New Orleans while the Army advanced down the Mississippi to the Gulf of Mexico. The Confederacy would then be split in two, with the populous areas of the

east denied the foodstocks of the west, and would be forced into submission.

However, most obvious plans have their weaknesses and "Anaconda" was no exception. Many of the South's merchantmen had been deliberately constructed with shallow drafts and were therefore able to operate from small ports and inlets inaccessible to more conventional warships. More fundamentally, at the outbreak of hostilities the North had virtually no blockade ships available, a problem compounded by the highly successful Confederate raid on Norfolk. Initially, the four blockading squadrons – the North Atlantic under Goldsborough, the South Atlantic under DuPont, the East Gulf under McKean, and the West Gulf under Farragut – were simply too weak to carry out their duties effectively. By mid-summer, however, the Federal fleet had grown sufficiently to enable it to take the initiative. In August 1861, two Confederate forts at Hatteras Inlet on the North Carolina coast were stormed and captured, and in November Port Royal, strategically positioned on the South Carolina coast between Charleston and Savannah, was attacked. Plans to mount a joint army–navy

The dress uniform with its dark blue frock coat, yellow braid and scarlet trim, although impressive, was discarded as impractical during active campaigning.

Headddress: A *chasseur-* pattern field cap with an infantry horn cap badge containing the letter ''M'' in its center was issued to all but the hybrid Mississippi Marine Brigade.

Jacket: Blue frock coats with plain high collars were worn by N.C.O.s and Marines ashore. N.C.O.s wore gold chevrons with red edging. At sea these were often discarded in favor of a blue pullover shirt.

Weapons: Generally Marines were too lightly equipped to fight successfully ashore, although they did take part in one or two major battles.

assault were frustrated when the transports carrying the landing craft were driven ashore in a storm. Unperturbed, DuPont determined to attempt an unsupported naval attack relying on the Marines under his command for limited military assistance. On 7 November, DuPont attacked and overwhelmed the hastily constructed earthen forts at Fort Walker and Fort Beauregard. In so doing, he secured the outer Port Royal Sound, denying the enemy future use of the port. General Lee at once withdrew inland, allowing the Union to consolidate its hold on the coastal islands.

Port Royal was merely the first of a long series of Union victories along the South Atlantic coast and in the Gulf of Mexico. By 1864, only Charleston, South Carolina and Wilmington, North Carolina, on the Atlantic seaboard, remained open to Confederate blockade runners.

Spurred on by the success of DuPont in the Carolinas U.S. Navy Flag Officer David Farragut, commander of the West Gulf Squadron, planned an assault on the Confederate stronghold of New Orleans. The key Confederate defenses consisted of Forts Jackson and St. Philip situated astride the Mississippi at Plaquemine Bend some 90 miles by river from the city itself. In addition, a boom of logs linked by heavy chains barred the way. Eager to enhance the navy's prestige, Assistant Secretary of the Navy Gustavus Fox vetoed initial plans for a

joint operation with the army and instead ordered a fleet of mortar boats under the command of Commander Porter to pound the forts into submission while Farragut's warships fought their way upriver. Porter's mortar boats began their bombardment on 17 April 1862, and a week later, Farragut's steam sloops forced their way through a break in the log boom. Unwilling to wait for a change of heart by the army and wishing to avail himself of the spring tide, Farragut immediately proceeded upriver to accept the surrender of New Orleans on 25 April. Yet again, the Federal navy, devoid of formal military help, had utilized its Marine contingent to the full to inflict a crippling blow on the enemy.

Not all unsupported naval actions were as successful. Soon after taking New Orleans, Farragut sailed with his fleet to Vicksburg. Although only a brigade defended the partially completed works, the Confederates refused to surrender. Farragut began a bombardment with his cruisers and gunboats, supported after 20 June by the newly arrived mortars, but to no avail. The siege was abandoned on 26 July when the navy, disillusioned by its first setback, returned to New Orleans and the Gulf.

The greatest single engagement of the war to involve the U.S. Marines was the dual between the ironclads *Virginia* and *Monitor* fought in Hampton Roads, Virginia on 9 March 1862. In their panic to

The U.S.S. *Cairo* patrols the Mississippi. Gunboats such as this did much to split the Confederacy in two.

evacuate Norfolk, the Union troops had failed to destroy completely the unseaworthy steam frigate *Merrimac*. The Confederates raised it, repaired it, coaxing life back into its damaged engines, armor-plated it and rechristened it *Virginia*. On 8 March, it steamed slowly but purposefully out of Norfolk harbor in search of the Federal flotilla. The *Cumberland* was rammed, the *Congress* sunk by gunfire, and a third major unit forced aground. By the sheerest of coincidences, as the *Virginia* returned triumphantly to her berth, the unsuspecting *Monitor* entered the far end of the sound. Designed by John Ericsson, an ex-patriate Swede, specifically to counter the ironclad threat, the *Monitor* was unique. Little more than an enormous raft, her superstructure, most of which was permanently below the waterline, was dominated by a single, huge, circular turret 20 ft (6m) in diameter and protected by 8-inch (20cm) iron plates. Firepower was provided by two 11-inch (28cm) Dahlgren smoothbore cannons, the mightiest conventional guns then at sea, manned by mixed crews of sailors and Marines. On 9 March, the two heavyweights joined ponderous battle. Neither was able to penetrate the armor of the other nor was the *Virginia* able to ram her adversary (she had, in any case, lost her ram when attacking *Cumberland* on the previous day). After four hours, dented and out of ammunition, the two giants disengaged, never to meet again.

Despite the relatively small size of the Marine Corps, its members enjoyed a wide variety of individual uniforms. Dress uniform was particularly impressive. The dark blue frock coat with its yellow braid and scarlet trim was embellished with gold or yellow worsted cuff lace to indicate rank. Field officers wore four gold lace loops, sergeant majors and quartermasters four of brass. Captains and sergeants wore three loops of gold and brass respectively, lieutenants and privates two. All ranks wore epaulettes on each shoulder, the width of the fringe indicating the rank. In addition, N.C.O.s wore gold chevrons edged with red. With the exception of staff officers who wore red, all ranks wore sky blue trousers embellished with a scarlet welt for officers and a scarlet stripe for senior N.C.O.s.

With the exception of the Mississippi Marine Brigade, created in November 1862 and comprising soldiers attached to the Mississippi fleet, which was therefore not a true Marine unit, all Marines wore a cap badge consisting of a gold wreath around a shield bearing an infantry horn with the Old English letter "M" within its loop.

For field purposes, all ranks wore dark blue frock coats with plain collars, although at sea enlisted men might wear a blue pullover-shirt over a white cotton shirt in preference. A dark blue *"chasseur"*-pattern field cap decorated with the infantry horn and the letter "M" was worn at all times. Inevitably, as equipment wore out, it was replaced with anything available, and as the war continued it was often difficult to differentiate between the Marines and the sailors with whom they lived and worked.

U.S. ARMY HOSPITAL STEWARD

Federal losses in the Civil War were horrific. Although exact figures are unavailable, an estimated 360,000 officers and men lost their lives. Of these, 110,000 – less than one-third of the total – were killed in action or mortally wounded. Of the remainder, a staggering 200,000 succumbed to disease, 25,000 died as prisoners of war, 10,000 were killed in accidents and 16,000 died from other causes. It has been suggested that a further 500,000 sustained non-fatal injuries, in many instances amputations. However, before hostilities began, no one could have anticipated the effect of modern weaponry on troops governed by the traditional tactic of the frontal assault.

At the outbreak of war, the U.S. Army Medical Department mustered a mere 115 officers and men, 27 of whom immediately resigned, all but three going to the South to form the embryonic Confederate Medical Department. As the war progressed, the Federal department grew in size and complexity until eventually it was led by a surgeon-general aided by an assistant surgeon-general. At its peak, it consisted of an inspector-general with 16 medical inspectors, 170 surgeons and assistants, 547 volunteer surgeons and assistant surgeons, 2,109 regimental surgeons, 3,882 regimental assistant surgeons, 85 acting staff surgeons and 5,532 acting assistant surgeons.

Surgeons were nominally commissioned as majors and assistant surgeons as captains. Both wore conventional staff uniforms with the added embellishments of a thin gold cord down each leg, medium or emerald green silk sashes and the letters "MS" interwoven in silver and gold into the epaulettes. In line with all staff officers, surgeons were permitted by an order of 22 November 1864 to remove their conspicuous epaulettes to make themselves less susceptible to sniper fire.

It was accepted that the professional surgeons could not hope to cater for the medical needs of tens of thousands of volunteers swelling the ranks of the army nor could they be expected to deal adequately with the huge numbers of injuries sustained in battle. At Chickamauga, for instance, an alleged 11,243 Federal troops, (20 percent of the combatants) were killed or injured, while at Antietam (Sharpsburg) – "the bloodiest one-day battle of the entire war" – a staggering 12,400 casualties were reported. Lengthy campaigns produced even greater carnage: in four weeks of bitter fighting in May and June 1864, encompassing the battles of Cold Harbor and Spotsylvania and the Wilderness campaign, treatment was given to 54,929 casualties, 52 percent of the Federal participants.

In an attempt to mitigate the resultant crisis, contract surgeons were occasionally hired, and

The evacuation of the wounded after the Battle of Seven Pines stretched Federal resources to the limit.

Frock coat: Stewards did not wear badges of rank on their otherwise traditional three-quarter length frock coats. Instead they wore a half-chevron of emerald green cloth with yellow edging bearing a badge of a yellow caduceus. A red worsted sash and broad crimson stripe along either seam of the trousers completed the specialist attire.

Knapsack: Wooden medical knapsacks containing medicines and a few crude surgical instruments were issued in 1862 and carried into the field by the stewards to ensure that the surgeons had supplies immediately to hand.

medical cadets (young men currently undertaking medical training) were enlisted. The contractees, jealous of their civilian status, retained their own clothes and were generally loath to operate beyond the relative protection of the large base hospitals. Even so, many, if unfortunately not all, performed excellent feats of surgery. Because of their youth and lack of experience, the cadets were often deployed further forward, assisting in the hospitals or dressing wounds in the field as circumstances required. Issued with the uniform of a second lieutenant, save for a forage cap in lieu of the less practical dress hat, and instantly recognizable by their green shoulder bars with a $\frac{1}{2}$-inch (1.3cm) gold strip running through the center, cadets unfortunate enough to be allocated to an active area of the front line must have offered tempting targets to the omnipresent enemy snipers. Details of their losses are, however, not recorded.

Many of the mundane duties at regimental level were delegated to the hospital steward – a senior non-commissioned officer tasked to assist the surgeon when and where required. Realistically, the steward's work must have brought him hourly into contact with the carnage of the operating table and the pandemonium of the make-shift post-operative wards, yet his official dress remained the somewhat impractical frock coat. A "half-chevron" of emerald green cloth with yellow edging bearing a badge of a yellow caduceus was worn on the upper sleeve as a badge of rank. Other embellishments consisted of a mixed green-and-buff cord around the otherwise conventional "Hardee" hat, a red worsted sash, and a broad crimson stripe along the outer seam of the trousers.

Medical staff at the front fought a constant and largely unsuccessful battle against disease. Lack of discipline and apathy combined with ignorance to make the military encampments hot beds of typhoid, smallpox, and other ailments usually associated with overcrowding and lack of sanitation. Regular units – and, notably, as the war progressed, black troops – invariably maintained at least minimum standards of hygiene. However, many of the younger volunteers shunned as unnecessarily regimental the washing and changing of clothes, with inevitable results.

As the war continued and numbers became critical, field commanders became increasingly uneasy at the high incidence of illness and disease within the ranks and at last began to heed the advice of their medical staffs. Discipline was tightened, the rudiments of hygiene enforced, and parades increased.

Conditions in the front-line trenches could not always be controlled. General Andrew Humphreys, then Meade's chief of staff and an accomplished engineer, reported plaintively after the Battle of Cold Harbor that, during the campaign, his troops had been forced to seek shelter in waterlogged trenches with little food and only tainted water to drink. The surrounding land was low, flat, and covered with the decaying bodies of the dead. Not surprisingly, malaria was rife.

Within 20 minutes of the storming of Marye's Heights, the wounded had been taken to regimental aid posts, leaving the dead alone, awaiting burial.

Evacuation of the non-walking wounded from the battlefield to the first aid dressing station was chaotic. Bandsmen were given the duty of stretcher bearers but were too few in number to carry out the task adequately. Their ranks were swelled by sections of ten men per regiment assigned to render assistance, but it soon became clear that the commanders were taking the opportunity of divesting themselves of their very worst men for this task. The wounded were often left for hours, and sometimes days, without help. Truces for the collection of the wounded from the battlefield were rare, and reports of men crying out in agony from no man's land for the want of water and shelter were common.

A few generals, notably Sherman, attempted as far as possible to retain the wounded at regimental level where they considered that care would be of a higher, more personal standard. However, an unfortunate parochialism ensued in which surgeons tended to ignore seriously injured men of other units to concentrate on the members of their own. Divisional hospitals – clusters of between 20 and 30 tents deemed sufficient to cope with the medical needs of 8,000 fighting men – were gradually established in the rear areas safe from enemy artillery fire. Eventually the regimental posts were disbanded, their staffs being assimilated into the less partisan divisional structure.

Initially, evacuation of the wounded was the responsibility of the Quartermaster Corps. However, numerous complaints that many drivers were simply refusing to enter the battle zone, compounded by several instances of horses being commandeered to pull guns or furnish remounts for the cavalry, led in August 1862 to the creation within the Army of the Potomac of an independent Federal Ambulance Corps. The standard ambulance, the so-called "rocker" type, was a four-wheeled vehicle pulled by two horses and manned by a driver and two stretcher bearers. As far as possible, each ambulance was self-contained, with a supply of fresh drinking water, cans of beef stock, bread and cooking apparatus carried on each vehicle. Three ambulances, under the overall command of a sergeant, were attached to each regiment. Brigade ambulances were the responsibility of a second lieutenant and, from 1864 onwards, divisional

The wounded gather at a field hospital after the Battle of Fredericksburg.

vehicles were under the charge of a full lieutenant. At first, Ambulance Corps troops wore caps with green bands 2 inches (5cm) broad around them and a green half-chevron above the elbow on each arm. All were armed with revolvers for self-defense. As the war progressed, the chevrons were reduced in size, and each command adopted the practice of designating its men with individual field insignia.

The most seriously injured soldiers were evacuated to huge permanent base hospitals. Transportation was invariably by train although, when convenient, ships were occasionally pressed into service. Hospital trains at first consisted of no more than a collection of empty boxcars provided with straw on which to lay the litters, but as time passed, conditions gradually improved. Conventional passenger rolling stock was gutted and refitted with bunks, while special cars were transformed into dispensaries and emergency operating rooms.

Civilians – and, in the latter stages of the war, an increasingly large number of women – were employed in the base hospitals to augment the meager military resources. Never popular with the conservatives, the women nevertheless played a vital role, adding a degree of compassion to an otherwise cold and frightening environment.

An ambulance train photographed in July 1863, en route to Harewood Hospital.

THE INDIANA REGIMENTS

At the outbreak of war, there were only six volunteer companies active in the entire state of Indiana. However, within a few weeks no fewer than six regiments of volunteers had flocked to the colors. Most joined initially for three months, but when it became apparent that this would be totally inadequate for the task ahead, they willingly re-enlisted for three years. Initially, the majority of troops were issued with a gray uniform dangerously similar at a distance to that of the Confederacy. The senior regiments, designated the 6th and 7th in deference to the 1st to 5th Regiments which had fought honorably in the earlier Mexican War, wore short gray padded jackets and gray trousers with blue flannel shirts, the 8th short light blue jackets and trousers, the 9th gray satinet jackets and trousers, and the 10th light blue jean jackets and trousers.

Under the patronage of its colonel-in-chief, Lew Wallace, previously the Governor of New Mexico and later author of *Ben Hur*, the 11th Indiana Regiment adopted the more picturesque if far less practical uniform of the North African Zouaves. Wallace, however, ensured that, unlike some of the ridiculously over-dressed Eastern Zouave regiments, the 11th never became a laughing stock. In his own words:

> There was nothing of the flashy, Algerian colors in the uniform, no red fez, no red breeches, no red or yellow sash with tassels big as

early cabbages. Our outfit was of the tamest gray, twilled goods, not unlike home-made jeans, and a vizor cap, French in pattern, its top of red cloth not larger than the palm of one's hand; a blue flannel shirt with open neck; a jacket Greekskin form, edges with narrow binding, breeches baggy, but not pettycoated; button gaiters connecting below the knee with the breeches and strapped over the shoe.

Despite their popularity with the men, the early uniforms of the various Indiana Regiments did not find favor with government officials in Washington who wrote to Governor Morton respectfully requesting that no further regiments be dressed in gray, "that being the color generally worn by the enemy." As a result, regiments raised subsequently wore standard Federal issue U.S. Army uniforms. However, many were issued with blue fatigue jackets similar in design to the original gray apparel, and with distinctive broad-brimmed black hats subsequently adopted by the Iron Brigade of the West in which the 19th Indiana was destined to play a prominent role.

Ever conscious of the need for practicality yet unwilling to allow the 11th to lose its identity completely, Wallace came up with a new uniform for his Zouaves in December 1861. A black Zouave-style jacket was introduced as were sky blue regulation uniform trousers and a dark blue uniform cap. A dark blue woolen vest was worn as an undergarment beneath the jacket. Surprisingly, the original red-topped fatigue caps, ideal targets for enemy snipers, continued to be worn instead of the blue fatigue caps, which were never issued.

In common with many regiments of the time, the majority of Indiana Volunteer N.C.O.s did not carry the impractical sword. They replaced it with a leather cartridge box worn on the belt to the right of the buckle.

Initially the state's early regiments were issued with the Model 1842 musket. Later, however, Indiana purchased 40,000 far superior P1853 Enfield rifled muskets with which it armed approximately half of its volunteers, equipping the rest with a modern mixture of domestically produced weapons, notably the M1855 "Harpers Ferry" rifle with its fiercesome sword bayonet.

In accordance with Federal military thinking, the Indiana regiments were not brigaded together but instead served independently under a number of commands. The 19th Indiana was arguably the most famous. Organized in Indianapolis on 29 July 1861, it arrived in Washington on 5 August to join the army then forming for an attack south into Virginia. Commanded at various times by Solomon Meredith, Samuel Williams, and John Lindley, it served throughout much of its existence as part of the Iron Brigade of the West. It first saw service at Lewinsville, Virginia (11 September 1861) as part of the Army of the Potomac, and subsequently fought at the 2nd Battle of Manassas (Bull Run), losing 259 out of 423 engaged, at South Mountain where it sustained 53 casualties, and at Antietam (Sharpsburg) where it lost a further 72 officers and

Major General Thomas Meagher, photographed here proudly wearing the "Hardee" hat of the Iron Brigade of the West.

Headdress: The wide-brimmed light-blue hats initially issued to the regiment were ultimately replaced by darker "Hardee" hats later to become the hallmark of the "Iron Brigade of the West."

Jacket: With the exception of the 11th Indianas who wore Zouave-style jackets and trousers, the regiment was issued with gray uniforms trimmed with black. Despite representations from Washington, these remained popular at grass roots level until the end of the war. The more realistic, however, changed to blue.

Weapons: Initially troops were issued with M1842 muskets. Later approximately half received the much improved British P1853 Enfield rifled musket.

men from the remaining 200 combatants. In 1863, the bloody Battle of Gettysburg cost it a staggering 210 killed, injured and missing out of a total of 288 engaged, while in the fighting from the Wilderness to Petersburg (5 May – 30 July 1864), a further 226 fell. Major Isaac May was killed at the head of his men at the 2nd Manassas, Lieutenant Colonel Alois Bachman died at Antietam, and, most tragically of all, Colonel Williams was killed at the Wilderness.

Many of the newer volunteer regiments, although lacking the prestige of the older units and the *elan* of the Iron Brigade, nevertheless fought bravely and well throughout their engagement. Under the command initially of Colonel William Brown and subsequently of Colonels John Wheeler, William Taylor and William Orr, the 20th Indiana served with distinction from its inception in July 1861 to Appomattox and the final victory. Tasked in the early stages with the uninspiring duty of guarding the railroad near Cockeysville, Maryland, north of Baltimore, against Confederate sympathizers and raiding parties, the regiment was moved on 24 September to Hatteras Inlet, North Carolina, and then to Fort Monroe, Virginia for the winter. While there, it witnessed the *Monitor-Merrimac* (*Virginia*) engagement (see p. 58), lining the banks to protect the disabled *Congress* from capture, but otherwise saw no direct action. Sent to reinforce McClellan's army on the Peninsula, the regiment was assigned to Brigadier Robinson's 1st Brigade, itself part of Major General Kearney's 3rd Division, III Corps. On 25 June 1862, while forming part of the army's left flank, the regiment experienced its first major fight, sustaining 125 casualties when the

The Indiana Regiment played a key role in the capture of Fort Donelson.

Confederates attacked in strength in the "Orchards" area. The regiment was again heavily engaged at Glendale, suffering ten fatalities, and at 2nd Manassas when a further 45, including Colonel Brown, were killed.

Due to its heavy losses, III Corps was withdrawn from the front immediately prior to Antietam and assigned to the defenses of Washington. From there, the 20th Indiana marched northwest to Gettysburg where, as part of Ward's Brigade, Birney's Division, it lost 156 all ranks, including Colonel Wheeler, in the ensuing battle. In 1864, during the final stages of the war, the regiment was transferred to II Corps where it sustained further heavy casualties in the Wilderness (33 killed), at Spotsylvania (18 killed), and at the siege of Petersburg, during which it suffered a further 22 fatalities including Lieutenant Colonel Meikel.

Under the inspired leadership of Colonel Silas Colgrove, the 27th Indiana left the state on 15 September 1861 to join Banks' command in Washington. As part of Gordon's 3rd Brigade, Williams' 1st Division, it first saw action in Jackson's campaign in the Shenandoah Valley in the summer of 1862. Assigned with the rest of the division to the newly formed XII Corps in September 1862, it fought with distinction at Cedar Mountain, losing 50 casualties, and at Antietam where it lost a further 209. In the thick of the fighting at Chancellorsville and at Gettysburg, where it suffered 150 and 110 dead and wounded respectively, the regiment constantly refused to yield ground, maintaining at all times the highest standards of morale. Uniquely, throughout its three years of service, while many units around it were all but disintegrating, the 27th lost only one man to desertion. As the war drew to a close, the regiment was posted to the West where, during its final formal engagement at Resaca, Georgia (13–16 May 1864), it was credited not only with capturing the colors and the colonel of the 38th Alabama Regiment but with inflicting five times its own casualties on the enemy. At a time when many regiments were beginning to scent victory and not unnaturally were demonstrating a marked reluctance to fight, the 27th continued to epitomize the fighting qualities of the Indiana volunteers as a whole by refusing to compromise the high standards which had made them so respected a part of the Union cause.

The 1855-pattern Harpers Ferry musket was produced in large numbers throughout the war.

U.S. MILITARY RAILROAD ENGINEERS

The military potential of the railroads had been exploited by several European powers well before the onset of the American Civil War. As early as 1830, the British War Office had experimented with moving troops by rail, and in 1842, Prussia had begun actively to consider the feasibility of constructing new lines which, while serving the day-to-day needs of the civilian population, would allow the rapid movement of troops from its eastern to its western borders or vice versa should both be threatened simultaneously. Within three years, tracks had been laid to both frontiers, and in 1846, the Prussian army moved 12,000 men from Potsdam, its headquarters on the outskirts of Berlin, east to Posen (now the Polish city of Poznán) in record time.

The first recorded use of railroads in war came in 1859 when France invaded Italy in response to a request for help from the Vatican. Within the space of 86 days, the French had moved 600,000 men and 129,000 horses to the border. Such efficiency, however, brought with it its own problems: large numbers of men and horses were deposited in isolated areas at railheads where they were forced to wait, hungry and militarily impotent, while their rations, ammunition, and other supplies were brought up by conventional mule train.

At the outbreak of the Civil War, there were approximately 22,000 miles of track in the North

compared with 9,000 miles in the Confederacy. At its best, Union track was excellent, far better than that in the South, but at its worst, it was wholly inadequate for the task ahead. Sleepers were generally laid straight on bare earth without any stone or gravel ballast; gradients were avoided as far as possible to minimize the strain on the under-powered locomotives; and lines were routed around hills to avoid the expense of constructing the cuttings and tunnels which would otherwise have been needed to keep the gradients below an acceptable minimum.

Due to the poor track, the large number of sharp bends caused by the rerouting around natural obstacles, and the relatively low power of the engines, few trains exceeded 25mph or pulled weights exceeding 150 tons. The lines themselves were owned by a multitude of small but fiercely competitive companies, few of whom had reached any form of commercial agreement with their rivals. Gages varied considerably, and each company operated its own depots, making uninterrupted long-distance travel all but impossible. Depots were often miles apart, necessitating the time-consuming transfer of passengers and freight by wagon before a journey might be continued.

Many Northern lines were too far to the north or west to become involved tactically; they simply carried on as before, growing rich on the increased

Heavy mortars were occasionally mounted on reinforced railroad trolleys and fired into the enemy's defensive positions from specially constructed tracks. Recoil was a constant problem.

Although strenuous attempts were made to bring the railroads, particularly those in the west, under Federal control, the majority of engineers remained civilian. Few if any wore uniform. Weapons were carried primarily for personal protection or to settle feuds. However the Confederate cavalry made frequent sorties against Federal lines of communication and danger was therefore never far away.

volume of traffic. Those closer to the battlefront became more directly a part of the war. Occasionally this led to a conflict of interests for the railroad directors – never more so than in 1861 when the president of the Baltimore & Ohio was threatened with both the confiscation by the Confederacy of his company's track laid within the jurisdiction of the Confederate state of Virginia if he carried Federal troops, and with an indictment for treason from the U.S. Secretary of the Interior if he refused.

Within days of the attack on Fort Sumter, Lincoln created the United States Military Railway Service with notional powers of seizure over all Northern lines. At first, very little was done to implement these powers, and the various companies were left to handle military traffic as if it were civilian. However, as the war progressed and the army swelled from under 20,000 to nearly 2 million men, the existing system with its multitude of owners and operating procedures, its plethora of gages, and, above all, its petty rivalries began to prove wholly inadequate. In August 1861, Thomas Scott, vice president of the Pennsylvania Railroad, was made Assistant Secretary of War with special responsibility for the military control of railroads. His first act was to appoint Daniel Craig McCallum, then the general secretary of the Erie Railroad, as military director and superintendent of military railroads in the West. A lively Scot and brilliant engineer, McCallum immediately set about the consolidation of the tracks under his authority, adding many miles to their existing lengths.

Shortly afterward Herman Haupt, a civil engineer and lecturer in mathematics at Penn College near Gettysburg, was appointed to a similar post in the East. Haupt's first task was to rebuild the elements of the Richmond, Fredericksburg & Potomac Railroad which had been comprehensively destroyed by the Confederates during their retreat before the advance of McDowell's troops on Richmond. The Union had been relying on the track for the transportation of all its supplies, and Haupt had the formidable task of assembling a construction force, gathering raw material, and repairing the line, all of which he completed in a record three weeks – a feat made all the more remarkable when it is realized that his duties included the rebuilding of a wooden bridge 400 ft (122m) long and 100 ft (30m) above the Potomac. Haupt was promoted to brigadier general in September 1862 but resigned less than a year later, expressing a willingness to continue without official rank or pay as long as no restrictions were placed on his work. Freed of government bureaucracy, he continued to serve the Union faithfully for the rest of the war.

Initially, the Confederacy utilized its limited rail resources far more successfully than the Union. Prior to the 1st Battle of Manassas (Bull Run), Jackson's entire brigade was moved by rail to Manassas Junction, allowing it to take up a strategic position ahead of the advancing Federals. (Ironically it would have been joined by Bartow's brigade of Georgians had the railroad workers not refused to work the overtime necessary to make a second trip). Lee made excellent use of the railroads during the Seven Days campaign in defense of Richmond in June/July 1862 and again in the recapture of Knoxville in September 1863.

Attempts by the Union to move its far larger

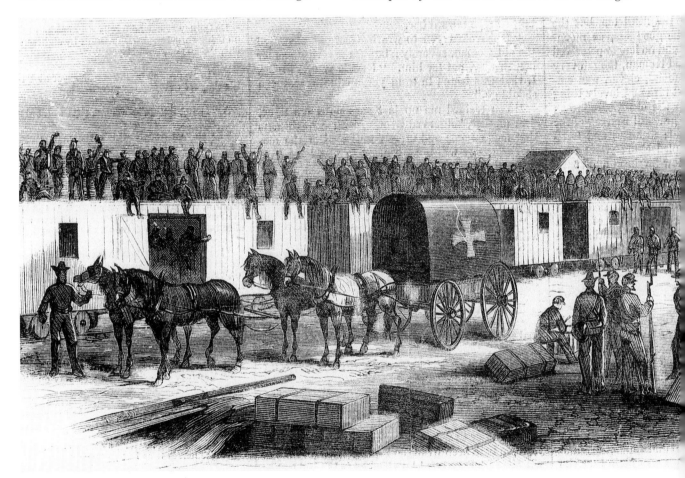

Federal reinforcements arriving by train during the battle at Peebles' Farm, September 1864. Acute overcrowding of rolling stock led to numerous derailments.

Herman Haupt in his personal locomotive, from which he supervised the construction gangs. He is standing on the footplate, by the circular window.

numbers of troops the considerable distances required were often frustrated by the railroad's total inability to cope. When Grant attempted to relieve Rosecrans' beleaguered troops in Chattanooga in October 1863, he found the Nashville & Chattanooga Railroad sadly lacking. In poor condition, inefficiently administered, and hazardous, its single track was simply incapable of moving the minimum of 30 supply trucks required daily to sustain the defenders. Eventually three existing one-track railroads – the Nashville & Chattanooga, the Memphis & Charleston, and the Nashville & Decatur – were linked to form a 200-mile one-way circuit which proved just sufficient for the task. Even this

could not operate until an entire infantry division had been allocated the task of repairing the southern perimeter of the arc, including no fewer than 18 bridges destroyed by raiding Confederate cavalry.

Sherman's famous "march to the sea" in December 1864 depended heavily on the railroad for the maintenance of its supply line which, toward the end of the campaign, stretched for over 450 miles. Divided into three sectors – Louisville–Nashville (185 miles), Nashville–Chattanooga (151 miles), and, eventually, Chattanooga–Atlanta (137 miles) – the track was constantly liable to attack by Confederate raiding parties and, forward from Chattanooga, had to be closely guarded by Federal troops who were badly needed elsewhere. Once the track was built as far as Chattanooga, finding sufficient locomotives and rolling stock proved a logistical nightmare. Sherman requisitioned every locomotive entering Nashville but even these were not enough, and it was only when engines were brought from the far north, civilian travel was banned, and movement of any kind was limited to the transport of essential food, ammunition, and equipment that supply at last outstripped demand.

The operation of the railroads was greatly facilitated by the growth in the use of the electric telegraph and the introduction of Morse code. Every station was connected to the system and could be used to relay orders to trains, which would be picked up at the next depot. In this way, trains could be requisitioned from great distances and moved along alien track with relative ease. Above all, stretches of track could be kept clear once a train had entered them.

Despite the tremendous improvements which the railroad system underwent throughout the war, it was never completely capable of fulfilling the tasks allotted it. Whether this was due to the inherent reluctance of the majority of the proprietors to relinquish control of their companies to the State, or whether it was due to the total inability of the higher command to comprehend the virtual impossibility of blending literally hundreds of often tiny and mutually distrustful organizations into one homogeneous unit remains a moot point.

UNION ARMY STAFF OFFICERS

Brevet Major General Rufus Ingalls, U.S. Cavalry, photographed wearing the uniform of a brigadier.

Not unnaturally, the miniscule pre-war staff which had ably served the peacetime army of 16,000 officers and men proved totally inadequate for the needs of the 2 million enlisted into war service. As a result, more soldiers were promoted to the rank of full general between 1861 and 1865 than had served in the entire Engineer Corps in 1860.

With the exception of army commanders, general officers were expected to lead from the front. Long supply lines were not encouraged nor was a reliance on second-hand information. Of the 583 officers appointed to the rank of general throughout the war, 47 were either killed in action or subsequently died of their wounds, a level of casualties unrivaled before or since.

Although regulations for the organization of staff and their duties did exist, these were largely ignored by many of the field commanders, who preferred to depend on the advice and assistance of a small nucleus of trusted personnel than on that of a large number of inexperienced and, on occasion, political appointees. When General Grant was promoted to the newly created rank of lieutenant general, he was authorized a personal staff of a brigadier general as chief-of-staff, four aides-de-camp with the rank of lieutenant colonel, and two lieutenant colonels as military secretaries. In the field, Grant supplemented these with two lieutenant colonels acting as assistant adjutant general and assistant inspector general, three staff captains, and two junior officers as A.D.C.s.

Unlike a modern headquarters, which differentiates totally between supply and administration, overall control of all aspects of staff work was

Headdress: Most senior staff officers interpreted dress regulations loosely. Their black felt hats were meant to be 6.25-in tall with brims of 3.25-in worn pinned up on the right, but most wore them slouched for comfort. However the cap badge with its silver embroidered letters "US" inscribed in Old English within an embroidered wreath seems to have been universally worn.

Tunic: Theoretically major-generals wore double-breasted frock coats with nine buttons placed in threes in each of two rows while brigadiers had eight buttons in each row placed in pairs. In practice many commanders wore far simpler sack coats with buttons of their choosing. Regulation standing collars were usually abandoned as impractical.

General Blanker, at the
head of his brigade,
covering the retreat from
Bull Run.

vested in the chief-of-staff. A.D.C.s were used to transmit orders direct from the commander to the troops on the ground with the result that, occasionally, intermediate commanders were circumvented. Inevitably this led to confusion, if not catastrophe. When in overall supreme command, Grant, a man renowned for direct action, frequently took personal control of elements of the Army of the Potomac, leaving its commanding general – the brilliant if irascible but fortunately loyal Meade – confused and impotent. Numerous attempts were made by Grant's staff to undermine Meade's status and position, but fortunately, although Grant listened attentively to their blatant disloyalty to a senior officer, he ignored their pleas for Meade's dismissal, allowing him to continue with at least the vestiges of authority.

General Andrew Humphreys, the chief-of-staff to General Meade and a highly competent and experienced regular officer, summed up the weaknesses of this dual command system when he later wrote of his experiences in Virginia:

> There were two officers commanding the same army. Such a mixed command was not calculated to produce the best results that either singly was capable of bringing about. It naturally caused some vagueness and uncertainty as to the exact sphere of each, and sometimes took away from the positiveness, fullness and earnestness of the consideration of an intended operation or tactical movement that, had there been but one commander, would have had the most earnest attention and corresponding action.

Left to his own devices in the West, Sherman was able to devolve a smaller, more intimate staff system. Doing away completely with the position of chief-of-staff, he ordered each of his regimental colonels to appoint a competent adjutant, a quartermaster, a commissary, and a team of three to four doctors to deal with the daily needs of each individual unit. Each brigade and divisional headquarters was given a similar team, the divisional HQ supplemented with a cadre of engineers. Unlike Grant who frequently interfered with the activities of his subordinates, Sherman accepted totally the need for delegation, granting his juniors immense power when necessary. In direct contrast to Meade, who admittedly was burdened with the execution of many of Grant's more mundane duties, Sherman's tactical headquarters typically consisted of no more than six wagons supported by a company of Ohio sharpshooters for protection and a company of Alabama irregular cavalry to provide orderlies and carry messages.

The greatest weakness in the Federal staff system lay in the fact that the quartermaster, commissary, and ordnance departments were all fiercely independent of the commander in the field, owing their allegiance direct to their masters in Washington. Although Grant complained bitterly of this anomaly, occasionally to Lincoln himself, nothing was done to subordinate these support units which remained independent throughout the war.

In the early stages of the conflict, staff officers, few of whom had any real military experience, were generally of a very low standard. Many commanders refused to commit their orders to writing, preferring to rely on verbal dissemination which frequently led to confusion – and occasionally on a gigantean scale. Exceptionally, Grant wrote out the majority of his orders and instructions himself, dispatching them via courier. Although this increased the possibility of compromise through loss or capture, it completely removed the fear of misunderstanding and added weight to orders which might otherwise have been ignored by independently minded subordinates.

Matters improved steadily as individuals gained in experience, so much so that the withdrawal of the Army of the Potomac from Cold Harbor across the James River in June 1864 is still regarded as one of the finest examples of staff planning and efficiency in the history of the United States army. Under the cover of darkness and in complete secrecy, the entire army disengaged and moved south, crossing the James River via a 2,100 ft (640m) long pontoon bridge constructed by Captain G.H. Mendell and 450 engineers in only eight hours. General Fuller described the entire exercise as "one of the finest operations of war ever carried out." Although this is certainly true, it must be remembered that had it not been for Lieutenant Colonels (later Generals) Comstock and Porter who, as Grant's A.D.C.s liaised with the subordinate commanders, reconnoitered the route, and planned the site for the bridge, so complicated a maneuver would almost certainly have ended in chaos.

The heavy losses among front line officers during the   bloody fighting of 1863 and 1864 did much to undermine morale, particularly among the new recruits, many of whom were conscripts without the commitment of the earlier volunteers. Low morale often manifested itself in indiscipline, malingering, and desertion, which occasionally reached horrific proportions. Immediately after the Fredericksburg campaign (November–December 1862), desertions from the Army of the Potomac reached 200 per day, and at one stage, 85,123 men from that army alone had gone AWOL. There can be no doubt that an injection of good replacement officers into brigades and regiments which had suffered badly would have done much for morale, yet inexplicably Washington refused to sanction such a move. Instead, regiments which were too far below strength to function properly were reduced to battalion status and their surplus officers discharged or offered the possibility of a commission in a newly formed regiment. In the words of Sherman:

If the worst enemy of the United States were to devise a plan to break down our army, a better one could not be attempted. Two years have been spent in educating colonels, captains, sergeants and corporals and now they are to be driven out of the service.

Standards of dress among general officers varied widely. Meade was a stickler for regulations, insisting that his officers wore regulation uniform although he occasionally allowed himself the luxury of an individualistic form of headdress. Grant, by contrast, regarded details of uniform as a tiresome irrelevancy and allowed his staff maximum personal discretion. Generals were issued with a double-breasted frock coat with a dark blue velvet collar and cuffs. Major generals wore twin rows of nine buttons in groups of threes, brigadier generals eight buttons in pairs. On formal occasions, a gold epaulette with silver stars (two for a major general and one for a brigadier) was worn on each shoulder. At other times, a black shoulder strap edged with gold embroidery and containing the same stars was substituted. The uniform was completed with a white shirt, black tie, dark blue waistcoat, plain dark blue trousers, and a black felt hat pinned up on the right side.

In the field, many senior officers wore dark blue variants of the civilian "sack coat" with turned-down blue collars and plain blue trousers. The hat was frequently "punched up" in the manner of a dunce's cap emphasizing the cap badge incorporating the Old English letters "us" within a gold embroidered wreath.

Some officers, notably Major General Warren, always maintained the highest personal standards in the presence of their men. Others, such as Burnside, dressed for comfort although rarely to the degree of Grant who frequently resembled an ill-kempt civilian rather than the supreme commander of the Union army.

Staff officers from the Adjutant General's, Inspector General's, Quartermaster and Pay departments wore the same basic uniform with plain blue collars and cuffs. Field-grade staff officers wore twin rows of seven buttons, junior officers one row. Epaulettes were marked with the wearer's corps insignia as well as his rank insignia.

Major General George G. Meade photographed with his staff officers.

TROOPER: U.S. VOLUNTEER CAVALRY

Prior to the outbreak of the war, the cavalry had played only the smallest part in the life and organization of the U.S. Army. It had none of the panache of the European hussars or lancers with their flamboyant uniforms and socially conscious officer corps, and lacked a sense of tradition both on and off the battlefield. Simplistically, the cavalry was regarded as an expensive irrelevancy by the military commanders of the day. Yet by Appomattox, the Union had brought into being no fewer than 258 cavalry regiments supported by a further 170 independent cavalry companies.

For the first two years of the war, the Union commanders demonstrated a marked lack of understanding of the potential of the massed mounted attack against raw infantry, preferring to commit the cavalry in small groups whenever and wherever they could be exploited in the short term. To compound the problem, individual cavalry units were frequently taken out of the line to act as escorts for convoys, guards for headquarters, military police, and even garrisons for captured enemy towns. However, by early 1864 it had at last been accepted that the Confederate use of cavalry *en masse* was far superior. Brigades and, later, divisions were formed and large scale maneuvers in all environments practiced. As the Union blockade of the South intensified, so the quality of the Confederate cavalry diminished, until by mid-1864, its indisputable superiority became a matter of history. The performance of cavalry is largely governed by the state of its mounts, and by the final winter of the war, Confederate horses were dying in large numbers from exhaustion compounded by malnutrition. Even so, by this stage the Union cavalry had improved so considerably that it is probable that its

better units would have proved more than a match for the vaunted forces of Jeb Stuart at their height.

Prior to the war, the role of the cavalry had been seen almost exclusively as the suppression of the Indian nations in the far West. When Texas voted to secede on 1 February 1861 and the 1st U.S. Cavalry was forced to retire in haste to the safety of Kansas, a void was left in the sparsely populated areas of the Midwest. Acutely aware of the very real danger of an Indian uprising, Congress authorized the creation of a number of volunteer regiments to take the place of the hard corps of regulars whose presence was required urgently for the battles to come.

Few of the Northern states had a sufficient surplus of horsemen, let alone mounts, to raise whole regiments without considerable difficulty, and they therefore tended to concentrate on the creation of new infantry regiments to the detriment of the cavalry. Furthermore, whereas local dignitaries tended to regard it as their patriotic duty to raise, arm, equip, and even train units which would later bear their names, few if any seemed inclined to support the cavalry. Consequently, few troops were raised until the autumn of 1861, and of these, hardly any were capable of active service until the following summer. Fortunately for the settlers, the Indians failed to take advantage of this critical period, preferring to concentrate on survival through the bitter winter, and thus denied themselves their greatest opportunity in decades to strike a blow against a weakened and divided enemy.

An indication of the lack of natural horsemen in the Northern states can be gained from a comparison of the number of infantry and cavalry regiments raised. Indiana, for instance, raised 13 cavalry and 152 infantry regiments, Illinois 17

By 1865 the Horse Artillery and Cavalry had learned to work together as a single potent entity, capable of exploiting the many weaknesses in the rapidly dwindling Confederate lines.

Headdress: Many officers wore the plain McClellan hat with its thin pointed peak in preference to the heavier regulation issue.

Jacket: Although the frock coat remained official wear for officers, many preferred the short plain jacket. Some, as here, even wore their dress jacket devoid of all formal accoutrements save for one or two rows of buttons.

Weapons: Uniquely, until 1863 the 6th Pennsylvania Cavalry carried a European-style lance. An excellent weapon in the hands of shock troops trained to fight in the close confines of continental Europe, the lance proved quite useless in the open plains of the United States and was eventually discarded in favor of the more conventional saber, pistol and carbine.

cavalry and 156 infantry, Iowa 9 cavalry and 51 infantry, Missouri (a relatively rural state) 32 cavalry and 266 infantry, and New York 32 cavalry and 254 infantry.

As the war progressed, Federal armies in the West made increasing use of mounted infantry, frequently including them with cavalry regiments in cavalry brigades. Illinois and Indiana, in particular, provided a large number of mounted infantry, suggesting that neither state had made full initial use of its available horsemen. The 17th and 72nd Indiana Infantry Regiments, for example, were mounted in February and March 1863 respectively and both dismounted in November 1864, while the 9th and 92nd Illinois Infantry were both mounted in March 1863 and retained that status for the rest of the war.

Pennsylvania provided perhaps the most unusual cavalry unit. Rush's Lancers (6th Pennsylvania

Cavalry) were armed with European-style lances, as well as pistols and the occasional carbine, until 1863 when they reverted to conventional weaponry.

Other unusual volunteer units were less successful. The 3rd New Jersey Cavalry – or "1st U.S. Hussars" as they preferred to be known – were quickly christened the "Butterflies" in response to the gaudiness of their uniforms, especially their heavily yellow-braided hussar jackets. Gentle mockery, however, turned to outright contempt when during a critical stage of the Battle of Yellow Tavern, six miles north of Richmond, on 11 May 1864, the entire unit retreated in disarray as soon as they came under enemy artillery fire. Suggestions by an embarrassed company commander that, the shells having stampeded the horses, the men had gone looking for them provoked an observer from the 7th Maine Infantry to exclaim in frustration, "We had many kinds of material in the Army of the

Officers and troopers of the 1st U.S. Cavalry rest after the Battle of Brandy Station during which, for the first time, they proved that the Confederate cavalry was not invincible.

Potomac and use for most of it, but not for the 'Uhlanen' (cavalry)."

More typical if less superficially impressive was the 1st Independent Battalion, Ohio Volunteer Cavalry. Raised in late 1861 and trained in Camp Dennison, Ohio, it was sent to Benton Barracks, Missouri in March 1862 and from there to Fort Laramie, Wyoming. Redesignated the 11th Ohio Volunteer Cavalry Regiment, the unit was subsequently split up between a number of posts including Fort Halleck, Sweetwater Station, and Fort Mitchell.

Throughout the war, over 20,000 volunteer cavalrymen were deployed in the West, although it was not until August 1862 that they were first called on to fight. A minor rising of the Wahpeton Sioux in Minnesota in which five settlers were killed quickly escalated into a general uprising in the area, during which the Redwood Agency was attacked and Fort Ridgley and the town of New

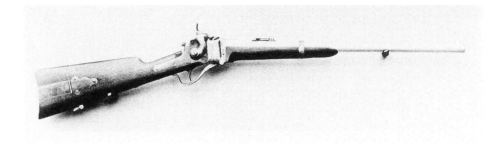

Ulm besieged. After relief units reached the area on 3 September and defeated the Indians at the Battle of Birch Coulee, a concerted attempt was made to pursue and destroy the remaining Sioux. A month later, the Indians suffered a heavy defeat at the hands of the Union infantry at the Battle of Wood Lake. However, their leaders escaped to the north chased by a volunteer brigade comprising three infantry regiments, an artillery company and the 1st Minnesota Mounted Rangers. Again battle was joined, on this occasion near Bismarck, North Dakota, and again the Indians were roundly defeated. Thereafter Brigadier General Alfred Sully with the 6th Iowa and 2nd Nebraska cavalry regiments was ordered to beat the remaining Sioux into submission, neutralizing them as a fighting force for the rest of the war. On 3 September 1863, a year to the day after the Battle of Birch Coulee, four companies of the 6th Iowa met and were surrounded by 4,000 Sioux braves in the region of Ellendale, North Dakota. A single cavalryman managed to escape the trap to bring word to Sully, who immediately advanced with the rest of his brigade, trapping the unsuspecting Sioux in a ravine. The Indians managed to fight off the cavalry until nightfall when the survivors escaped, leaving some 3,000 warriors dead, wounded, or prisoner. The cavalry lost 22 killed and 50 wounded in the engagement, which subsequently became known as the Battle of Whitestone Hill, and inflicted upon the Sioux their greatest ever defeat at the hands of the U.S. Cavalry.

In July 1864, Sully – his brigade now reinforced by the 7th Iowa Cavalry, two companies of Dakota cavalry, Brackett's Minnesota Cavalry Battalion, the 2nd Minnesota Cavalry, and some assorted infantry – advanced along the Missouri River intent on destroying once and for all the final vestiges of the Sioux nation. Battle was joined at Killdeer, near the Spring River, on 28 July, and a force of 1,600 braves was routed by a spirited saber charge by Brackett's Minnesotans. Sully continued his relentless advance, reaching the Yellowstone River on 12 August, Fort Berthold on 28 August, and Fort Rice on 8 September.

As the Civil War approached its conclusion, cavalry volunteers from the East, who in the main had enlisted specifically to fight the Confederacy but who were now largely stationed many hundreds of miles from home in the barren wastes of the West, began to agitate to return home. However, not one unit mutinied, while some, notably the 11th Ohio Cavalry which was not disbanded until 12 July 1866, remained in uniform long after the South had surrendered.

Sharps carbines proved popular with the cavalry on both sides.

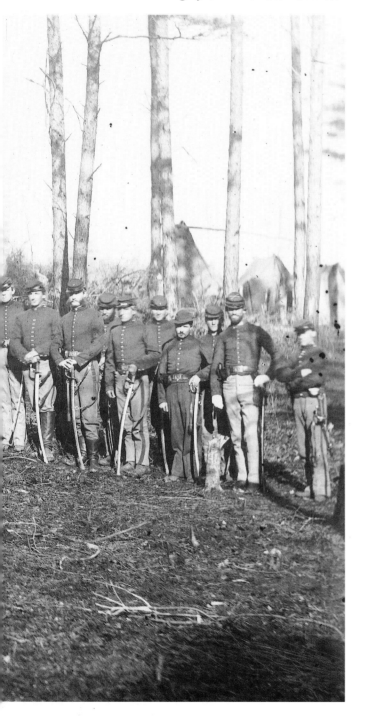

THE PENNSYLVANIA RESERVES

Few units in the Federal army epitomized so precisely the effects of the inefficiency and petty mongering of the politicians of 1861 as did the Pennsylvania Reserves. Within days of the attack on Fort Sumter, literally tens of thousands of loyal Unionists offered their services to the colors. The administration, both nationally and at state level, was simply overwhelmed. Anticipating a longer war than that envisaged by the over-optimistic central government, Governor Andrew Curtin of Pennsylvania continued to accept men into service long after Secretary for War Simon Cameron had declared the state's allocation filled. When the jealous and ambitious Cameron refused to accept the new regiments, Curtin "adopted" them by authorizing the creation of a Pennsylvania Reserve Corps, assuming (correctly) that they would soon be inducted into the regular army. Originally designated the 1st to 13th Pennsylvania Reserves, this unique division was eventually accepted into the Union army and renamed the 30th to 42nd Pennsylvania Volunteers. Most soldiers, however, insisted on keeping the old names, causing administrative havoc and confusion wherever they went.

Although it was originally intended that the Reserves would adopt uniforms similar to those of the regular forces, at the time of their induction supplies were exhausted, with the result that the units were forced to remain in "cadet gray" until the end of the war. Quite how many Pennsylvanians were mistaken for the enemy and shot by Union snipers because of this administrative nonsense has never been recorded.

Initially, all 13 regiments were grouped into three brigades and one large division. (The 1st

Pennsylvania Cavalry and 1st Pennsylvania Light Artillery were at first also attached to the Reserves Division but were transferred out within a few months.) Originally part of McDowell's I Corps, the division transferred to Porter's V Corps prior to the Peninsula campaign but returned to I Corps in the late summer of 1862, remaining with it throughout the battles of 2nd Manassas (Bull Run), Antietam (Sharpsburg), and Fredericksburg. Having sustained heavy losses, the division was ordered to Washington later that year for rest and recuperation. Almost immediately McCandless's 1st and Fisher's 3rd Brigades requested to be returned to the Army of the Potomac to help in the defense of their own native Pennsylvania which by then had come under serious threat from Lee's advancing Army of Northern Virginia. Assigned to Meade's (later Sykes') V Corps, they were redesignated the 3rd Division under the command of General Samuel Crawford and, as such, fought tenaciously at Gettysburg and in subsequent campaigns. The last action of the Reserves as a unit was at Bethesda Church near Richmond on 1 June 1864.

When the Reserves were mustered out later that month, a large number re-enlisted. Reorganized along with new recruits into the 190th and 191st Pennsylvania Volunteers, collectively designated the Veteran Reserve Brigade, they fought as part of Ayres' Division, V Corps, at Cold Harbor.

Confusingly, brigade organization within the division did not remain a constant. At the Battle of Fredericksburg, McCandless's 1st Brigade incorporated the 1st, 2nd, 6th, and 13th Regiments, Magilton's 2nd Brigade comprised the 3rd, 4th, 7th, and 8th, while Fisher's 3rd accounted for the 5th, 9th,

An attack by the Pennsylvania Bucktails, led by Colonel Thomas Kane, against Stonewall Jackson's Virginians in the woods near Harrisburg, Virginia, on 7 June 1862.

Headdress: As a concession to common sense all Pennsylvania Reserves were issued with standard issue Federal blue kepis.

Tunic: By late 1862 the majority of reserves wore blue tunics although a number retained the original "cadet gray" blouses and the majority still wore gray trousers.

Weapons: Many reserve units, notably the 13th, were recruited from the backwoods and included an unusually large number of excellent shots. Many carried personally acquired sporting rifles in preference to issue muskets. As the war progressed and hand to hand fighting became more common, the once maligned bayonet became more evident.

Company F, 114th
Pennsylvania Infantry,
pose for a photograph.
Note the camouflaged
encampment at the rear.

10th, 11th, and 12th. The 1st and 3rd Brigades reformed with the same regiments when they rejoined the Army of the Potomac prior to Gettysburg, whereas the 2nd disbanded. Of its former members, the 3rd and 4th fought with the Army of West Virginia, distinguishing themselves at Cloyd's Mountain (9–10 May 1864), while the 7th and 8th were assigned to the 1st and 3rd Brigades respectively, acquitting themselves with their customary zeal during the Wilderness campaign. Although they were supposed to take part in the same battle, the 9th was found to be so depleted prior to the campaign that it was returned to Washington in May 1864 for premature discharge.

Throughout its history, the Reserves Division was blessed with excellent commanders. Formed initially by George Archibald McCall, a veteran of the Seminole and Mexican wars and an excellent

tactician, command passed to John Fulton Reynolds on the division's induction into the Army of the Potomac (although, strangely, it continued to bear McCall's name). General George Meade, later to be victor at Gettysburg, commanded for a short period before his promotion, after which the division passed to Crawford. Although the most famous of its commanders, Meade was arguably the least effective, if only because of his irascible temperament. In the words of General Grant, Meade was "an officer of great merit ... brave and conscientious," yet he "was unfortunately of a temper that would get beyond his control at times ... making it unpleasant at times, even in battle, for those around him to approach him even with information."

To comprehend fully the extent of the Reserves' involvement throughout the war, it is necessary to analyze in more depth the part played by individual regiments.

The 8th Reserves, 37th Pennsylvania Volunteers, was formed in the steel city of Pittsburgh on 28 June 1861. Initially seconded to outpost duties in northern Virginia, it later joined McClellan's forces on the Peninsula. It sustained 230 casualties during the Seven Days' campaign, mainly at Gaines's Mill, and subsequently fought in every major engagement undertaken by the Army of the Potomac throughout the rest of the year. It lost 131 men, almost half its remaining strength, attacking Marye's Heights during the Battle of Fredericksburg. After a short respite in Washington, the regiment rejoined the army, fighting with distinction during the Wilderness campaign and at Spotsylvania, where it lost 17 killed.

The 10th Reserves, 39th Volunteers, were drawn from the intelligentsia of the western part of the state, with "teachers and pupils serving in the ranks together." Company "D" recruited exclusively from the students of Jefferson College, and Company "I" from their rivals at Allegheny College. In the fight for Gaines's Mill, 134 officers and men fell.

The 11th Reserves, 40th Volunteers, suffered the heaviest losses within the division, the eighth highest *pro rata* losses of the entire Union army. Formed in western Pennsylvania, it too fought at Gaines's Mill where it was cut off and forced to surrender. Exchanged in August 1862, it rejoined the Army of the Potomac before it left for the Peninsula. It subsequently sustained such losses during the battles of 2nd Manassas (Bull Run) and South Mountain that it mustered at Antietam (Sharpsburg) fewer than 200 combatants strong. Bolstered by a few recruits and the return of the wounded, the regi-

ment fought at Fredericksburg with 394 officers and men, of whom 211 were killed or wounded.

The 13th Reserves, known as the "Bucktails," were perhaps the most colorful of all the Pennsylvania regiments. Drawn from the farmers and lumbermen of the outer state, many of whom were excellent shots and insisted on providing their own weapons, the outfit was originally known as the Pennsylvania Rifles or the Kane County Rifles after its first colonel; Thomas Kane. Tradition has it that Private James Landregan of "I" Company, spying a deer's hide hanging outside a butcher's shop in Smethport, Pennsylvania where the regiment was then quartered, crossed the street, pulled out a knife, cut off its tail, and tucked it into his hat. Upon his return to headquarters, Colonel Kane, a man well endowed with a sense of humor and with an eye toward creating a tradition, decreed that in future the unit would be known as the "Bucktails." Thereafter every recruit was required to bring with him, as an indication of his marksmanship, the tail of a buck which he had shot. Four companies were seconded with Colonel Kane to the Army of the Shenandoah (against "Stonewall" Jackson), rejoining the regiment prior to the 2nd Battle of Manassas.

The gray uniforms worn by the Reserves differed greatly in style and texture, varying in color from drab or tan-gray to "cadet" light gray. Of the 13,000 pairs of "linen duck" and "undress brown linen" trousers purchased by the state, some would inevitably have found their way to the Reserves. From late 1862, individual members of the 1st to 13th were issued with blue jackets and virtually all with U.S. army dress hats in an attempt to prevent obvious confusion with the enemy, although some remained clad wholly in gray throughout the war.

The gallant charge of
Humphrey's Division,
including the
Pennsylvania Reserves,
at Fredericksburg.

GUNNER: HEAVY ARTILLERY

Despite the terrifyingly destructive power of heavy artillery, so aptly named the "God of War" by Napoleon, it was rarely used to its full potential by the Union army. At the outbreak of war, the North had 4,167 pieces of ordnance in its armory, of which a mere 163 were field guns and howitzers. Between 1861 and 1866, 7,892 cannon of all sizes were issued, 1,700 of which were forged in the massive Cold Spring Foundry.

Pre-war artillery techniques were sadly lacking, owing more to the lessons of the Mexican and Seminole wars than to modern innovation. Matters did improve somewhat when Major William Barry, a veteran of both wars and the spirited commanding officer of the 5th U.S. Artillery during its brilliant and successful defense of Fort Pickens at Pensacola, Florida (May 1861), was promoted and appointed Chief of Artillery within the Army of the Potomac. With the full support of McClellan, if not initially of Congress, Barry gathered together every regular artillery unit that could be spared from fortress duties and outlying areas, concentrating them under one command. By the time the Army of the Potomac was ready to take to the field in August 1861, it contained over half of all professional artillery units in the Union army.

Barry was never able fully to convince his masters of the need for independence of thought and action within the artillery. Although, after the Battle of Chancellorsville, the four batteries attached to each division were concentrated into brigades under direct corps command, with a reserve of 100 fieldpieces and 50 heavier guns set up as a reserve to enhance concentration of fire, the peculiar administrative needs of the guns were never fully understood. Staff structure within the artillery simply did not exist, with the result that planning had to be undertaken by experienced officers from the batteries, leaving actual command of the guns to inexperienced juniors or officers considered incompetent for staff duties. Well after the 1st Battle of Manassas (Bull Run), batteries in action were rarely if ever commanded by officers above the rank of major.

Immediately prior to the war, the rifled barrel had been developed and demonstrated but had been almost universally discounted by the ultra-conservative and all-powerful Congressional military lobby. Nor had it been accepted by the field commanders, who felt that the heavy forests where they considered most battles were likely to be fought would render useless the tremendous increase in range and accuracy afforded by rifling. To the traditionalist, artillery was a defensive weapon. Such smoothbores as the 12-pounder Napoleon, introduced from France and built in great numbers in the North, could project an exploding shell 1,200 yards (1,100m) if required, but

A battery of 12-pounder Napoleons dug into a coastal defensive position. As the war progressed, many such sites were abandoned and the guns transferred inland.

84

Headdress: Heavy artillery N.C.O.s and gunners were issued with standard blue kepis. However, the traditional Jäger horn insignia was replaced by large brass crossed cannon.

Tunic: Conventional trousers and tunics were issued. Red N.C.O.s' chevrons, trouser stripes, officers' frock-coat trim and shoulder tabs and hat cords demonstrated the wearers' membership of the artillery.

Weapons: All ranks were issued with short (26-in) swords. Usually these were abandoned as impractical although in some cases they were replaced with privately acquired cavalry sabers. Most officers carried pistols.

this was never regarded as their prime function. More importantly, and unlike rifled artillery, they could fire grapeshot 400 yards (365m) and canister 200 yards (185m) into the packed ranks of advancing infantry. It was accepted that smoothbore artillery was of little use in the attack. It could not fire into the protected positions of the defenders immediately prior to an attack without inviting heavy counter battery fire nor could it advance with the infantry without severe losses among the crews at the hands of accurate enemy rifle fire.

The standard U.S. heavy artillery at the outbreak of war consisted of:

- 12-, 24-, and 32-pounder howitzers, capable of throwing an explosive projectile high into the air, which would then fall steeply behind breastworks or walls where it might do most damage to an undefended enemy.
- 12-, 18-, and 24-pounder siege guns.
- 8-inch (20cm) and 24-pounder siege howitzers.
- 8-inch, 10-inch (25cm) and 24-pounder siege mortars.
- 32- and 42-pounder coast defense guns.

- 8- and 10-inch Columbiad coast guns.
- 8- and 10-inch coast howitzers.
- 10- and 13-inch (33cm) coast mortars.

The vast majority of heavy guns in use in the mid-19th century were not only smoothbore in manufacture but were constructed of bronze. Attempts had been made to substitute iron for bronze but successes had been rare. Notwithstanding this, and conscious of the large reserves of good ore to be found in the North and West, Washington persevered with the development of cast-iron barrels, commissioning a number of private gunsmiths to carry out independent experiments.

Many of the results were excellent. Captain Thomas Rodman patented the idea of casting an iron smoothbore gun around a water-cooled core, enabling the metal forming the inner part of the barrel to cool and harden first; as the outer layers cooled, it compressed the inner metal, giving it extra strength to withstand the explosive discharge of the shell. Trials carried out by the War Department in the late 1850's, in which a battery of conventional ordnance was tested against a battery of Rodmans, proved conclusively that the new cast-

A battery of heavy mortars, although relatively short-ranged and inaccurate, could deliver a murderous barrage against an enemy defensive emplacement.

iron barrels had a life expectancy more than eight times that of bronze guns. From 1859 onward all larger guns were cast on the Rodman system. Attempts were subsequently made to upgrade existing iron barrels, which until then had exhibited a dangerous propensity for blowing up, by retrofitting iron hoops over the breech ("Brooke" guns), but as is so often the case with stop-gap measures, success was limited.

As the war progressed, the effectiveness of heavy artillery as an offensive force was at last conceded. The traditional smoothbore having neither the range, accuracy, nor versatility for such a role, the necessity for rifling was begrudgingly accepted. Initial attempts by Colonel James and others simply to cut grooves in existing bronze smoothbores merely succeeded in weakening the barrel with inevitable catastrophic consequences for the crews. The most successful rifled gun of the time was the "Armstrong," designed by William Armstrong, an English lawyer turned hydraulic engineer. Wrought-iron hoops were heated and shrunk, one upon another, over the weakest part of the rifled iron barrel to give it additional compressed strength. More fundamentally, and for the first time in the history of heavy ordnance, the weapon was loaded from the breech rather than the muzzle. Although slow and cumbersome by modern standards, the Armstrong was revolutionary for its day and quickly became the model for a series of subsequent Union designs.

The heaviest guns served by the field artillery were the siege mortars: massive stubby weapons transported ponderously about battlefields on simple wooden carriages or, where possible, floated into position on large rafts. When fired from the land, mortars were usually positioned on a flat timber bed to spread the recoil and to offer as smooth a working surface as possible. The direction of fire was roughly estimated by the commander, who aligned a piece of weighted string, held vertically at arm's length and in the direction of the target, with a line painted along the top of the barrel. As the barrel was constantly at a given elevation, usually between 45 and 50 degrees, it was only possible to determine the range by altering the quantity of powder in the cartridge. Perhaps because of, rather than despite, their obvious indiscriminate fall of shot, siege mortars invariably had a devastating effect on civilian morale.

A particularly famous 13-inch siege mortar, nicknamed "Dictator" by its crew, was used by Company "G," the 1st Connecticut Heavy Artillery, between 9 and 31 July 1864, during the Siege of Petersburg. Mounted on a specially constructed railroad flatcar and positioned on a bend in the track to afford it lateral adjustment of fire, the monster hurled 45 200-lb rounds an average distance of 3,600 yards (3,292m) into the heart of the enemy position.

A number of heavy artillery regiments were formed from existing infantry units. The 8th New York Heavy Artillery was formed in December 1862 from the 129th New York Infantry, itself formed the previous August from volunteers from the New York State counties of Niagara, Orleans, and Genesee. Many heavy artillery units on garrison

duty converted or, in the case of the 8th New York, reverted to the infantry in May 1864 to assist Grant in his final push against Richmond. In that capacity, despite their obvious lack of training for the role, many served outstandingly. In ten months of action, the 8th New York lost 1,010 in action, of whom 361 were killed, 14 percent of the total complement of 2,575 officers and men. The 1st Maine Heavy Artillery took more casualties than any other unit during the Wilderness campaign losing 600 out of 900 participants in one charge alone.

Unlike their brasher light infantry colleagues, the heavy artillery wore a uniform very similar to that of the basic infantry save for the red of the N.C.O.s' chevrons, trouser stripes, and frock-coat trim, and officers' shoulder straps and hat cords. All ranks were entitled to carry a short, stubby sword based on a French variant of the Roman infantryman's sword, but few bothered. Officers, however, tended to carry a pistol. Large brass crossed cannons were worn in lieu of the infanteers' Jäger horn as a cap badge.

The English 600-pounder Armstrong gun was among the largest to see action during the war.

The interior of Fort Sumter during the initial bombardment.

U.S. SIGNAL CORPS

Despite the obvious necessity for the speedy transmission of orders and intelligence, the Union army did little to exploit the full potential of the telegraph until comparatively late in the war.

At the outbreak of hostilities, the War Department requested the American Telegraph Company, with its established system along the eastern seaboard, and the Western Union Telegraph Company, then expanding westward through the Allegheny Mountains, to provide military communications in the east. Control was vested in Anson Stager, the former general superintendent of Western Union and a close friend of Secretary of War Edwin Stanton. With the willing assistance of Stanton, himself a former director of the Atlantic & Ohio Telegraph Company, but contrary to the wishes of the military who increasingly demanded control of "tactical" or battlefield communications, Stager managed to keep the entire operation civilian. The Federal Military Telegraph System, as it became known, remained answerable to the Secretary of War throughout the conflict, and at no time was control relinquished to the generals.

At its height, the service employed approximately 12,000 telegraphers, transmitted over 3,000 messages a day and maintained 15,000 miles of wire. Attempts were made in March 1864 to force the telegraphers to wear an informal uniform consisting of a dark blue blouse with staff officer's buttons and dark blue trousers with a silver cord down each leg, but there is no evidence that this edict was taken very seriously, particularly in the more remote areas.

Albert James Myer entered the army in 1854 as a medical graduate but soon realized that his talents lay in the embryonic field of communications. Working closely with E.P. Alexander, who was later to transfer his allegiance to the Confederacy, he experimented in depth with Morse code, eventually introducing the "wigwag" signal system. On 27 June 1860, he became the army's first signal officer, a post created by Congress as a reward for his achievements. He at once set about the creation of a formal military Signals Corps. With the advent of war, Myer clashed heavily with Stager whom he regarded as a commercial opportunist. Stager called upon the assistance of his political allies in Washington, as a direct result of which Myer was relieved of his command in November 1863 and was transferred to the West where, it was felt, his views would be less influential. By then, however, the Signal Corps had been firmly established and was proving its worth on every battlefield.

Direct lines were laid from Washington to the principal army headquarters, enabling orders to be transmitted instantaneously. Further lines were laid from army to corps headquarters. Field crews – either civilian or military – accompanied the Corps to ensure that communications were re-established immediately after the headquarters moved into a

A Military Telegraph battery wagon deployed close to the front line in June 1864.

Headdress: All ranks wore conventional blue kepis. Officers wore a cap badge consisting of an embroidered Signals Corps flag with the letters "US" above the cross within a wreath. Men assigned to the balloon corps often wore the letters "AD" for Aeronautic Department or "BC" for Balloon Corps on their hats.

Tunic: Signallers wore plain dark blue cavalry jackets and trousers and were armed with Colt revolvers. Square crossed flags on 3-in long staffs, one red within a white border, the other white within a red border, were worn on the right upper arm to signify the branch of service.

Crow's nest signals stations were set up behind the front line to ensure the speedy transmission of orders from the rear headquarters.

90

new position, in this way denying the more maverick of the commanders any excuse for excessive independent action.

Communications to divisions and regiments, at this level totally the prerogative of the military, worked less formally. Telegraphy was used if the terrain permitted and the battle was static, but otherwise traditional visual means were resorted to. Signal officers were attached to each headquarters, to the major artillery batteries, and to observation posts to ensure that details of potential targets reached the guns with minimum delay. Responsibility for the laying and maintenance of lines, often eight miles in length, was delegated to cable detachments commanded by senior N.C.O.s. Reels of field cable were transported on wagons and, because the insulation of the wire was often poor, normally secured to short poles or trees. Mounted telegraphers tapped into the main telegraph routes where possible and attempted thereafter to keep the lines open and secure.

When troop movement was anticipated or the battlelines were fluid, visual signaling – lamps by night and flags by day – was preferred. Although the system had the advantage of simplicity, observation was an obvious drawback. By their very nature, relay posts had to be in the clear line of sight of the recipient and were therefore invariably overlooked by the enemy. Surprisingly, neither semaphore (the use of flags held at different angles to the signaler's body) nor Morse code appear to have been developed within the Signal Corps. Instead, a superficially simple, if chronically slow, system was adopted that demanded the use of only three flag positions in which letters were indicated by reference to the numbers 1, 2, or 3. To indicate the number 1, the signaler would move the flag in a semicircle down to his left. A corresponding movement to the right would indicate 2, and to the front, 3. Letters, and where possible phrases, were represented by a sequence of numbers. Thus "1.1" represented the letter "A," "1.2.2.1" "B," and "3.3" "end of message."

Although this simple expediency was sufficient to protect a message from a casual observer, it could easily be unraveled by anyone with the time and determination. Primitive ciphers, such as that utilizing twin overlapping wheels each with the alphabet inscribed in jumbled form around its edge, were often employed to afford primitive protection. When greater security was required, formal codes were introduced. Given sufficient time and, ideally, the aid of a computer, most codes of today are not considered difficult to break. Fortunately for the Union, however, the Confederacy lacked both the technique and facilities for serious analysis, with the result that the North's communications were never seriously compromised. At night, torches – or less commonly, Coston lights, a series of 20 colored lamps, each with a previously designated meaning – replaced the flags.

Whereas the Confederacy introduced the telegraph system, Union commanders such as Ulysses S. Grant made it their own. Taking his loathing of verbose letters and lengthy reports to its logical conclusion, Grant had whenever possible a telegraph installed in his field office where he would

During Sherman's campaign into Georgia, the Military Telegraph was fully stretched maintaining communications. Here the line is extended to Ackworth, Georgia.

spend much of his time talking by wire to all parts of his command. Each of his brigade headquarters was allotted a line team consisting of two men, a mule and reel of insulated wire; each team was expected to make it its business to maintain contact at all times with army command.

Without doubt, the most unusual application of the telegraph was in conjunction with the "lighter than air" balloon. Thaddeus Lowe, a well-known pre-war balloonist, offered his services to the Union, and in 1861, the Balloon Corps was authorized. The following year, seven balloons accompanied McClellan in the Peninsula campaign and soon proved their worth both as intelligence gatherers and as spotters for the guns. Each balloon required a squad of men to maintain its generator (which used a dangerous combination of sulfuric acid and iron filings to generate the hydrogen gas), fill the canopy and attend to the tethering ropes. Initially, these men were drawn from the ranks of the Topographical Engineers on the dubious premise that map-making seemed an obvious application, but soon administration passed first to the Military Telegraph Corps and then to the Quartermaster's Department before inevitably reverting to the Signal Corps. Shortsightedly, the Corps complained to the War Department that it had neither the men nor the finances to run the balloons, as a result of which the Balloon Corps was disbanded. The Confederacy breathed a sigh of relief and the Union lost one of its finest assets.

There was very little to differentiate a signaler from a line soldier except for the former's $\frac{3}{4}$-inch (12cm) square crossed signals flags – one red within a white border, the other white within a red border – on 3-inch (7.5cm) long staffs that were worn on the upper sleeve. In the field, the men wore standard cavalry jackets and trousers and were armed with Colt revolvers for personal protection. Officers wore a cap badge consisting of embroidered Signals Corps flags surmounted by the letters "us" within a wreath. Troops attached to the balloons would occasionally provide added panache by wearing the letters "AD" denoting ("Aeronautic Department") or "BC" for ("Balloon Corps") on their hats.

THE IRON BRIGADE OF THE WEST

Few units served the Union cause as bravely or tenaciously as the Iron Brigade of the West. Originally comprising the 19th Indiana and 2nd, 6th, and 7th Wisconsin regiments and later joined by the 24th Michigan, the brigade recruited exclusively from the Midwest. Over half of its membership consisted of native Americans, 40 percent were Scandinavians or Irish, the residue being of German or English extraction.

The brigade saw action at the 1st and 2nd Battles of Manassas (Bull Run), sustaining one-third casualties, and throughout the Maryland campaign, where during three weeks of bitter fighting it lost 58 percent of its remaining strength. At Antietam (Sharpsburg), a war correspondent, sickened by the carnage yet mindful of the considerable part played by these Midwestern troops in the North's first victory, christened the brigade the "Iron Brigade," ignorant of the fact that that title had earlier been bestowed on Hatch's New Yorkers; nevertheless, the name stuck. After fighting at Fredericksburg and Chancellorsville, the Iron Brigade threw itself unreservedly into the Gettysburg campaign, losing two-thirds of the 1,800 who fought on Seminary Ridge. The soul if not the body of the Iron Brigade of the West died at Gettysburg, and although it continued to function as an independent unit, it was destined not to play any further major part in the war.

Throughout its existence, the brigade was blessed with several brilliant commanding officers. Responsibility for its initial formation was delegated to Rufus King, a retired railroad engineer, newspaper editor, and one time Attorney-General for New York State. In 1861, King had been appointed Minister to the Vatican but, fortunately for the Union, had delayed his voyage, sensing that his services would soon be required closer to home. According to the traditions of the day, King was given command of his brigade leading it successfully until his promotion to major general in March 1862. Brigadier John Gibbon, who succeeded King, was without doubt one of the finest tacticians of the war. A veteran of the Seminole War and a former West Point artillery instructor, Gibbon denied his family ties at the outbreak of hostilities, turned his back on his three brothers then fighting for the Confederacy, and threw in his lot with the North. Initially gazetted commanding major of Battery "B," 4th U.S. Artillery in support of King's brigade, Gibbon was soon appointed Chief of Artillery, Army of the Potomac. Promoted to brigadier general in May 1862, he assumed command of the brigade, a post which he retained until his elevation to major general the following November. Although subsequently badly wounded, Gibbon refused to retire from active service, returning to the fray with renewed vigor after a period of

The Iron Brigade of the West sustained one-third casualties during hand-to-hand fighting at Bull Run.

Headdress: By 1862 a standard Federal blue uniform had been issued to the brigade. This included a large black "Hardee" hat which earned the brigade its alternative nickname, "The Black Hat Brigade."

Hat badge: As supplies ran out, the original ornate regimental hat badges were replaced by more conventional Federal issue. Company B, the 6th Wisconsins depicted here, sustained horrific losses at Spotsylvania.

Footwear: Issue white gaiters were soon abandoned as impractical. Cheap and uncomfortable issue boots were usually replaced by civilian footwear purchased privately or looted from Confederate prisoners.

93

sick leave. Appointed one of the surrender commissioners at Appomattox and breveted for his actions at Antietam, Fredericksburg, Spotsylvania, and Petersburg, Gibbon returned to the postwar regular artillery in the rank of colonel, seeing extensive service on the frontier. One of his final actions as an officer was to lead the relief column to the Little Big Horn in 1876 to bury the mutilated remains of his friend, Colonel (formerly General) George Custer.

Gibbon having been promoted, command passed to Solomon Meredith, a pre-war public office holder and a blatant political appointee. Meredith had, however, successfully led the 19th Indiana since its inception, had been wounded while leading his troops from the front at Groveton, and turned out to be an excellent choice. Described by a colleague as "six feet six inches in height, of commanding presence, and a ready speaker," he was seriously injured on the second day of Gettysburg and never

fully recovered from his injuries nor from the fact that two of his three sons serving with the Union were killed. Mustered out in May 1865, Meredith accepted the post of Surveyor-General of Montana before retiring to a farming life.

Each of the commanders stamped his own authority on the individualistic and somewhat eccentric dress of the brigade. Although officers were issued with standard U.S. army uniforms, there was insufficient material to clothe all the volunteers in blue on the outbreak of war. The 2nd Wisconsin were therefore equipped with plain, single-breasted gray frock coats, gray trousers with a black cord down each leg, a gray kepi trimmed with black and a gray overcoat trimmed with black piping and pockets. The 6th Wisconsin originally mustered in a motley assortment of civilian dress comprising a colorful mixture of cloth and headwear totally inappropriate to war. Before leaving their home

Antietam Bridge, where the Iron Brigade lost 72 out of 200 fighting men during one fierce battle.

state, they were issued with gray single-breasted jackets with black shoulder straps, cuffs, and collars, plain gray forage caps, gray trousers with a black strip down each leg, and a gray overcoat. The material was, however, of such poor quality that within a month the majority of uniforms were in shreds, compelling the 6th to enter Washington once again civilianized save for a "uniform" consisting of "gray hats trimmed with green."

Inevitably, the volunteer gray uniforms of both regiments were often mistaken for the more regulated apparel of the Confederate infantry, with dire results: during the 1st Battle of Manassas (Bull Run), the 2nd Wisconsins were forced to withdraw in disorder, having declined until too late to fire on the advancing enemy under the misconception that they were friendly reinforcements. After the battle, the entire brigade was quickly issued dark blue frock coats and sky-blue trousers. Gibbon, on

The Iron Brigade at Gettysburg. Note the distinctive headgear of the leading officer.

taking command, had the brigade issued with distinctive black "Hardee" hats and white gaiters. The ravages of battle soon took their toll, and by 1863, over half of the brigade had abandoned the frock coat in favor of the more durable fatigue coat. The impractical gaiters were soon discarded as were the ornate hat badges, but the "Hardee" hat itself remained as a jealously guarded and distinctive feature, earning the unit the nickname of the "Black Hat Brigade." Inexplicably, some officers preferred the kepi while the 24 Michigan, which was posted in immediately before Antietam, remained loyal to the conventional uniform of fatigue cap and blouse.

Few brigades fought in as many campaigns or sustained the losses of the Iron Brigade of the West. Organized in Indianapolis on 29 July 1861 following the briefest of training, the 19th Indiana joined the main army in Washington on 5 August. It lost 259 out of a strength of 423 at 2nd Manassas, 53 at South Mountain, and 72 out of 200 combatants at Antietam: 210 officers and men from a total of 288 engaged fell at Gettysburg, and a further 226 in the fighting from the Wilderness to Petersburg. (For more information on the 19th Indiana, see p. 64.) The Wisconsin regiments fared no better, the 2nd suffering the highest percentage of losses in the Union army: 19.7 percent killed. Of a total enrollment of 1,203, the regiment lost 753 killed and wounded, 132 missing or captured (of whom 17 died in prison), and 60 non-battle casualties from disease and injury. After Spotsylvania, losses were so great that the regiment, now reduced to fewer than 100 active men, was ordered home and mustered out, the survivors being transferred to Companies "A" and "B" of the 6th Wisconsins after a period of initial recuperation serving, in the opinion of the men rather wastefully, as a headquarters provost guard with the 4th Division. The Iron Brigade of the West should not be confused with John Porter Hatch's "Iron Brigade," comprising the 2nd U.S. Sharpshooters and the 22nd, 24th, 30th, and 84th New York Volunteers, with whom they served as part of King's division at the 2nd Battle of Manassas. Hatch's "Iron Brigade" was broken up in May 1863 when the 22nd, 24th, and 30th New York were mustered out at the expiration of their two years' service.

SUPPORT TROOPS

Within four years of the outbreak of war, the US army grew from a parochial force of 16,000 officers and men to a monolithic 2 million. Standards of support and administration which had sufficed for a professional army in peacetime were simply inadequate for the logistical needs of a part-volunteer, part-conscript force in time of war. Men who would never have passed the stringent medical examination for the regulars were accepted *en masse*, straining to breaking point the limited medical facilities available. Those who would once have been forced through age or injury to retire were now posted to the Veteran Reserve Corps to guard strategically important posts.

Although the troops became hardened and professional by their experiences in combat, and some became brutalized, it was important for the maintenance of their morale to ensure that they retained, whenever possible, memories of home and the cause for which they were fighting. Newspapers did much to bring the full extent of the war to the civilian population. Circulation among the great Northern dailies increased considerably as each tried to outstrip its rivals in the production of timely and accurate war news. Corps of "special" correspondents followed the armies and the navy, providing volumes of information and vivid feature items which were read as avidly by the troops – the vast majority of whom, in the best traditions of

As the war progressed, limited Federal supplies were often supplemented by booty captured from the Confederacy.

fighting men, had little idea of where they were, where they were going or why – as by those back home. Graphic battlefield maps, usually better than those available to the army, were compiled by highly skilled cartographers and reproduced faithfully on the front pages of such papers as the *New York Herald*. Overt censorship appears not to have existed, but then neither was there much to censor, although whether this was due to journalistic patriotism or the readerships' jingoistic refusal to accept detailed criticism of such notables as President Lincoln remains a moot point.

The spiritual welfare of troops facing death and mutilation on a regular basis was not forgotten. In all, 2,500 chaplains were employed by the Union army, of whom 11 were killed in action. On 22 July 1864, one of their number, the Rev. Milton Haney attached to the 55th Illinois Infantry, was awarded the Congressional Medal of Honor, the highest award for valor in the face of the enemy, for his part in the Battle for Atlanta. In 1862, for the first time in United States military history, Jewish rabbis were allowed into the chaplains' ranks.

Under the terms of an order promulgated on 25 November 1861, chaplains were to wear plain black frock coats with a standing collar and a single row of nine black buttons, plain black pantaloons and a plain unadorned black hat or forage cap, the last item replaced by a plain *chapeau-bras* for

Headdress: Plain unadorned black hats, decorated after August 1864 with a staff officer's cap badge, were replaced by a *chapeau-bras* on ceremonial occasions.

Frock coat: Chaplains were expected to wear plain black frock coats with standing collars and a single row of nine black buttons. However, as they were expected to purchase their own clothing, many elected to appear in far more eccentric attire.

Weapons: Although not obligatory, a number of chaplains carried straight swords. Many chaplains saw active service; eleven were killed in action and one awarded the Congressional Medal of Honor.

ceremonial purposes. On 25 August 1864, this rather plain uniform was enhanced by the addition of "herring-bone" or black braid around the buttons and button holes and a staff officers' cap badge. In reality, however, as chaplains had to equip themselves and were usually considered as an unwanted impediment by all but the most devout commanders, they were rarely taken to task for wearing non-regulation uniforms, and they soon gained the unenviable reputation of being the most eccentric dressers in the army. Since chaplains received the pay of a cavalry captain, many wore captain's shoulder straps which, together with the straight sword favored by some, made them look faintly ridiculous. In the words of the lieutenant colonel commanding the 127th Pennsylvania Volunteer Infantry on seeing his new chaplain Captain Gregg approaching the camp for the first time, resplendent in "a new uniform with prominent shoulder straps, a regulation hat with a gold circulet, and a gold cord, sashed, belted and spurred, and with a sword dangling at his side: 'What damn fool is that?' "

The regular supply of fresh food and water was of cardinal importance if the troops, particularly the less-acclimatized urban dwellers, were not to succumb to disease which, despite precautions, accounted for a staggering 224,586 Union army deaths throughout the war. Military store-keepers, or "suttlers", were appointed to each camp to regulate the supply of provisions. Inevitably, with the huge possibilities for fraud and corruption, particularly in the early stages of the war, standards varied greatly. Store-keepers were authorized "a citizen's frock coat of blue cloth, with buttons of the department to which they are attached; round black hat; pantaloons and vest, plain, white or dark blue; cravat or stock, black." There is evidence, however, that many, particularly those serving in outlying areas, reverted to civilian apparel.

Pay, although never high, was critical to morale. Nevertheless, although soldiers in the field were meant to be paid every two months, most considered themselves lucky if they received payment at four-month intervals, while delays of six and even eight months were not unusual. Union privates received $13.00 per month until June 1864 when this paltry sum was increased to $16.00. N.C.O.s received, on average, an additional $3.00 per rank scale, although specialists, notably engineers received considerably more. Second lieutenants in the infantry or artillery received the far more rewarding salary of $105.50 per month increasing to $115.50 for captains, $169.00 for majors, $181.00 for lieutenant colonels and $212.00 for colonels. General officers of one-, two- and three-star status received $315.00, $457.00 and $758.00 respectively, while staff officers received an average enhancement of $15.00 per month. Little if any benefit seems to have been set aside for retirement or invalidity.

Nearly everything needed by the army, save for weapons and food, was supplied by the Quartermaster Bureau. Uniforms, greatcoats, shoes, haversacks, canteens, mess kit, and blankets were all issued as were barracks, horses, pack mules, and forage. Fresh water for drinking and wood for fuel were brought forward by wagon or, where possible, by ship to insure that the troops at the front remained at all times functional. Invading Northern armies had to maintain long supply lines of wagon trains, railroads, and port facilities. With the exception of those few instances in which the troops lived off the countryside, an invading Union army required one wagon for every 40 men, and one horse, including cavalry remounts, for every two or three men. A campaigning army of 100,000 therefore required no fewer than 2,500 supply wagons, at least 35,000 animals, and over 600 tons of supplies per day.

Control of the Quartermaster Corps was vested in Montgomery C. Meigs, a brilliant and resourceful engineer who assumed the appointment of Quatermaster General in the rank of brigadier on 15 May 1861. Throughout the war, Meigs oversaw the spending of $1.5 billion, virtually half of the North's entire budget. He forced the field armies to abandon their large and heavy Sibley and Adams tents in favor of the far more practical portable shelters known affectionately as "dog" or "pup" tents, introduced standard graduated measurements for uniforms, and pioneered the introduction of the Blake-McKay leather-sewing machine which did much to improve the standards of footwear, particularly among the enlisted ranks of the infantry.

Food and forage were supplied by the Commissary Department. Initial allocations were made by the Commissary-General to the commissaries of armies, which were responsible for the distribution downward to the individual corps, divisions, bri-

The Quartermaster's Office, Fort Fisher.

gades, and regiments. Rations varied but usually consisted of ham, bacon, beef (salted or on the hoof), beans, flour, salt, sugar, coffee, hardtack, and occasionally, especially in the later stages of the war, bread freshly baked by mobile bakeries. Salt was issued in large quantities to prevent fresh meat from putrifying in the heat. Except when it could be pillaged from enemy farmsteads or bought locally, fresh fruit seemed to be wholly lacking, a factor which almost certainly helped the spread of disease.

Artillery, small arms, and all types of ammunition were supplied by the U.S. Ordnance Board. An ordnance officer or sergeant was posted to each regiment and tasked with the completion of weekly returns showing the state of arms, and ready-use and stored ammunition. Most ordnance N.C.O.s were highly experienced and, in many instances, were veterans. Usually they wore full infantry dress uniform with red chevrons surmounted, in the case of fully trained ordnance sergeants, by a distinctive red star.

A Federal supply column is drawn up awaiting orders to advance. The sheer logistics of moving so vast a force were horrendous.

THE PRISONER OF WAR

In four years of bloody and protracted fighting, an estimated 60,250 prisoners of war died in captivity, the vast majority during the final few months of hostilities. During the early stages of the war, prisoners were not a problem. Obsolete forts, derelict factories, converted warehouses, and even county jails were used as makeshift stockades to hold the prisoners while highly informal local arrangements were made between the respective field commanders for their exchange and ultimate release.

As the war progressed and prisoners became more of a burden, the South, already suffering the first privations of the blockade, pressed the Union for a more formal exchange cartel. Initially, Lincoln refused to agree, arguing that to do so would be to recognize the legitimacy of the Confederate government. However, massive Federal losses in the winter battles of 1861–62 heightened Northern public opinion in favor of regularized exchanges, forcing the President to enter into a formal agreement with the enemy army, although technically not with its government. Under the terms of the cartel, which was promulgated on 22 July 1862, each rank was awarded a weighting. An N.C.O. was equivalent to two privates, a lieutenant to four, a captain to six, a major to eight, a lieutenant colonel to ten, a colonel to 15, a brigadier to 20 and a

general to 40. Surprisingly, the worth of a commanding general was deemed to be only 60 times that of his newest recruit. Prisoners were exchanged on a one-for-one basis and were subsequently allowed to return to the ranks. Any surplus of prisoners held by either side were released as parolees and, as such, were not allowed to return to active service until formally exchanged. This somewhat unusual system worked so smoothly over the next few months that by the spring of 1863 it was reported that the prisons were empty of all except those too sick or wounded to travel.

The cartel was suddenly suspended in May 1863 when the Confederate Congress endorsed a policy of re-enslavement or execution of black soldiers captured in Union uniform. Although informal exchanges continued thereafter, the whole policy was abandoned by Washington later that year when it was discovered that a significant number of the 30,000 parolees "freed" by Grant after his capture of Vicksburg in July had been returned to duty without formal exchange, in blatant breach of their parole conditions.

Subsequent attempts to renew the cartel foundered when the Confederacy refused either to admit its culpability over the Vicksburg incident or to treat freed slaves within the Union army as bona

Federal prisoners captured during the Second Battle of Bull Run. Virtually no resources existed for their welfare.

Prisoners were held at the mercy and whim of their captors. Many had the better items of their clothing, together with their personal possessions, looted at the time of capture, and were forced to make and mend and even steal from the dead to survive. Medical facilities were largely non-existent. Unknown thousands died needlessly of starvation, disease and neglect on both sides. In 1866 Henry Wirz, the commandant of the Confederate prison at Andersonville, was tried and became the first United States citizen to be executed for war crimes.

fide prisoners of war. Indeed, there is a strong suggestion that attitudes hardened considerably throughout the South, even among the more liberal non-slave-owning urban majority, when it was realized that the Union was willing to use freed slaves against it. As a belated gesture, the Confederate Bureau of War did offer to treat properly black soldiers lawfully freed at the time of their enlistment (but not runaways), but by this stage Northern attitudes were such that no compromise was accepted.

Actual treatment of black prisoners at the hands of the Confederacy varied. Indeed, because the South refused to recognize the status of Negro captives, precise records were not kept and it is therefore virtually impossible even to gain an approximation of how many there were. Some Confederate commanders treated all prisoners alike, while others condoned – and in a few instances, actively organized – massacres. Hundreds of blacks were murdered at Poison Spring, the Crater, and elsewhere. In the two days of carnage which followed the Confederate recapture of Plymouth, North Carolina in April 1864, every black person found in a Union uniform or suspected of supporting the North was slaughtered. Black prisoners spared immediate execution were often returned to their previous masters or occasionally sold to a new one. While awaiting transportation, many were put to hard labor repairing and constructing Confederate defenses.

The worst instances of racial brutality took place on 12 April 1864 after Brigadier General James Chalmers with 1,500 troops recaptured Fort Pillow in western Tennessee from a mixed Union force under the command of Major Lionel Booth. The

exact circumstances of the final assault on the fort which immediately preceded the massacre are hotly disputed, but there is some suggestion that Union troops either deliberately or inadvertently fired on a flag of truce. What is certain is that in the ensuing fighting, 231 Union troops were killed and 100 seriously injured for the loss of 14 Confederates killed and 86 wounded. Southern reports suggest that the Union sustained the majority of its losses when its troops attempted a last desperate retreat to the safety of a gunboat patrolling the Mississippi. Federal reports, however, claim that the Union troops, recognizing the impossibility of their position, surrendered as soon as the perimeter defenses of the fort had been breached, and that thereafter the Confederates entered into an orgy of killing, murdering black prisoners, burying others alive, and torching the hospital tents containing their wounded. Whatever the truth, from the moment the story of Fort Pillow became common knowledge until the end of the war, black troops fought the Southern enemy with a previously unknown hatred and ferocity.

President Lincoln was placed on the horns of a dilemma by such Confederate activities. At first, he threatened an eye-for-an-eye retaliation including the execution of a number of Southern troops drawn at random in response to the Fort Pillow massacre. Then he prevaricated and, finally, he did nothing, arguing that such executions would inevitably involve innocent parties and would only serve to strengthen Southern resolve and probably lead to greater and worse retaliation. Despite this, certain Union field commanders in South Carolina and Virginia did carry out their own form of reta-

Castle Pinckney prison camp after Bull Run. At this stage most prisoners could hope for parole. As the war progressed, however, they were condemned to neglect and untold suffering.

liation. When black prisoners were put to work repairing Southern defenses under fire, an equal number of Confederate prisoners were put to work on Union defenses under the same conditions until the practice ceased.

Whereas threats of retaliation did little to help recaptured runaways, there is evidence to suggest that it did much to alter the attitude of the Confederacy toward black freedmen. During the final months of the war, as a prelude to the introduction of conscription among its own slave force, the Confederacy changed its policy toward black prisoners, granting them all prisoner of war status (although not always equal treatment). However, by then it was too late to undo the damage caused by four years of overt racism.

Conditions in Confederate prison camps deteriorated considerably as the North's grip on the South tightened and food became even more scarce. Although there is evidence that prisoners often ate as well as their equally hungry guards, the former inhabitants of the Industrial North seemed less robust than their Southern rural enemies and many died of starvation.

The camp at Andersonville in southwest Georgia came to epitomize the very worst of prison life. Hastily built in February 1864 to accommodate captives previously held on Belle Isle in the James River near Richmond, Andersonville soon became overcrowded with prisoners from Sherman's army as well as from the eastern theater. Initially it was intended that the compound would cover 16 acres and contain sufficient hutted accommodation for 10,000 prisoners. When it was captured in April 1865, it encompassed 26 acres, much of it swamp, and held over 33,000 men. No huts were ever built.

Instead, the inmates tried to protect themselves from the heat of the Georgia sun by manufacturing shelters from branches taken from the trees used to construct the outer perimeter fence. The water supply consisted of a single stream which ran sluggishly through the center of the camp, sanitation was provided by a single open sewer, and medical supplies were non-existent. No one knows exactly how many died of starvation, disease, and neglect in Andersonville, although 12,912 bodies lie in the adjoining national cemetery. After the war, the camp commandant, a Swiss immigrant named Henry Wirz, was tried and executed for war crimes.

Not all Confederate prisons were inhumane. Food, sanitation, and accommodation at Camp Ford, built near Tyler, Texas in 1863, were so good that it was not considered necessary to construct a separate hospital block.

Despite the far better living conditions in the North, Federal stockades were often little better than Andersonville. Elmira Prison in New York was designed to hold 5,000 prisoners but in reality held twice that number. Half enjoyed hutted accommodation but the rest were forced to live in tents with not even one blanket each, even during the rigors of mid-winter. Five percent of the inmates per month died of cold and starvation.

Although it is popular to regard Confederate prisons as far worse than those in the North, it should be remembered that the vast majority of postwar historians on whom we must rely for a proper analysis were strongly pro-Union. It is perhaps enough to note that 13 percent of Southern prisoners died in Northern camps compared with only 8 percent of Northerners in Confederate camps.

New York Zouave prisoners at Castle Pinckney prison camp. The sign above the door would indicate that, despite everything, they were able to keep a sense of humour.

THE CONFEDERATE ARMY

Few Southerners sought open confrontation with the Federal government. By 1860 they had developed their own unique lifestyle and simply demanded the right to be left in peace. The vast majority did not own slaves – indeed many quietly accepted the inevitability of eventual abolition. Only three countries in the Americas – Brazil, Cuba and the United States – continued to practice slavery, and it was clear to all but the most reactionary that this status quo could not continue forever. However, as the powerful northeastern states fell increasingly under the influence of European immigration, the gulf between the North and South grew until eventually many Southerners began to believe that nothing short of total independence could protect their way of life. Southern leaders began to argue that the Union of 1789 was no more than a contract between each state and the Federal government, which could be rescinded by either party. The rights enshrined in the Declaration of Independence had, they argued, never been surrendered, and in consequence, each state had the option of going its own way should it for any reason find the actions of the central government unacceptable.

In 1861, 11 states exercised this option, seceded from the Union and formed themselves into a new nation which they named the Confederate States of America. Almost at once they denied the theory on which their own creation was based: at the Montgomery Convention which followed, they declared the Confederacy to be a "permanent government" from which none had the right to withdraw. When Washington threatened to restore Federal rule by force of arms, Southerners flocked to the cause of the fledgling government. Many officers – including Robert E. Lee, who had earlier been offered command of the Union forces ordered to suppress the rebellion – resigned their commissions and offered their services to the Confederacy.

Southerners believed – and many Northerners agreed – that their way of life gave them a great advantage over the enemy. Their tradition of military service was strong, their rural lifestyle meant that most were natural horsemen and excellent shots, and their leaders possessed powers of man management born of generations of slave owning. They went to war in 1861 with an arrogance resulting as much from a belief in themselves as in their cause.

As was the case with the Union, volunteers flocked to the states rather than the central government to offer their services. Although the Confederacy initially did not introduce formal dress regulations (with the notable exception of a few regiments), most of the troops were issued with vaguely similar uniforms. Louisiana, with its strong French traditions, produced a number of Zouave units, notably the Louisiana Tigers with their striking striped pantaloons. New Orleans fielded the lavishly attired Washington Artillery and South Carolina the Charleston Light Dragoons with their European-style plumes and epaulettes, but most wore some vestige of gray.

More than any other fighting unit, the Confederate cavalry epitomized the South's attitude to war. Each man supplied his own horse and tackle, only established horsemen were accepted, and conventional military discipline was kept to a minimum. For two years the cavalry swept all before it, gaining a reputation for invincibility which led to complacency and, ultimately, to its undoing. At Brandy Station it met a new generation of Northern cavalry: well trained, well equipped and, above all, drilled in the art of modern warfare. The Southern cavalry suffered the first in a series of defeats which sent shock waves reverberating through the Confederate military command. At Gettysburg, the North, which had always enjoyed a vast industrial and numerical superiority, proved that it was now at least the equal of the South in tactics and leadership. From then to the inevitable surrender at Appomattox two years later, the South could do no more than engage in a series of delaying and rearguard actions in the hope of foreign intervention or a qualified peace.

It was during this period that the ordinary Confederate soldier came into his own. Invariably hungry, his clothing in tatters and often inadequately armed, he fought tenaciously for every inch of his land. As uniforms wore out or were destroyed in the fighting, soldiers whose homes were not under the control of the advancing Union armies asked their families for civilian replacement clothing. Others simply looted the bodies of the Union dead or stole from prisoners of war. By 1864 few Confederate regiments retained any outward semblance of order although, as the Union forces frequently discovered to their cost, their fighting spirit remained unabated. Butternut replaced gray as the color of the day as conventional dyes became all but impossible to obtain. Inevitably some troops went too far in their use of captured equipment, and at one stage the Union had to threaten to shoot as spies any enemy troops captured wearing Federal clothing. Indeed a few even abandoned uniforms completely, forming themselves into bands of bloodthirsty irregulars, although fortunately such instances were comparatively rare.

In many ways, the Confederate army was an enigma. Highly motivated, it shunned internal politics. Suspicious of any outward manifestation of class (many soldiers refused to salute officers whom they regarded as equals in the struggle for independence), it displayed to the bitter end an unwavering loyalty to its leaders in general and to Robert E. Lee in particular. A lesser army would have disintegrated when defeat became inevitable. Instead the Confederates remained a cohesive force even when denied the cohesive factor of proper uniforms. After the war many Southern troops joined the newly reformed Union army, in numerous instances gaining high office within its ranks. Today the South can boast a higher number of senior army officers *pro rata* than any other quadrant of the United States – proof that the fighting spirit of the 1860s, which enabled an ill-equipped, poorly armed and vastly outnumbered army to survive four years of bloody warfare, did not die at Appomattox.

ROBERT E. LEE

Socially, politically, and culturally, Robert E. Lee was the complete antithesis of his rival in war and one-time companion Ulysses S. Grant. Born in 1807, the fourth son of "Light Horse Harry" Lee, a veteran cavalry leader during the Revolutionary War and former Governor of Virginia, Lee could trace his ancestory through many of the great original families of America, including that of George Washington. Although Lee had married well and despite his aristocratic connections, he was not in fact a rich man. His somewhat eccentric father had an advanced sense of honor but little financial acumen and, dying when Lee was still relatively young, left a widow and seven children with a social position but without the necessary resources to maintain it. His son Robert was deeply influenced by his gentle and dignified mother, adopting many of her characteristics in later life. Above all, he gained from her a desire to excel at whatever he did.

Unable to afford a university education, Lee obtained a place at West Point from which he graduated second in his class, having been appointed corps adjutant, the highest honor available to an officer cadet. Commissioned into the elite Engineering Corps in 1829, Lee later transferred to the cavalry in search of promotion but found little to inspire him in the peacetime army. During the Mexican War (1846–48), he served as a captain on the staff of General Winfield Scott, during which time it is more than likely that he had his first encounter with Grant. Unlike the latter, who then returned to anonymity, Lee concluded the war with one wound, three brevets for gallantry, and a mushrooming reputation which prompted General Scott to describe him as "the very best soldier I ever saw in the field."

As Superintendent of West Point between 1852 and 1855, Lee continued steadily to enhance his reputation. In October 1859, while on compassionate leave at his home in Arlington, Virginia, he was ordered to Harpers Ferry to suppress a pro-secessionist insurrection led by the tempestuous John Brown. The latter's ill-conceived capture of the Federal arsenal and armory was contained by the time that Lee and the company of Marines under his command reached the area, leaving him with little to do but make a final and virtually bloodless assault on the thoroughly confused and demoralized abolitionists. The fact that the insurrection had been led by a group of whites made Lee realize that open confrontation could not be avoided for long. Avidly anti-secessionist and a non-slave owner himself, this placed Lee on the horns of a dilemma.

He had returned to his command in Texas when, on 1 February 1861, that state became the seventh to secede, and the state government ordered all Federal troops to vacate its lands forthwith. Now devoid of a command, Lee returned to Arlington to await events in Virginia. On 18 April, at the instigation of General Scott, Lee was ordered to Washington and offered command of an army then being formed to return the seceded states to the Union. Bitterly opposed to civil war, Lee refused, stating that "he could take no part in an invasion of the Southern states." When Lincoln called on Virginia to furnish troops for the invasion, the state legislature refused and instead joined the secession. Lee resigned from the army which he had served faithfully for 36 years and at once offered his services to the defense of his homeland.

Surprisingly, Lee was not initially given field command but instead was appointed military adviser to the Confederate President Jefferson Davis, in which role he was able to plan a cohesive defense for the Confederacy. Working in unison with Thomas (later "Stonewall") Jackson, he spent the early part of 1862 putting together a strike force from a number of static garrisons in northern Virginia, using it to excellent effect in an audaciously conceived attack into the Shenandoah Valley. Fearful of the threat to Washington, Lincoln was forced to hold back General McDowell's large corps for the defense of the capital, denying McClellan and the Army of the Potomac sufficient troops to execute an encircling movement around Richmond.

On 31 May 1862, General Joseph Johnston, in command of the Confederate field forces, was seriously wounded. Lee was appointed in his place and at once set about rebuilding the Army of Northern Virginia into one of the most potent fighting units of the war. Discipline and command were tightened, morale improved, and control returned to headquarters. Not willing to surrender the initiative, Lee linked with Jackson to the north, and, in a series of bloody skirmishes known

General Robert E. Lee resplendent in the uniform of a Confederate Lieutenant General. This photograph was taken by Matthew Brady in 1865.

collectively as the Seven Days' Battles, inflicted a humiliating defeat on the Union forces. For bringing the Confederacy its first major victory since Manassas (Bull Run) and for halting the Federal advance on Richmond, Lee became universally acclaimed in the South and the subject of much veneration among his own troops.

Ever a realist, Lee knew that he could not hope to beat the North in a conventional war. Instead he spent the next two years trying to keep the enemy from the industrial heartland of Richmond and from the rich farmlands of northern Virginia, at least while the crops were being harvested. In an attempt to destroy the Federal will to win, and in the hope of attracting European support for the Confederate cause, Lee embarked on a series of battles in which he relied on speed, initiative, and the sheer motivation of his men to defeat the vastly more powerful enemy. Twice expelling the Federals from his beloved Virginia, Lee won notable vic-

Lee, in the company of his staff, surveys the battlefield at Fredericksburg. Note the comparative simplicity of his dress compared to that of his subordinates.

tories at the 2nd Battle of Manassas (Bull Run) on 29–30 August 1862, at Fredericksburg on 13 December 1862, and at Chancellorsville on 1–6 May 1863 when, outnumbered by more than two to one, he split his forces and encircled the enemy. In an attempt to shift the battlefield from the Confederacy, and with a view to enlisting support from Southern sympathizers, Lee crossed into Maryland but met overwhelmingly superior forces at Antietam (Sharpsburg) and was forced to retire back across the Potomac.

Conscious of the stalemate in Virginia and unable to influence the series of Confederate reverses in the West in the summer of 1863, Lee once again advanced into the North in a last desperate attempt to carry the war to the enemy – this time into Pennsylvania. However, unlike the Federals who had the luxury of constant reinforcements, Lee was unable to replace his losses. His veteran troops were exhausted, and many of his finest subordinates lay dead – notably "Stonewall" Jackson, killed by mistake by his own troops at Chancellorsville. Inevitably Lee was defeated at Gettysburg (1–3 July 1863), and his dejected troops were forced to retire once more behind their own defensive lines.

In May 1864, Grant assumed overall command of the Union forces and began a relentless two-pronged drive into the Confederacy. Overwhelmed by superior numbers, Lee could do little but fight a series of delaying actions, all of which only served to deplete his already scarce resources. The Confederates fought valiantly during the Wilderness campaign, at Spotsylvania, and at Cold Harbor, inflicting over 50,000 casualties on the enemy, but to no avail. Eventually Lee was forced to deploy the remnants of his exhausted troops in defensive positions outside the remaining strongholds of Richmond and Petersburg to await the inevitable outcome. Even then, for nearly a year Lee's brilliantly engineered defensive works frustrated every attempt to storm them.

The end came on 2 April 1865 when the defensive lines surrounding Richmond broke under a massive assault, forcing the remaining defenders to leave the protection of their trenches and make a last desperate break for freedom. On 9 April, Lee accepted the inevitable and surrendered his army to Grant at Appomattox Courthouse, an ordeal made easier by the magnanimity of Grant and his staff.

After the war, Lee spent several months recuperating from the rigors of the final retreat, although he never fully recovered his health. Conscious of the need to provide for his wife and seven children (the Arlington plantation that his wife had inherited had been confiscated by the Union) and mindful of the need for setting a good example to the thousands of unemployed soldiers, he accepted the position of president of Washington College (now Washington & Lee University) in Lexington, Virginia. As well as being a progressive and enlightened lecturer, Lee also placed the college on a sound commercial footing, instilling a sense of purpose into its students, many of them former soldiers from his Army of Northern Virginia.

Robert Edward Lee died in his home at Washington College in 1870 at the age of 64, and now lies buried in its grounds.

Although Lee traditionally favored long cavalry boots and a large utilitarian black hat, both shown here, it was not until after Gettysburg that he began to appear regularly in the full uniform of a Confederate States general. Even then he invariably kept the adornments of rank to a minimum.

THE LOUISIANA TIGERS

Louisiana was never naturally a part of the United States. Initially settled by the French, it remained part of their empire until 1803, when the Louisiana Territory (which extended from the Mississippi to the Rockies) was purchased by Thomas Jefferson from the impecunious revolutionary government for $15 million. Fifty years later, the bulk of the citizens of the state of Louisiana (which had been admitted to the Union in 1812) remained insular, refusing to abandon either their traditional ways or, in the case of those in the southern part, their highly personalized Creole dialect. Few felt any allegiance to Washington, D.C. or the Federal government. Many settlers had, however, gained considerably from the growth of New Orleans as a major seaport and from the resultant increase in agricultural productivity within the state's hinterland, and they were determined to protect their new-found affluence. When therefore Louisiana seceded from the Union on 26 January 1861, they gave the newly formed Confederacy their absolute support.

The harsh realities of war came quickly to Loui-

siana. Within weeks of the attack on Fort Sumter, the Union navy began a highly successful blockade of the Gulf ports, effectively starving the South of most of its imports. In April 1862, New Orleans was attacked, forced to surrender, and placed under a strenuous regime of martial law designed to break, once and for all, the spirit of rebellion in the area. General Benjamin Butler, appointed military governor of the city on 1 May 1862, said:

> I find the city under the dominion of the mob. They have insulted our flag – torn it down with indignity. This outrage will be punished in such a manner as in my judgment will caution both the perpetrators and abettors of the act, so that they shall fear the stripes if they do not reverence the stars of our banner.

Within weeks, Butler had hanged a prominent citizen for removing the Union flag from a public building, had passed a law classifying as a prostitute any woman who by her actions, manner, or deeds in any way attracted the attention of the occupying forces, and had brought the British government to the brink of intervention on behalf of the Confederacy.

Starke's Louisiana Brigade storming the Federal lines near "Deep Cut." Stones replaced muskets when the ammunition ran out.

108

Headdress: Many Louisiana regiments favored the straw hat, often inscribed with patriotic logos, rather than the originally issued red stocking cap.

Trousers: Whereas most regiments abandoned the bright red shell jackets, nearly all retained the striking red, white and blue striped pantaloons reputedly manufactured from bed-ticking.

Gaiters: White leather gaiters were issued to all enlisted men and were worn throughout the war.

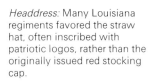

More fundamentally, he had hardened the resolve of the entire population of Louisiana to fight to the finish rather than yield to Northern domination.

Most volunteers joined one of the numerous independent regiments which were formed into two brigades within the Army of Northern Virginia. The first, officially designated the 8th Brigade of General Dick Ewell's Division, was commanded by Dick Taylor, the son of Zachary Taylor, 12th President of the United States, and, according to a leading critic, "the one Confederate general who possessed literary art that approached first rank." Taylor had been educated in Edinburgh and France and at Harvard and Yale before taking over the administration of his plantation in Louisiana. Pro-secession, he was appointed commander of the 9th Louisiana but failed to see action at the 1st Battle of Manassas (Bull Run). Appointed brigadier on 21 October 1861, he was given command of the Louisiana Brigade under Jackson in the Shenandoah Valley campaign and during the Seven Days' Battles. Although ill during the final stages of the latter, he showed his true grit and determination by directing his troops from the back of an ambulance. Promoted major general in July 1862, he was given responsibility for the defense of western Louisiana, halting Bank's advance in the Red River campaign of 1864. In May of that year, Taylor was further elevated to the rank of lieutenant general and given the responsibility of protecting eastern Louisiana, Mississippi, and Alabama – a hopeless task which he performed to the very best of his ability until the very end, after which he surrendered with honor rather than inflict further suffering on his troops.

The brigade itself, one of the finest in the Confederate army, comprised Seymour's 6th Louisianas, Hay's 7th, Kelly's 8th, Stafford's 9th and Roberdeau Wheat's Louisiana Special Battalion whose nickname, the "Tigers," was eventually adopted by the entire brigade. The 2nd Louisiana Brigade, comprising the 2nd, 9th, 10th, 15th, and, later, the 1st and 14th Regiments, was commanded by Brigadier Stafford until his death on 5 May 1864 during the Wilderness campaign, after which the remnants of both brigades were merged.

Whereas Louisiana troops tended to be better equipped than most in the Confederacy, they did not enjoy a statewide uniform. Troops raised in the immediate vicinity of New Orleans tended to wear a predominantly blue uniform, often with a red flannel stripe attached to the left shoulder to differentiate them from soldiers of the Union army. Rural companies, however, favored gray trimmed in a variety of colors.

Many of the original volunteer regiments remained true to their French heritage and adopted Zouave or *chasseur* uniforms. The Confederate State Zouaves (St. Leon Dupeire's Louisiana Infantry), the Louisiana Zouaves and the Zouaves and *chasseurs* all vied with each other during the first few months of the war to create the most stunning uniforms with no thought paid to their obvious impracticality in the field. The 1st Battle of Manassas however, brought home to all concerned the realities of war, and by early 1862, Taylor was able to boast a brigade "over three thousand strong, neat in fresh clothing of gray with white gaiters,

bands playing at the head of their regiments."

One of the most distinctive of the early uniforms was that issued to the Louisiana Special Battalion – the original "Tigers." It was essentially a typical Zouave costume, consisting of a red stocking cap with a blue tassel, a dark brown jacket with red braid in one of a number of patterns, and a red shirt decorated with several sashes. The colorful trousers – either blue with white stripes or a mixture of red, white and blue – were made from bedticking and earned the regiment its unusual nickname. The heavy jacket was often discarded in battle, enabling the troops to fight in their shirtsleeves, while the stocking cap was invariably replaced by a more popular wide-brimmed straw hat, itself often inscribed with such patriotic mot-

toes as "Tigers Win or Die," "Tiger Looking for Old Abe," and "Tiger Always." To add to the mystique of the regiment, each company had its own exotic title. Thus Company "A" became "Walker Guards," Company "B" "Tiger Rifles," Company "C" "Delta Rangers," Company "D" "Catahoula Guerrillas" or "The Old Dominion Guards," and Company "E" "The Wheat Life Guards."

The 7th Louisiana – nicknamed "The Pelicans" because of the design of the state seal often borne on their waist-belts – was another Zouave unit although, in this instance, the officers exchanged the conventional sleeved waistcoat for a shell jacket with a standing collar and badges of rank sewn on the sleeves. Available photographs of Zouave units show the enlisted men wearing con-

ventional black boots or shoes protected by calf-length white gaiters, occasionally of leather but more usually of webbing.

In the best Zouave tradition, many of the regiments (including "The Tigers") recruited *vivandières*, or female sutlers, to accompany them. Such women usually wore short wool jackets of the same color and trim as those of the men, wide-brimmed plumed hats, and heavy skirts over trousers made of wool below the hemline and cotton above. Unlike their European equivalents, who often had an unenviable reputation for promiscuity, the Southern *vivandières* were well respected. Many placed themselves in the line of fire to bring water and administer first aid to the wounded, and several were killed.

The Louisiana Brigade fought tenaciously, if against hopeless odds, during the Battle of Spotsylvania.

CONFEDERATE INFANTRY: 1862

The Army of Northern Virginia was one of the finest fighting forces of the 19th century. Constantly outnumbered, ill-equipped, and usually hungry, it held the Union steamroller at bay for three long years before eventually yielding to overwhelming force.

The Army had its roots in the far smaller and less sophisticated Army of the Shenandoah formed in early 1861 to defend the Confederacy against Union intervention. Initially most troops were supplied, armed, and equipped by the individual states, all of which introduced their own standards of dress and uniform. As the war intensified, the unsophisticated state administrations were simply overwhelmed, necessitating central government intervention, but by then thousands of troops had been organized into a mass of regiments, battalions, and even independent companies. Some – notably the 1st Virginia Regiment, the Washington Artillery of Louisiana, and the Clinch Rifles of Georgia – had been formed, fitted out, and trained well before the war and were thus able to offer themselves to the Confederacy as fully competent fighting entities. Others, such as the Georgia Hussars who spent $25,000 on their initial outfits, lacked military training but at least had the financial ability to insure that they went to war equipped with the best (and gaudiest) that money could buy.

The Confederate government tried to equip the thousands of volunteers who enlisted in the spring and summer of 1861 for an initial period of 12 months, but gave up when it realized the impossibility of the task. Instead, volunteers were given a basic equipment list and ordered to furnish their own clothes. Potential cavalrymen were even expected to provide their own mounts, saddles, and tackle. This led to an inevitable, if unfortunate, feeling of superiority among the urban units (many of which were equipped by local subscription) when they compared themselves to their less affluent country cousins.

An attempt was made during the summer of 1861 to bring a degree of uniformity to the Confederate ranks. Many states had based their own local uniforms on existing U.S. army patterns, with the result that a disconcertingly large number of Southern troops were still clothed almost exclusively in Federal blue. When this had led to confusion in the ranks, such as during the 1st Battle of Manassas (Bull Run), the South had invariably gained, but its legislators were realistic enough to know that this would not always be the case and strove to introduce as soon as possible a drab gray uniformity. Certain of the more outlandish units, notably the Zouave regiments, initially showed a marked disinclination to relinquish their bright

The Confederate Infantry withstands a massed Federal attack during the Battle of Fair Oaks, 31 May 1862.

Jacket: Issue gray double-breasted tunics were unpopular and were usually replaced with civilianized gray single-breasted jackets.

Side arms: Whole units abandoned the bayonet in favor of privately acquired hunting and Bowie knives. These were subsequently found to be totally inadequate in the face of massed Federal bayonet charges which became more common as the war progressed.

Personal equipment: Greatcoats and other heavy equipment were often abandoned in the summer without a moment's thought for the future. Great hardships resulted in the subsequent winter with several units having to be declared non-operational due to their inability to fight in the cold. The soldier here has at least retained his blanket roll and canteen.

and gaudy uniforms, although eventually even they were forced to concede the impracticality of red pantaloons and scarlet jackets in the proximity of enemy sharpshooters.

On 6 June 1861, General Order No. 4 was issued governing the distribution of the coats for officers and other ranks. Cadet gray double-breasted tunics with a long skirt extending halfway between the hip and the knee, a standing collar and twin rows of large brass buttons were introduced, but these soon fell from favor with ordinary soldiers, many of whom quickly replaced them with short-waisted single-breasted jackets requested from home. Initially officers were ordered to wear gold collar insignia – one to three gold bars (second lieutenants to captains) and one to three stars (majors to colonels) – but it was rapidly realized that, again, these made excellent targets, and on 3 June 1862, a further order was promulgated allowing officers to dispense with the insignia in the field. Self-preservation being a great spur to insubordination, there is ample evidence that many officers had unilaterally discarded their badges of rank well before

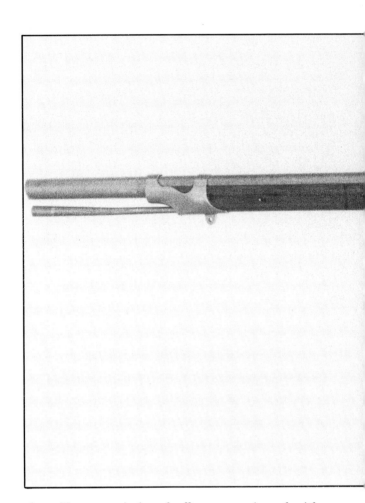

Below: Two Confederate privates pose informally for a photograph. The soldier on the left carries a Bowie knife, much favored by backwoodsmen in the early stages of the war.

then. Non-commissioned officers were issued with chevrons in branch-of-service colors but there is photographic evidence to suggest that the great majority of N.C.O.s either wore no badges of rank or introduced small, black homemade variants. As the war progressed and the effects of the blockade became more apparent, it became less possible to maintain standards in design and color so that, by late 1862, jackets were varying in hue from dark to a brownish gray and were being issued with from five to ten buttons. No longer able to control the design of their troops' uniforms, many states still attempted to preserve their local identity by issuing individually designed buttons and belt buckles, although these were not always universally available.

Waistcoats were not regulation issue. They were, however, a popular item of contemporary civilian attire and were thus often worn as supplements to the jackets, particularly in the cold winter months. Troops were issued with overcoats, but many contrived to "lose" these during the hot summer months without any thought for the future, making the waistcoat all the more important when the weather deteriorated.

Despite an undertaking given by the Confederacy as early as 19 April 1861 to provide regulation steel gray trousers for its troops, comparatively few actually seem to have been issued and most that were were sky blue. As early as the latter part of 1862, it was not uncommon to see troops in home-woven brown or butternut civilian breeches heavily patched to extract the last vestige of wear and preserve at least an element of dignity for the soldier. Typically trousers were made of wool

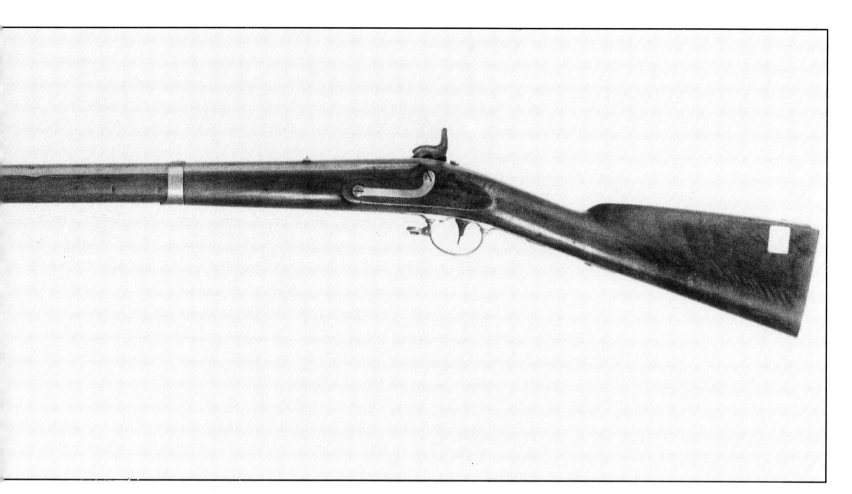

although gray denim material was common in the West. In the summer of 1862, some enterprising soldiers even resorted to the manufacture of remarkably smart (if coarse) trousers from blankets.

Shoes and boots were a constant bone of contention. At first, many volunteers provided their own heavy boots into which they tucked the tops of their trousers. After a few miles of forced marching, however, the massive high heels attached to these boots were found to be a positive liability: when the insteps wore down, the wearer was left with an uneven walking surface. Furthermore, the poor-quality leather lost all shape in the rain and actually froze solid in the winter, rendering the boots all but unwearable in inclement weather. "Jefferson" boots, either Southern-made or imported from England, were given a trial but generally proved little better than useless. Imported shoes were lined and filled with stiff paper, causing them to disintegrate in the wet, while domestically manufactured products comprised green leather which cracked in the heat. As early as the winter of 1862, frantic orders were issued to the worst-equipped troops to collect hides from the military slaughter pens for the manufacture of moccasins but, at best, this could only provide a temporary respite from a problem which was destined to plague the commissaries for the rest of the war. Many infantrymen resorted to homemade wooden clogs as the only viable alternative.

In theory, each soldier was to be issued three flannel shirts and four pairs of woolen socks, but in practice, these were often simply not available. Many issue shirts were imported and were thus in a variety of colors. Few had collars or pockets,

although certain more formal patterns were designed to be worn in lieu of uniform jackets in the summer months, particularly in the early stages of the war.

All ranks wore a variety of black or brown belts, either secured with Confederate ordnance plates depicting the letters "CSA" or with clasps of locally manufactured state design. Cartridge boxes were secured with similar plates, but these were expensive to produce and became a rarity after 1862.

Most infantrymen were issued with bayonets and scabbards of various designs, although most found them to be heavy, cumbersome, and of little use. In true Confederate tradition, many regiments discarded the weapon *en masse* without a thought for the future, although ironically a number tried to rectify this mistake once they had experienced the impact of a Union bayonet charge. Many volunteers supplemented their issue armaments with personally acquired revolvers and Bowie knives in anticipation of vicious hand-to-hand fighting, but these, too, were soon discarded as heavy and impractical as soon as the realities of actual warfare were appreciated.

By the advent of 1863, shortages were taking their toll at all levels. Troops were reduced to wearing homespun dyed civilian clothing and, in some cases, hand-me-downs. Many were forced to resort to pillaging the Federal dead and robbing prisoners, so much so that Washington felt it necessary to threaten to treat as spies Confederate soldiers captured in predominantly Union uniform: (some were actually tried and shot.) Despite this, the Army of Northern Virginia continued to function, fight, and occasionally win for two more terrible years of war.

The M-1841-pattern musket was carried by many Confederate regiments.

4TH ALABAMA REGIMENT

Alabama was one of the most conservative states in the deep South. The third state to secede from the Union (on 11 January 1861) its capital, Montgomery, saw the establishment of the Confederacy in February of that year and was the seat of government until its removal to its permanent base in Richmond in July.

General Orders No. 1, containing dress regulations for the newly formed "Alabama Volunteer Corps," were issued on 28 April 1861. Although there is considerable evidence that many units ignored these, the majority complied within the realms of administrative possibility. Dark blue frock coats were to be worn as were gray wool trousers and West Point-style shakos. The letters "AVC" (the "C" standing for "Corps" and not "Cadets" as has been erroneously suggested) were placed on the cap below the national eagle. Also issued were woolen overcoats of jeans material lined with heavy checked or striped osnaburg, beautifully warm in winter but heavy and totally impractical in the wet. Approximately 10,000 distinctive black felt hats with the brims looped and buttoned on the left side were ordered and became a popular item of dress when introduced.

As the "Alabama Volunteer Corps" grew and demand for uniforms began to outstrip supply, gray became the most common coat color. In August 1861, Governor Andrew Moore introduced a simpler outfit including a gray wool jacket with seven brass military buttons down the front, shoulder lapels, two belt straps, and a double, thick, standing collar lined with osnaburg. Gray trousers and a gray wool overcoat, the latter with buttons similar to those of the jacket, a detachable lined cape secured to the collar by five small brass buttons, and an adjustable waist band (a luxury for the times) completed the outfit.

By the end of 1861, the highly efficient state quartermaster's department had acquired 7,416 complete uniforms including checked or striped flannel shirts, woolen underwear, socks, gloves, shoes, and blankets. In March 1862, the central Confederate government assumed responsibility for supplying the state's troops, after which Montgomery restricted its activities to clothing reserve and militia units. Nonetheless state buttons and the ubiquitous slouch hat remained popular with volunteers, who continued to wear them long after they ceased being regulation issue.

During the same month, troops of the 1st Alabama Infantry, about to leave Montgomery to take their place in the line, were each issued with an enameled cloth knapsack, haversack, and cedar canteen. As an existing unit, they were not, however, issued with the new Confederate uniform

Porter King resigned as a judge in 1861 to take command of the Marion Light Infantry, mainly comprised of students from Howard College. The company was subsequently absorbed into the Alabama Regiment.

Headdress: The U.S. Military Academy-style shakos were adorned with a state eagle, a blue and white plume and the letters "AVC." By 1863 most troops had been issued with conventional Confederate gray kepis.

Frock coat: The dark blue three-quarter length frock coats with their high collars, light blue piping and ostentatious epaulettes were soon replaced by more practical gray cloth coats.

Weapons: Most Alabama Volunteers were armed as here with the M1842 smoothbore 0.69-caliber musket and M1840 model bayonet.

which was still in short supply, and they thus presented a motley impression as they marched to war, each wearing his personally supplied variant.

Due in part to the French influence from Louisiana, a number of the first volunteer units to be formed in Alabama adopted the Zouave style of uniform, although due to cost and impracticality in the field, most soon reverted to the anonymity of Confederate gray. The Alabama Zouaves (Law's Company), the Tallapoosa Zouaves (Smith's Company), and the Eufaula Zouaves (later Company "K," the 15th Alabama Infantry Regiment) were among the most famous.

The 4th Alabamans were the first troops from the state, and indeed among the first from the Confederacy, to experience formal battle. Under the command of the vastly experienced Evander Law, they were deployed as part of General Barnard Bee's Brigade when news reached General Beauregard, who was in overall command of the Confederate forces in the area, that a large Union army was approaching Manassas from the direction of Washington. Determined to hold his position until Johnston could arrive with reinforcements, Beauregard ordered Nathan Evans with the 4th South Carolina Regiment, the 1st Louisiana Special Battalion, and a squadron of cavalry to secure the river crossings, while his remaining troops, including Bee's Brigade, were ordered forward to the high ground in the vicinity of Henry House Hill, some two miles south of Bull Run. A fervent believer in taking the offensive, Evans delayed the progress of the vastly superior Federal forces for over an hour by leading a series of charges against the confused and shaken Northern ranks. Forced at last to withdraw, the remnants of Evans' troops retired to a fresh position between Bull Run and Henry House Hill where they were joined by Bee's 4th Alabamans and 2nd and 11th Mississippians and by Bartow's 7th and 8th Georgians who had force-marched to their assistance. Despite their hunger and thirst – 21 July was a blazing hot day – Bee's men were not allowed to rest but instead were deployed forward to within 100 yards (91.5m) of the enemy. Once in position, they halted and fired a series of withering volleys into the enemy lines, lying on the ground for protection against returning fire while they reloaded.

Although outnumbered three to one at 10:30 a.m., in an effort to buy yet more time until the bulk of Johnston's reinforcements could arrive, the jubilant Confederates took the initiative, rising *en masse* to charge the by now thoroughly disillusioned Northern divisions to their front. Although Bartow's Georgians on the right flank took the worst casualties (they subsequently named the area "the place of slaughter"), Bee's men suffered severely. In the words of Captain Thomas Goldsby of the 4th Alabama, "Our brave men fell in great numbers, but they died as the brave love to die – with faces to the foe, fighting in the holy cause of liberty." Whether the 30 percent casualties suffered by one Alabama company or Lieutenant Colonel Jones who died in agony, his leg shattered by enemy fire, would have agreed with those sentiments is doubtful. During the morning, every field officer of the 4th Alabama was killed or injured.

When Evans' weary men on the left and Barstow's Georgians on the right were forced to give ground, Bee found his flanks exposed and his position untenable. Forced to withdraw under heavy fire, his men now made a tragic error. Seeing a gray-clad regiment some distance off and assuming it to be part of the long-awaited reinforcements, an officer from the 4th Alabama made a recognition signal which he mistakenly thought was answered. The Alabamans moved to re-form next to the newcomers, who were in fact the gray-uniformed vanguard of Sherman's 2nd Wisconsin Regiment. Immediately the unsuspecting Southerners unfurled their colors, they were met by a murderous fire. Out of control, they abandoned their position and fled south toward Henry House Hill where the 600 South Carolinians of Hampton's Legion had formed in reserve. Eager for glory, Hampton advanced his troops toward the enemy and, for a while, found himself all alone and in the forefront of the battle. Within minutes, the South Carolinians were cut to pieces and forced to join the general retreat.

Meanwhile the Confederate rear had been reinforced by Jackson's five regiments of Virginia infantry. Despite strong protestations from Bee, Jackson refused to advance his troops in support of the shattered front-line brigades, although he did order his artillery to fire into the advancing Federals. Exasperated, Bee turned, rallied the exhausted remnants of the 4th Alabamans, and led them back over the crest of Henry House Hill toward the enemy. It was a gallant but hopeless effort. The Union artillery battered the Alabamans so badly that, once again, they broke and ran. In a desperate attempt to hold his command together, Bee turned and charged the enemy. A few seconds later, he was shot off his horse, mortally wounded. Exhausted but unbowed, the few remaining Alabamans re-formed around their regimental banner and, under the command of a color sergeant, were at last able to take up a position in reserve on the right of the now heavily reinforced Confederate line.

Evander Law, the lieutenant colonel of the 4th Alabama at 1st Manassas, was severely wounded during the fighting. Fully recovered, he was elected colonel on 8 October 1861 and given command of Whiting's Brigade, which included his old regiment. Having led the brigade during the Peninsula campaign and at Malvern Hill, 2nd Manassas, and Antietam (Sharpsburg), he was promoted brigadier general on 3 October 1862. He led his brigade in the attack on the Round Tops during the Battle of Gettysburg, assuming command of the division when Hood was wounded. He again succeeded Hood at Chickamauga but reverted to brigade command during the Wilderness campaign and at Spotsylvania, North Anna, and Cold Harbor where he was again badly wounded. Sent to the Carolinas to recuperate, he assumed command of Butler's cavalry brigade in February 1865.

After Law's injury at Cold Harbor in June 1864, control of his old brigade, which then constituted the 4th, 15th, 44th, 47th, and 48th Alabama Regiments, passed to Brigadier General Perry who retained command until the final surrender.

ALABAMA.

PRESENTED BY THE LADIES OF THE CANEBRAKE.

A memorial to the Canebrake Rifles, later to become Company 'B' of the 4th Alabama Regiment.

THE CONFEDERATE IRREGULAR

As the war progressed and the Federal blockade tightened, many Confederate troops were, of necessity, forced to wear irregular items of clothing. The lucky ones – the so-called "Butternuts" – were issued with apparel made from cheap, mass-produced, coarse gray cloth which at least resembled uniform. The less fortunate were compelled to supplement their existing uniforms with captured or looted items of Union kit. Most confined their pillaging to anonymous items of clothing such as shirts, underwear, socks and shoes, although articles such as overcoats and raincoats and even jackets and trousers were widely worn. Where possible, the strictly military items of kit were dyed gray or butternut.

The acquisition and use by the Confederates of essential clothing items was accepted by the Federals as inevitable and justifiable. However, the wearing of their uniforms by spies and pro-Confederate guerrillas was not tolerated.

Matters came to a head in 1863 when the tide of battle began to turn convincingly against the South. On 26 January, General Grant, in command of the Department of the Tennessee, ordered that: "guerrillas or Southern soldiers caught in the uniforms of Federal soldiers would not be treated as organized bodies of the enemy but would be closely confined and held for the action of the War Depart-

Union troops recapturing a wagon train from a group of Confederate guerrillas in Virginia, September 1863.

ment. Those caught within the lines of the Federal army in such uniforms or in civilian clothing would be treated as spies."

On 29 March, the commander of the Department of Maryland went further, formally ordering that any officer or soldier of the Confederate army found within Federal lines wearing clothing or accouterments of the United States would be dealt with as a spy. The Southern authorities threatened retaliation, arguing that such clothing and accouterments were legitimate bounty under the rules of war and might therefore be worn by the capturing forces. In an attempt to defuse the volatile situation, Adjutant General Francis Lieber issued a series of general orders expounding clearly Washington's attitude toward enemy troops captured in Federal uniform. General Order No. 100, dated 24 April 1863, stated:

Troops who fight in the uniform of their enemies, without any plain, striking, and uniform mark of distinction of their own, can expect no quarter. If American troops capture a train containing uniforms of the enemy, and the commander considers it advisable to distribute them for use among his men, some striking mark or sign must be adopted to distinguish the American soldier from the enemy.

After 1863 resupply became increasingly difficult for the Confederate forces. Many troops resorted to civilian homespun while others supplemented their uniform from items of kit looted from prisoners and the dead. A few irregulars fought unashamedly for plunder. Though subject to summary execution if caught, they frequently resorted to Federal uniform to gain the element of surprise. Although their greatest excesses were disowned by the Confederacy many, notably William Quantrill, held Southern commissions.

Lieber's well-considered statement had little immediate effect on the Confederates. Only four days later, the commander of the 8th Missouri Cavalry reported the murder of seven of his men by "rebels dressed in Federal Uniform who rode up to them as friends," stripped and murdered them and then, as a final insult, threw them into a heap "like so many hogs."

On 30 August 1863, Sherman complained to Grant that his troops had recently captured two men professing to belong to the Confederate cavalry. Neither wore uniform nor indeed anything to suggest the mark of a soldier, although both were fully armed and had taken active steps to avoid the Northern patrols. The fate of these men is unknown, although others like them met unfortunate ends. Private Dodd of the 8th Texas Cavalry was shot as a spy on 5 January 1864 when caught wearing United States uniform, and three days later, the Department of Ohio issued an order directing corps commanders to execute by firing squad any Confederate soldier caught wearing Federal uniform within Union lines. However, despite the obviously strong feeling of the commanders on the ground, Washington showed a marked reluctance to support such strong measures. In several instances, field orders that sentenced to death "spies" in hybrid uniform were revoked.

Not surprisingly, the government was far less compromising in its attitude toward the bushwacker. Vicious, blood-thirsty, and self-centered, the bushwacker, or raider, fought far more for himself than he did for the Confederacy, although a number were awarded protective commissions in the Southern army. Prevalent in the border states, particularly Missouri and what was to become West Virginia, he was detested by most and feared by all. Captain Charles Leib, an officer in the Union army, described a group of raiders whom he encountered in western Virginia:

Imagine a stolid, vicious-looking countenance, an ungainly figure [clothed] in a garb of the coarsest texture of homespun linen or linsey-woolsey, tattered and torn, and so covered with dirt as not to enable one to guess its original color; a dilapidated, rimless hat or cap of some wild animal covering his head, which has not been combed for months; his feet covered with moccasins, and a rifle by his side, a powder horn and a shot-pouch slung around his neck ... Thus equipped, he sallies forth with the stealth of a panther, and lies in wait for a straggling soldier ... to whom the only warning given of his presence is the sharp click of his deadly weapon.

The most notorious raider, William Clarke Quantrill, was not even a Southerner. The son of an Ohio schoolteacher, he had drifted around the West until the advent of the war had given him the opportunity to practice his particular talents. Despite his lack of Confederate ties, he chose to support the cause of the South because of the potential afforded him to attack the symbols of Missouri authority which he had grown to detest.

Quantrill gathered about him a gang of psychopathic killers, including four men who were later destined to become infamous in their own right: Frank and Jessie James, and Cole and James Younger. Initially theirs was a relatively conventional war in which Union supply lines and bases were attacked in conjunction with more orthodox Confederate military operations. In August 1862, Quantrill's band captured Independence, Missouri as part of a Southern cavalry raid against Arkansas, and as a reward, Quantrill received a captain's commission in the Confederate army. Thereafter he referred to himself as "Colonel" as if to imply the respectability of regimental status for his group.

Quantrill was totally unscrupulous. Capable of double crossing his own men, of murder in cold blood, and of every type of subterfuge, he insured that his men were well mounted and armed by stealing from enemy and neutral alike. On one occasion, he pretended to support a pro-abolitionist attack aimed at freeing slaves while, at the same time, fore-

Confederate irregulars rarely if ever wore a uniform and therefore could expect little quarter if captured. Denied an amnesty after the war, many turned to crime as a way of life.

warning the plantation owner of the raid. The attackers were massacred, leaving Quantrill and his gang free to plunder their dead bodies.

Quantrill's most blood-chilling raid began before dawn on 21 August 1863 when, with about 450 men, he attacked and sacked the town of Lawrence, Kansas, a center for abolitionism and therefore a special target for the Confederates. At the time of the raid, the guerrillas were in a highly vengeful mood. In an attempt to prevent the outlaws' wives and sisters feeding and sheltering their kinfolk, Thomas Ewing, the local Union commander, had ordered the arrest all adult female relatives and their transportation under guard to Kansas City. There, on 14 August, a building housing many of the women collapsed, burying five of them beneath the rubble.

The carnage began immediately the band crossed the Kansas border. Ten farmers were kidnapped to guide the guerrillas toward unsuspecting Lawrence; they were murdered, one by one, as soon as their usefulness was over. Quantrill's only order to his followers was to "kill every male and burn every house" – instructions which they carried out with alacrity. The first of the Lawrence residents to die was a United Brethren clergyman shot through the head while milking his cow. During the next three hours, 182 men and boys were murdered, many in

full view of their mothers, wives, and children, and 185 buildings destroyed. At about nine o'clock in the morning, a column of advancing Union cavalry was spotted by a lookout, and the gang made good its escape without sustaining a single injury.

Only the most partisan were unmoved by this shocking occurrence. A manhunt for Quantrill's followers netted a number who were summarily hanged or shot, but most escaped into the Missouri backwoods. General Ewing ordered the forcible removal of over 10,000 civilians from the four Missouri counties bordering Kansas and declared the area a war zone in the hope of cutting off the guerrillas from their supplies.

In October 1863, while on their way to Texas and winter quarters, Quantrill and his men, dressed in stolen Union uniforms, met a group of Federal troops en route for Fort Baxter Springs, Kansas. Taking the Northerners by surprise (they had assumed that Quantrill and his men were a welcoming party), the guerrillas slaughtered without mercy the majority of the young, unsuspecting soldiers.

The trail of murder and carnage continued until May 1865 when the 27-year-old Quantrill was surprised by Union troops in Kentucky and mortally wounded. When he died a month later, few mourned his passing.

John Morgan's "highwaymen" were notorious. Here they are shown sacking a peaceful town in the west.

THE CONFEDERATE ENGINEER

From the point of view of engineering, the Confederacy began the Civil War at a distinct disadvantage. The vast majority of the officers and men comprising the small but efficient regular army Corps of Engineers and Corps of Topographical Engineers elected to remain loyal to the Union, leaving the South without a nucleus of professional experience on which to build. The Confederacy did, however, have two saving graces: her comparative lack of size and the unswerving support of Robert E. Lee, himself a military engineer of some stature. With the exception of the ill-fated Gettysburg campaign, Confederate armies were never called on to advance deep into enemy territory or to sustain themselves far from the presence of sympathetic civilians, and therefore they never experienced the very real problem of maintaining long lines of supply and communication. They had to repair rather than build bridges and military highways, and were able to rely on an existing (if small) network of railroads for communication. Unlike the Northern railroads which were largely dependent on coal, most Southern locomotives were wood burners and, as such, were far easier to provision.

As early as 1860, Virginia formed its own state Corps of Engineers from the few professional engineers available, utilizing their skills in the construction of a line of coastal and frontier forts. Initially, this unit remained independent, dressing in the standard U.S. officers' dark blue uniform with white belt, gold badges of rank, and state buttons and cap badges according to the Virginia dress regulations of 2 March 1858. However, when the Confederate government moved to Richmond the following year, this small cadre, which consisted totally of officers, merged into the Confederate Corps of Engineers.

Initially, the Corps remained small and exclusive. The actual construction of fortifications, roads, and bridges was undertaken by unskilled labor drawn from available infantry units placed under the temporary command of engineering officers or civilian sub-contractors employed for specific tasks. During the Peninsula campaign (March–July 1862), the system was regulated somewhat, and in June of that year, the Chief of Engineers of the Army of Northern Virginia was directed to take 300 men from each division to form a Corps of Pioneers

Confederate defenses, such as these at Fort Sedgewick, did much to frustrate the Northern streamroller and to prolong the war.

Headdress: Initially officers were instructed to wear "fore and aft" staff officers' hats. However as the war progressed they tended to wear whatever they could find. Cap badges comprising a pair of silver-plated crossed flags were occasionally issued.

Tunic: The staff officer's uniform with buff facings and red sashes, which officially constituted an Engineer Officer's dress, was rarely worn. Instead most favored gray or brown jackets with matching trousers. A variety of infantry-pattern swords, pistols and carbines were carried for personal protection.

to work under the direct control of the engineers. Despite the bravery and diligence of the Pioneer Corps, there were too few of them and they were too lacking in skill to be truly effective. On occasion, they were simply not available, in which case the engineer in charge of a project was entitled to use his initiative and resort to available resources. In one instance, an officer, tasked with bridging the James River near Richmond and finding that the Pioneers had been deployed elsewhere, had 500 civilians rounded up by the Provost Marshal and marched under guard to do the job.

In late 1863, as the battered remnants of the Army of Northern Virginia retreated south into the Virginia hinterland, the necessity for a regularly constituted Corps of Engineers comprising enlisted men as well as officers was at last conceded. Two regiments – the 1st and 2nd Regiments of Confederate States Engineers, each consisting of ten companies of 100 men – were authorized by the Confederate Congress and formed in time for the intended 1864 offensive. The 1st Regiment and two companies of the 2nd served with the Army of Northern Virginia, while the remainder were posted to the West.

Initially, few staff officers fully understood the potential of the new Corps, so much so that much of the 1st Regiment spent its initial engagement fighting as infantry, a duty which it performed more than adequately. However, as the war continued and the need for punitive, slowing action became more apparent, the engineers became more accepted in their true role of building fortifications and defending them with equal ease and ability. As the retreat to Appomattox progressed, engineer elements were constantly to be found at the head of the army, building bridges to facilitate its continued withdrawal, while their colleagues brought up the rear and held off the enemy by destroying the same bridges once their usefulness had been served.

Inevitably, skill comes with age, and because of this, the Corps of Engineers did not consist of young men. Most were between the ages of 25 and 35 and married, and were skilled artisans in their own right. Field and company officers were engineers by profession in civilian life, as were many of the junior officers.

Officers of the Corps of Engineers wore regulation staff officers' uniforms with buff facings, red sashes, and (when available) buttons depicting the Old English letter "E." However, during the latter stages of the war when uniform became difficult if not impossible to acquire, most resorted to conventional officer attire supplemented where necessary by civilian clothing. Enlisted men did not have an authorized button but instead wore general service ones and, toward the end, even plain wooden buttons. Typically, they wore waist-length gray or brown jackets with matching trousers, brown boots and belts, gray regulation kepis, cloth haversacks, and water canteens. Non-commissioned officers wore either buff or white chevrons and, in more established posts, a white cotton stripe down each leg. In keeping with their dual role as artisans and infanteers, most engineers carried rifles and ammunition pouches as well as the ubiquitous shovels.

The massive fortifications built for the defense of Petersburg and Richmond owed much to the inspirational genius of General Lee, himself an accomplished engineer. Built in 1862 and regularly strengthened thereafter, they withstood the concerted might of the Army of the Potomac during the final stages of the war and might well have enabled the garrisons of both cities to continue their resistance almost indefinitely had Lee not been forced to withdraw the bulk of his troops westward in a final desperate attempt to avert defeat. As it was, Petersburg held out until 2 April 1865 while Richmond was abandoned, rather than fell, to the enemy.

Immediately on taking overall command in 1862, Lee had ordered the creation of a network of defensive lines around Richmond. Each divisional commander was allocated a sector and ordered to

Confederate fortifications at Vicksburg, although largely built by unskilled labor, were brilliantly conceived and in many instances bore the hallmark of Robert E. Lee himself.

construct defenses along its length utilizing all raw material available. Initially, these defenses comprised a confused mixture of trenches interspersed with areas of wooden revetments, but as the months went by, the line was developed into a complex arrangement of fire steps, artillery positions, and support trenches as sophisticated as any constructed during World War I.

More worldly wise than their Union foes, Confederate soldiers quickly became skillful in the construction of impromptu defensive trenches. Within an hour of halting – and without goading – regiments would construct shelters made of fences, stones, and logs supplemented by earth and sods, which were proof against all but artillery. They would dig full rifle pits in a day and parapets with fire steps and shelters within two. With the help of trained engineers, these localized defenses were often turned into veritable fortresses to the extent that, during the last few months of the war, seven out of eight Union frontal assaults failed despite the North's overwhelming superiority in numbers and firepower.

The Confederate States Corps of Engineers fought its greatest battle at a time when defeat was imminent. Between 29 March and the final Confederate surrender at Appomattox on 9 April 1865, the remnants of the Army of Northern Virginia fought desperately in an attempt to link up with Johnston's forces retreating from Sherman in North Carolina. Harried by Sheridan's cavalry and pursued relentlessly by Grant's overwhelming forces, the hard-pressed, starving, and exhausted Southerners fought a series of desperate rearguard actions in an attempt to buy time. While the cavalry stood and fought at Namozine Church (3 April) and Amelia Courthouse (5 April), the rest of Lee's forces retreated north, crossing the Appomattox River. During the last few hours of the war, the engineers desperately supported Ewell's infantry at Sayler's Creek and High Bridge (6 April) and at Farmville (7 April). Bridges were blown and obstacles built but to no avail. After the brief but bloody engagements at Appomattox Station (8 April) and Appomattox Courthouse on the following day, Lee sought unconditional surrender. Exact losses during this final campaign are unclear due to the large number of desertions. What is certain is that, to the bitter end, no corps served the cause of the Confederacy more ably than its Corps of Engineers.

The task of the engineer was as much to rebuild as to destroy. It became the common practice of all armies to retreat to lay waste the communications around them without giving much thought to the possibilities of counter-attack.

THE CONFEDERATE BUTTERNUT

Few of those who advocated secession at any price in the heady days of 1860 had any real conception of total war. Many accepted that Washington would fight for the restoration of the status quo, but the overriding feeling was that the Federal government would agree to an equitable compromise after a limited period of saber-rattling. Total warfare encompassing entire communities – male and female, combatant and civilian – was simply beyond the comprehension of even the greatest pessimist. When war broke out a year later, early Confederate victories shrouded the reality of the growing casualty lists and the inevitability of a Union victory. The battles of Seven Pines (Fair Oaks) and the Seven Days fought in May and June 1862 within a few miles of Richmond shocked the final residue of the complacent South to the core, but by then it was too late. The United States – North and South – was experiencing absolute warfare, and the Confederacy was fighting for its very existence.

The South was never able to clothe or provision its mushrooming army adequately. Although it controlled the cotton plantations, the mills were either under Union control or across a hostile ocean patrolled by a powerful blockading fleet. Furthermore it needed to export its entire cotton harvest throughout the war simply to pay for essential arms and ammunition.

Initially most troops were clothed and equipped by the individual states, relieving the central government of the responsibility. However, as the various units were gradually merged into a single army, it became increasingly clear that there would simply not be enough official pattern gray uniforms to go around. This problem was compounded by the total inability of the average Southern soldier to look after what little he had. From the outset, discipline within the Confederate army was appalling. Of proven excellence in battle, the Southern troops, particularly the cavalry, saw little reason to be regimental at other times. Officers were voted into their commands rather than appointed on merit, and as a result, they rarely risked crossing their subordinates by inflicting what they as well as their men saw as tiresome irrelevancies. When an item of equipment, however valuable or scarce, became momentarily useless, it was treated as an impediment and discarded even though its presence might be crucial in the future. Cold weather gear was abandoned *en masse* with the coming of hot weather in the summer of 1862 as if to negate the ferocity of the winter that would inevitably follow.

Such a grave irresponsibility on the men's part had ramifications well above regimental level, never more so than during the Mine Run campaign (November–December 1863). Meade, with the Army

Confederate troops pose for an impromptu photograph at a base camp in Warrington Navy Yard, Pensacola, Florida, in 1861. The lack of formal uniform is all too apparent.

Headaddress: Felt hats, gray or blue kepis, anything which would offer protection from the elements, were pressed into action.

Jackets: Uniformity was virtually non-existent. Original uniforms were merged with looted Federal gear and civilian clothing to offer a modicum of decency. Outfits were coarse, patched and ragged. Those without boots simply tucked their trousers into their socks.

Equipment: Personal effects were reduced to a minimum, all surplus articles being discarded. Most troops carried a haversack, canteen and tin mug but little else. Even cartridge pouches were abandoned, it being considered easier to carry ammunition loose in the pockets.

of the Potomac, had earlier taken the initiative and attempted to maneuver Lee out of his strong position on the Rapidan River. He executed a successful crossing with five corps at Germanna Ford and then turned west toward Orange Courthouse. Lee's cavalry, skirmishing far ahead of his lines, detected the movement immediately, allowing the Confederate Army of Northern Virginia plenty of time to dig in along strong points in the Mine Run area. Finding no obvious weaknesses in the enemy position, Meade ordered a general withdrawal without a fight and went into winter quarters around Culpeper. Sensing the confusion and indecision in the Federal command, Lee at once ordered a general advance behind Northern lines, only to be told that his men had thrown away their overcoats and could not therefore operate in the harsh winter cold beyond the protective mantle of their base camp, with its hot food and fires.

Clothes that were issued were rarely properly cared for – once again demonstrating the inability of company officers to instil minimum standards of appearance. Soap had become a sought-after luxury by 1862, with the result that little if any was squandered on the washing of clothes. Shirts, socks, and undergarments became vermin infested for the want of a hot scrub. Comparatively new clothes were frequently abandoned as unwearable even though a soaking in boiling water would have restored them to near-pristine condition. Strangely, even when the Confederates were fighting close to their own cities, matters did not improve, there being no obvious attempts made by the civilian authorities to set up improvised central laundries.

The Confederate soldier's tenacity, independence, and unshakeable belief in his cause were his greatest assets yet, at the same time, his greatest enemies. Proud of their reputation as hard fighters and never men prone to inquiring too far into the future, the Confederates simply did not see the need for discipline. As long as they kept their weapons clean and their powder dry and turned up when and where their presence was required, what did it matter how they got there or what they looked like? There were, of course, exceptions to this generalization. "Stonewall" Jackson commanded the finest light infantry in the world during the campaigns of 1862–63, but he would not have been able to execute the complex and lengthy maneuvers that he did without a strong sense of motivation assisted by excellent discipline. Even so, his troops were often likened to scarecrows and tramps as they appeared suddenly and unexpectedly behind enemy lines.

Kit replacement became a near impossibility from late 1862 onward. Many Confederate troops

The Confederate charge on Missionary Ridge during the Battle of Chattanooga. Sheer determination did much to overcome the chronic lack of supplies.

relied upon Federal equipment pilfered from prisoners or the dead to augment their own meager issue, but this became unpopular when rumors began to spread that the North was treating Southerners caught in Union uniform behind its lines as spies. Many families attempted to send what they could from home, but inevitably, clothing provided domestically was civilian in nature and left the soldiers resembling armed farm boys rather than soldiers.

The most realistic solution lay in the wholesale issue of a new homespun uniform made of cheap, durable cloth. Never popular with the Confederate authorities, who perpetually strove to establish at least some degree of formality within their forces, the new issue was intended to supplement rather than replace the traditional gray. Nevertheless by 1865, few units were wearing anything but the new issue.

The new uniform quickly attained the universally accepted nickname "butternut" after a group of farmers from Ohio, Indiana, and Illinois who had thrown in their lot with the Confederacy. Violently anti-"Yankee," these smallholders had, during the previous 50 years, evolved a corn–hog–whiskey economy in the rural south of that region. Totally divorced from the more affluent settlers of New England heritage who farmed to the north, theirs

was a totally isolated society. They dressed in homespun clothes dyed with the oil of walnut or butternut trees, and hence acquired the generic name "Butternuts."

Butternut first appeared extensively at South Mountain (14 September 1862), when it was noticed that hundreds of the Confederate dead were wearing the new, coarse uniform. Production was simple and ideally suited the home economy then being forced by necessity on the South. Wool and cotton were carded together and spun into yarn. This was then dyed with walnut or butternut oil and woven into cloth on homemade looms. The cloth was then dyed again until it became a reddish brown, after which it was cut and sewn into uniforms.

Any carpenter could make a loom and any woman could operate it. As the Northern soldiers marched deeper into the South, they were amazed to see the extent of manufacture of butternut. Many houses had improvised looms, and those that did not invariably had the means to card the wool and cotton, and spinning wheels to turn them into yarn.

Always short of clothing and equipment, the Southern soldier was in many ways the author of his own discomfort. Nevertheless had it not been for the resilience and productivity of his womenfolk at home, he might well have been in a far worse predicament.

The charge of the 6th Missouri Regiment at Vicksburg. The lack of formal uniforms did nothing to reduce the fighting potency of these gallant men.

THE VIRGINIA CAVALRY

Not the first state to secede from the Union, Virginia was nonetheless politically and economically the most powerful in the Confederacy. It contained the Confederate capital, several strategically important ports, many of the railheads, and much of the South's industrial output. Its greatest weakness lay in its geographical position as a border state, a problem which was severely compounded when the disenchanted pro-abolitionist mining communities across the Blue Ridge Mountains voted to form the independent state of West Virginia and return to the Union in 1863. Virginia's main rail link with the west passed through Manassas Junction which was relatively close to the Maryland border and less than 40 miles from the outskirts of Washington. More crucially, the northern part of the Shenandoah Valley – the aptly named "breadbasket of the Confederacy" – lay dangerously exposed to marauding Federal cavalry parties.

During the early stages of the war when the Confederacy was in the ascendancy, none of this mattered. Two battles fought for the control of Manassas Junction – the 1st and 2nd Battles of Manassas (Bull Run) – both ended in comprehensive Southern victories, and by early 1862, it was Washington rather than Richmond which faced the possibility of capitulation. However, as the war

progressed and the sheer industrial might of the North began to take its inevitable toll, the situation began slowly but steadily to change. In early 1864, the Shenandoah Valley was comprehensively sacked by vengeful Union troops, and from then until the final Confederate surrender, Virginia was destined to suffer severely at the hands of an increasingly uncompromising enemy.

With the exception of western Virginia, which provided no fewer than 12,688 volunteers to the Union cause in 1861 alone, large numbers of men from all parts of Virginia flocked to enlist in the Confederate army. Initially organization and training of the state troops were delegated to an erratic and somewhat eccentric professor from the Virginia Military Institute, but in mid-May control passed to General Joseph Johnston. A West Point graduate, a veteran of the Seminole and Mexican wars and a trusted friend of Robert E. Lee, Johnston assumed command of all facets of training in the South once the Virginian forces were absorbed into the Confederate army.

Initially Johnston's Army of the Shenandoah consisted of 10,000 officers and enlisted men organized into four brigades, each with its own artillery battery but all sharing the services of the 1st Virginia Cavalry under the command of Colonel

The "Black Horse Cavalry," as it was known, did much to snatch victory from defeat at Manassas on 21 July 1861 when they held, and eventually routed, the New York Fire Zouaves.

132

Headddress: Many Virginians adorned their irregular slouch hats with feathers as if to emphasize their éliteness.

Jackets: Jackets of all kinds were worn with or without regulation Confederate collar and cuffs. Officers wore badges of rank on their shoulders and sleeves, N.C.O.s on their upper arm.

Firearms: Issue sabers were soon abandoned as impractical. Troops were given pistols but usually supplemented the firepower of these with privately purchased carbines and even in a few instances with shotguns.

Jeb Stuart. As the army grew and the cavalry expanded, the latter was re-formed into an independent brigade, but it never really lost its strong Virginia bias.

When first established, the 1st Virginia Cavalry (or "Black Horse Cavalry" as it was locally known) consisted of four troops of 100 men each, but by the summer of 1861, it had grown to a full regiment of ten troops. Its members regarded themselves as a social and military élite. All were accomplished horsemen used to hard riding and most were excellent shots. The regiment served with the Army of Northern Virginia throughout the war, performing invaluable reconaissance duty as well as undertaking several daring raids deep behind enemy territory. It was present at the 1st and 2nd Battles of Manassas, at Fredericksburg and Chancellorsville, and at the great cavalry action at Brandy Station. After Stuart's death at Yellow Tavern, the regiment continued in service, finishing the war as part of Munford's Brigade.

At no time did the 1st Virginians show their true worth more than during the 1st Battle of Manassas when the presence of these superb horsemen did much to turn defeat into victory. The rebel line was being hard pressed when Stuart and his regiment arrived from the south to take up a position on the extreme Confederate left flank below Henry House Hill. Well deployed in a patch of woods, the Virginians managed to keep their presence concealed from the Union troops until the latter had been committed to a frontal assault up the hill against what they assumed to be the remnants of the rapidly disintegrating Southern army. In a spirited charge, a squadron of Stuart's 1st Virginians tore into the unsuspecting lines of the 11th New York Fire Zouaves, leaving the latter, and with them the entire Union right flank, shaken and demoralized. The Union assault quickly wavered and, within minutes, disintegrated into a general withdrawal. Panic set in among the raw Union troops, turning an orderly retreat into a full-scale rout. The Confederate cavalry was not disciplined enough to pursue the enemy and were thus unable to exploit their victory to the full. Nonetheless, in two hours of bloody fighting the Virginian cavalry earned for itself a reputation for invulnerability which it was to retain at least until Brandy Station.

Members of the 1st Virginian wore gray or butternut uniform adorned with numerous troop and personal variations. Many troopers sported long, flowing hair despite its impracticality in the field.

Others wore often ornate plumes and feathers in their non-regulation slouch hats. Shell jackets, double-breasted fatigue blouses, and Federal-style fatigue dress, with or without the regulation Confederate yellow collar and cuffs, were all worn. Where possible, officers retained the elaborate cuff braiding, or "chicken guts," on their long frock coats or shell jackets. Commissioned rank was indicated both by insignia worn on the collar and by the design of the sleeve braiding: lieutenants, captains, field officers, and generals wore from one to four strands respectively. N.C.O.s wore yellow chevrons and $1\frac{3}{4}$-inch (4.5cm) stripes on the outer seams of their light blue trousers. Theoretically senior N.C.O.s also wore distinctive yellow sashes, but these were regarded as both an unnecessary encumbrance and an invitation to enemy sharpshooters and were invariably discarded.

A wide variety of high boots were worn, usually over but occasionally under the light blue or gray corduroy trousers. The black leather belt with its pistol holster and ammunition pouch was fastened with a circular Virginia state buckle.

The Virginians were among the first cavalry troops to abandon the saber, although whether this was due more to its impracticality or to its rarity is a moot point. Carbines and pistols of every kind were provided by the individual troopers and carried into battle. Although this ameliorated considerably the initial problems of supply, ultimately it made ammunition replenishment a logistical nightmare. In the absence of carbines, sawn-off, double-barreled, muzzle-loading shotguns were found to be most effective, although the indiscriminate discharge of such weapons by excited troops in the heat of battle did tend to endanger both friend and foe alike.

As the war progressed, Virginia continued to provide the bulk of the Confederate cavalry. In August 1864, Fitzhugh Lee's entire division consisted of seven Virginian regiments, the 1st to 4th of which formed a veteran brigade under the irrepressible Brigadier General W.C. Wickham. Wickham was typical of the cavalry leaders of the time. A graduate of the University of Virginia, he devoted his pre-war energies to his legal practice and to the running of the family plantation. Although opposed to secession, he volunteered and fought for the Confederacy at the 1st Battle of Manassas during which he served as a captain in the élite Hanover Dragoons. Promoted lieutenant colonel and placed in command of the 4th Virginia Cavalry

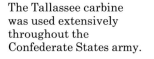

The Tallassee carbine was used extensively throughout the Confederate States army.

in September 1861, he was severely wounded by a saber thrust in hand-to-hand fighting during the Battle of Williamsburg (4–5th May 1862). While convalescing at home, he was captured by McClellan but subsequently exchanged for his wife's relative, Thomas Kane of the Pennsylvania Bucktails. Restored to command of the 4th Virginia and promoted colonel in August 1862, he led his regiment at the 2nd Battle of Manassas, at Boonsborough, at Antietam (Sharpsburg), and on Stuart's raid into Maryland and Pennsylvania. Wounded while in temporary command of Fitzhugh Lee's Brigade at Upperville, Wickham recovered in time to lead his men at Fredericksburg, Chancellorsville, and Gettysburg. Appointed brigadier general on 1 September 1863, he served under

Fitzhugh Lee in the Mine Run operations, at Brandy Station, and at Buckland Mills before repelling Kilpatrick's raid on Richmond in February 1864. Thereafter he commanded his unit during the Wilderness campaign, at Spotsylvania and Yellow Tavern, and during a number of minor engagements, before retiring to take up his seat in the Confederate Congress on 9 November 1864.

By April 1865, Fitzhugh Lee's Division consisted almost exclusively of Virginians. Munford's Brigade, the successor to Wickham's Brigade, contained the 1st to 4th Virginians, Payne's Brigade comprised the 5th, 6th, 8th, and 36th Virginians, while Gary's somewhat assorted unit contained the 24th Regiment. No state could have given more to its beloved Confederacy.

To many Virginians, John Brown's stand at Harpers Ferry proved the inevitability of war and hastened the break-up of the Union.

HOOD'S TEXAS BRIGADE

The Lone Star State of Texas seceded on 1 February 1861, less than 15 years after being admitted to the Union. The governor, Sam Houston was firmly against the split but was forced to concede when a state convention voted by 166 to 8 to throw in their lot with the South.

Texas did not immediately call for volunteers but instead decided to bide its time and await events. Impatient for action and despairing of the state government's inactivity, many Texans moved east to offer their services to the newly formed Confederate army. Several infantry units were formed, and on 12 November 1861, the 3rd and 5th Texas Infantry Regiments, under the commands of John B. Hood and J.J. Archer respectively, linked with the 18th Georgia under W.T. Wofford to form the Texas Brigade. Overall command initially passed to Colonel Lewis T. Wigfall of the 1st Texas Infantry, but when he was elected to the Confederate Senate, his place was taken by the newly promoted Brigadier General Hood.

A blond giant with doleful eyes and a quiet, unassuming manner, John Bell Hood was without peer as a brigade or divisional leader, at which level he was able to subordinate his lack of basic intelligence to his sheer charisma and will to win. In less than six months, he turned his brigade into, in the words of Lee, "the best combat troops in the Army of Northern Virginia." When Hood was promoted major general and posted to command of the 2nd Division on 10 October 1862, the Texans paid him the highest compliment possible by retaining his name as part of the brigade title. From then to its disbandment at the very end of the war, it remained "Hood's Texas Brigade."

Under Hood's inspired leadership, the brigade was blooded at Gaines's Mill (27 June 1862) after which its numbers were supplemented by the addition of Colonel M. Gary's Hampton Legion. Despite its somewhat grandiose title, the Legion in fact consisted of six companies of South Carolina infantrymen formed, paid for, and maintained (together with four cavalry companies and a battery of artillery) by the immensely wealthy Wade Hampton. The entire Legion was led by the inexperienced Hampton at the 1st Battle of Manassas (Bull Run) during which it fought with distinction but sustained 20 percent casualties. Thereafter it was broken up, the artillery being redesignated Hart's South Carolina Battery, the cavalry joining Rosser's cavalry regiment, and the infantry joining Hood.

Prior to relinquishing command to Colonel Jerome Bonaparte Robertson of the 5th Texan Infantry, Hood again led his brigade during the 2nd Battle of Manassas and at Antietam (Sharpsburg).

Longstreet's Texans retaking the outer line of entrenchments on the south side of the James River.

Headdress: Officially the Texas Brigade wore Federal pattern kepis. However as the war progressed many abandoned these in favor of slouch hats often adorned with a feather. As if to emphasize Texan independence, troops of all ranks tended to favor the Lone Star hat badge, although the trooper here has retained the more orthodox crossed sabers.

Jacket: Many of the first companies formed adopted styles and patterns later associated with neighboring states. In this instance the trooper is wearing a Mississippi-style jacket with high collar and several rows of stripes across the chest.

During the later stages of 1862, the brigade was restructured to return it to full strength, the 1st, 4th, and 5th Texan Regiments being joined by the 3rd Arkansas under the command of Colonel Van Manning.

When Robertson received his third wound during the Battle of Gettysburg, when the Texans fought as part of Hood's Division, he was temporarily replaced by Colonel P. Work. Reinstated when the brigade moved to the West, Robertson led his men into action at Chickamauga (19–20 September 1863), but by then he had lost the support of General Longstreet. When Jenkins replaced Hood as divisional commander, Robertson lost his one remaining ally and was removed from command, his place being taken by the Texan John Gregg. Returning to the East, the brigade once again distinguished itself during the Wilderness campaign, during which, on 6 May 1864, it lost over 400 men out of 711 in action during a single unsupported attack.

Lieutenant General John B. Hood, after whom the famous Texas Brigade was named.

Gregg was killed on 7 October 1864 during the Petersburg campaign, after which command passed in quick succession to Colonels Winkler, Bass and Powell, the latter holding the position until the final surrender.

At no time did Hood's Texan Brigade conduct itself more bravely than during the three days of bitter fighting at Gettysburg (1–3 July 1863). Realizing that the Confederacy could not hope to win a protracted war, Lee had advanced deep into Federal territory to draw Meade's Army of the Potomac away from Virginia. Gambling on the belief that a Southern victory on Northern soil would strengthen the growing peace movement in the North and

Oates with 500 men from the 15th and 47th Alabama successfully took the Devil's Den with few losses. However, fate now turned against the Confederacy. During the few minutes which Oates allowed his men to draw breath before turning north to cross the saddle separating them from Little Round Top, the Federals brought forward reserves, including Battery "D" of the 5th U.S. Artillery, pre-empting a further Confederate advance with considerable loss of life. During a confused afternoon of gallant fighting, the Southern brigades mounted a series of costly individual assaults against the by now heavily defended Federal positions on Little Round Top.

Privately-purchased hunting rifles with reinforced barrels and crude sights were carried by marksmen of both armies.

might encourage Britain's intervention on behalf of the South, Lee began the movement of his troops north from Chancellorsville on 3 June. There followed a month of balance and counter-balance in which both sides attempted with little success to cut the other's lines of communication.

By late June, both armies faced each other in the area of the Gettysburg railhead. The Union forces enjoyed the advantage of the ridge of high ground to the south of the town, but the Confederates were better placed to take the offensive. The Texan Brigade, as part of Hood's Division and Longstreet's Corps, was positioned on the extreme right of the Confederate line facing III Corps led by Federal General Sickles. Denied the eyes and ears of Stuart's cavalry still some miles away on a fruitless foraging expedition, Lee lacked information on the terrain and enemy dispositions and was therefore unable to formulate a complete tactical plan.

On 1 July 1863, believing the main enemy defensive line to be further north than it was, Lee ordered Longstreet with two divisions (Hood on the right and McLaws on the left) to move south under cover of dead ground and thereafter to turn and advance north, rolling up the Federal flank in his path. Ironically, Sickles, in contravention of orders and against all military logic, had moved the leading elements of his corps forward to high ground in the path of the intended advance and now commanded the strategically important high ground north of the Round Tops. When Longstreet reached the forming-up point for his assault, he realized to his horror that instead of facing an understrength regiment supported by a battery of guns as he had anticipated, an entire corps now blocked his advance. Longstreet immediately requested permission to call off the attack, but permission was denied, and at approximately 4:00 p.m., Hood's Division attacked toward the Round Tops.

The four regiments of the Texas Brigade did all humanly possible to drive the Federals from their vantage point. The 1st Texas and 3rd Arkansas assailed the Devil's Den, a craggy promontory a little to the west of the Round Tops, while the 4th and 5th Texans supported Evander Law's Alabama Brigade in an assault on Little Round Top itself. At one stage, the Southerners reached the summit of the hill only to be slaughtered by the massed guns of Smith's 4th New York Battery, firing into them at point blank range. Eventually, exhausted and cut to pieces, the remnants of Longstreet's Corps, including the brave Texans, were forced by the sheer weight of enemy firepower to retire, leaving the Federal's much battered left flank intact.

No one was fully aware of it at the time, but on 2 July 1863, the Confederacy had reached its high water mark. The battle raged all that day and for another, but eventually Lee was forced to retreat and ultimately to retire southward into the safety of Virginia. Yet Hood's Texan Brigade could not have done more. In the words of Private Giles of the 4th Texas: "Every fellow [in the battle for the Little Round Top] was his own general. Private soldiers gave commands as loud as the officers; nobody paying any attention to either."

Texans were as independent in their dress as they were in all matters relating to discipline or regulations, and it was some time before the Texan Brigade adopted a universal uniform. Until then, all wore gray although the cut and shade varied greatly. Many wore frock coats, some with stripes across the chest in the manner of the Mississippi regiments, and most sported kepis. As the blockade took effect and replacement kit became more difficult to obtain, slouch hats of every color and design began to replace the kepis, while items of civilian wear and looted Federal equipment became more prevalent. As if to emphasize Texas' unique status as a previously independent republic, many of the troops displayed "Lone Stars" prominently on their pouches, headdress, and buckles.

CONFEDERATE STATE ARTILLERY

During the heady days of mass enlistment in the summer of 1861, few of the tens of thousands of Southerners who flocked to the newly raised Confederate colors considered service in the artillery. Spurred on by the reassuring presence of their friends and neighbors, most joined the local infantry battalions. Others who could ride, and who owned a suitable mount, favored the cavalry. Only a few ex-regular soldiers with previous gunnery experience willingly volunteered for the artillery.

Such batteries as were formed were usually neither numbered nor lettered but instead were generally identified by their commander's name. Others were either called after the area in which they were formed or were dedicated to a local hero. This led to confusion and did little to enhance a feeling of national identity among the gunners. Commanders were elected, invariably from among the social elite who, uniquely among the Southerners who fought in the War between the States, regarded service with the guns as prestigious.

Lee showed his disdain for artillery in 1862 by leaving the majority of his guns behind when embarking upon his invasion of the North. Nevertheless, after the Battle of Chancellorsville, he was forced to concede the necessity for massed artillery

and, in 1863, ordered a general reorganization of the 66 batteries within the Army of Northern Virginia. The six batteries of horse artillery were formed into a single battalion, although, thereafter, they rarely fought as such. The remaining artillery was grouped into 15 battalions of four batteries; each battalion being commanded by a lieutenant colonel with a major as second in command. Two or three battalions, when grouped together, were commanded by a colonel. Five battalions, under the command of a brigadier general, comprised a division, one of which was allotted to each of the three army corps. Within each corps, one battalion was allocated to each of the three infantry divisions. The remaining two, under the command of a colonel, formed the reserve.

Despite this reorganization, the battery, not the battalion, remained the pivot of Confederate artillery. For example, the men of Lieutenant Colonel Carter's battalion attached to Rodes's Division of II Corps continued to regard themselves as belonging to four strictly independent entities: Carter's Virginia Battery (King William Artillery), Fry's Virginia Battery (Orange Artillery), Page's Virginia Battery (Morris Artillery), and Reese's Alabama Battery (Jefferson Davis Artillery).

A battery of Confederate 12-pounder Napoleons captured at Missionary Ridge. The South could ill afford the loss of such magnificent weapons.

Headdress: Conventional Confederate gray kepis adorned with a red cap band and cover were worn by all enlisted gunners.

Jacket: Although many gunners retained the traditional double-breasted frock coat others favored the simpler shell jacket.

Webbing: Issue Confederate haversacks designed to carry ammunition forward proved unpopular and were often replaced by looted Federal-issue waterproof leather bags. Swords were issued to all gunners but were often abandoned as impractical.

Most batteries were either self-financing or were sponsored by the regions from which they took their names. As the blockade bit deeper, horses, limbers, and accouterments became virtually impossible to obtain, necessitating the reduction in size of most batteries from six guns to four. Losses from counter-battery fire and from enemy snipers armed with the latest generation of long-range rifled muskets were occasionally so great that infantry companies were transferred *en masse* to serve the guns. None of this helped to preserve the *élan* usually associated with artillery regiments, with the result that traditional pride in unit, which so often manifested itself through smart appearance and discipline, was as a rule sadly lacking.

Distinctive items of dress which had originally served to give the individual batteries an air of independence were often abandoned as impractical after a few weeks in the field. Most batteries resorted to orthodox Confederate dress adorned with red chevrons and a red band around the kepi. Ironically, many photographs of enlisted men show them wearing regulation double-breasted frock coats long after these had become a rarity in other branches of service. When required, gunners would secure a primer pouch to their leather belts, in which they would store the friction primers needed to fire the cannon. Others would carry haversacks slung across their shoulders in which they would transport the heavy shells from the limber to the gun. Confederate haversacks were made of white cotton or drill and, at about 11 inches (28cm) square, were virtually useless for the needs of the gunners, most of whom abandoned them at the first opportunity in favor of plundered waterproof leather Federal-issue bags.

All ranks in the artillery were issued with swords, although most found these so heavy and

impractical that they discarded them. The majority of swords in the South were of domestic manufacture although a number were imported from Europe and others were captured from the North. Locally produced items were of poor quality. Grips were often wrapped in oilcloth or brown leather secured by a single or, at best, double strand of untwisted copper or brass; hilts were crudely cast, and scabbards badly stiched. Short broad-bladed stabbing swords, no more than 18 inches (46cm) long and therefore of particular use in the tight confines of a battery position, became popular with those who could acquire them from civilian sources. Muskets were rare, although pistols, particularly copies of the ubiquitous Colt, were carried by all officers and a sizeable number of the men.

A few elite units retained high standards of discipline and dress throughout the war. Rutlidge's Battery, raised in Nashville, Tennessee in May 1861, later became Battery "A" of the 1st Tennessee Light Artillery, at which time its commander, Captain A.M. Rutlidge, was assigned to General Polk's staff. Seeing action at Mills Spring and Shiloh, the battery's losses in the latter engagement were so heavy that it was found necessary to amalgamate it with McClure's Battery. Despite its subordination, its losses, and its subsequent merger, it never completely lost its identity, and to the end, its members continued to wear their distinctive battery letter "A" on their collars and the crossed cannon barrels on their shoulders and hats.

Without doubt the most famous artillery unit to fight for the Confederate cause was the Washington Artillery. Organized in 1838 as the "Native American Battery" (Company "A" of Persifal Smith's Regiment), it fought with distinction in the Mexican War. Reorganized in 1852 as the Washington Artillery of New Orleans, its new recruits consisted entirely of wealthy and prominent citizens of that city. In 1857, command passed to Colonel J.B. Walton who did much to improve its standards. Under the command of Judah Benjamin, it offered its services to the Confederacy and was mustered in on 26 May 1861. The unit was fortunate to receive much of its equipment, including six 6–pounder cannon with ammunition, from the seizure of Baton Rouge Arsenal on 11 April 1861.

Four batteries of the Washington Artillery fought with the Army of Northern Virginia, helping to turn the tide during the 1st Battle of Manassas (Bull Run), and another fought with the Army of Tennessee. The Washington Artillery particularly distinguished itself in the defense of Marye's Heights during both the Fredericksburg and Chancellorsville campaigns. Commanded successively by Walton, Benjamin Eshelman, and William Miller Owen (the author of the emotive *A Hot Day on Marye's Heights*), the battalion, as it later became, fought in every major battle contested by the Army of Northern Virginia.

It is perhaps indicative of the Confederate attitude toward commissioning through the ranks that, despite their obvious social and academic advantages, few soldiers from this quite outstanding battalion were commissioned and posted elsewhere.

After the war, in a unique recognition of its fighting ability it was given permission by the victorious Federal government to form the "Washington Artillery Veterans Charitable & Benevolent Association Inc." Using this organization as a cover, it held secret drills, assembled weapons, and, in 1870, "rose" to drive the carpetbaggers and their supporters among Longstreet's Metropolitan Police off the streets. In later years, the Washington Artillery sent a battery to fight in Cuba during the Spanish-American War, and served with distinction in both World Wars.

The Washington Artillery wore distinctive blue uniforms, officers having frock coats and other ranks shell jackets. In line with both Federal and Confederate practice, a distinguishing red trim was worn on the upper part of the kepi, on the jacket trim, and along the seams of the trousers. Other ranks wore pipe-clayed leather belts, their headdress bearing crossed-barrel cannon badges with the letters "WA" in brass. Officers wore a broad red sash with the bobble secured on the left, red epaulettes with gold edging, and conventional gold patterning on the lower sleeves. There were other Confederate artillery units that also bore the name "Washington Artillery." Captain G.H. Walter's South Carolina Artillery (Company "A" the Hampton Legion), Captain P.W. Bibb's Tennessee Artillery (the Washington or Hampton Artillery, although originally called Company "K" the 32nd Virginia Infantry and later Company "A" the 1st Virginia Artillery) and finally the Washington Mounted Artillery (Company "A" the 7th Battalion South Carolina Infantry) all aspired to the name. None, however, could match the original unit for panache, professionalism, and sheer determination.

The storming of the Confederate guns during the Battle of Nashville.

THE CONFEDERATE NAVY

At the outbreak of war, the Confederacy had neither a fleet nor a naval tradition. It did, however, have a long and vulnerable coastline liable to attack or blockade and an enemy increasingly reliant on imports from Europe. In 1860, John B. Floyd, the pro-secessionist U.S. Secretary of the Navy, sent the majority of the ships under his command on lengthy goodwill flag tours as far from their home bases as possible to give the South the opportunity to mobilize her limited naval resources without retaliation. When, on 16 March 1861, the Confederate government ordered the creation of a fleet to harry Northern commerce, Washington was able to do little to prevent it. By late 1864, when the Confederate force was at its zenith, the fleet numbered 700 commissioned and warrant officers, 3,674 enlisted men, and a land brigade formed specifically for the defense of Richmond. Due to its lack of raw materials and shipbuilding facilities, the South concentrated on quality rather than quantity. She built a total of 37 ironclads, including the revolutionary *Virginia* (*Merrimac*), (see p.59) and is generally considered to have had a far superior fleet of coastal sloops.

Appointed Confederate Secretary of the Navy on 21 February 1861, Stephen Mallory acted tirelessly throughout the war to insure that the Confederate fleet operated as efficiently as possible. Born in Jamaica but raised in Florida, Mallory qualified in the law, was appointed a judge at an early age, fought in the Seminole War, and served in the U.S. Senate until his resignation in 1861 upon the secession of his adopted state. He quickly realized that the motley collection of volunteers who were coming forward to man his new ships were simply too inexperienced to operate the privateers with which he intended to harass the Northern merchantmen on the high seas. Offering the command of these ships to the few seasoned seamen available, many of them foreign sympathizers, he retained the majority of his new recruits for the defense of his home waters.

As if to emphasize the lack of naval tradition within the Confederacy, several of the constituent states initially recruited their own naval forces. Virginia was the first to create a state navy, dressing it in conventional Federal uniform save for the inclusion of Commonwealth of Virginia buttons. Georgia followed suit soon after. Its officers, too, were issued with standard blue Federal uniforms with state buttons, but the sailors were more strikingly attired. Volunteers received a red flannel shirt with a sky blue falling collar and cuffs, both edged with white, conventional navy blue trousers,

15-inch Radman guns played a key role in Federal coastal defense. As the war progressed, many of the crews were transferred to light guns and sent to the front.

Headdress: Straw hats were initially issued to members of the Mobile Squadron as a concession to the heat, but were later tolerated in all commands.

Badges of rank: Rank and service were indicated by shoulder straps rather than by the more conventional epaulette rings favored by the North.

Weapons: Officers were issued with French-made Le Mats or domestically-produced Colt pistols. Deck officers often supplemented these with a British Royal Navy-pattern cutlass.

and a dark blue vizorless cap. Both forces were merged into the Confederate navy within months of their inception, as a result of which the apparent impracticality of the Georgian uniform was never put to the test.

Brought into being specifically for the defense of the Mississippi River, the Louisiana state navy lasted somewhat longer, commissioning its own ships and retaining its independence well into the war. Initially, officers and men were dressed in Federal blue, although later, gray double-breasted jackets were issued to certain officers.

Uniforms worn by the Confederate navy were initially similar to those of their Union opponents, save for the badges of rank which, in the case of officers, comprised gold stripes worn on the cuff. Until the introduction of formal regulations in 1862, sailors tended to dress for comfort. Thereafter

all wore new standard steel gray uniforms, necessitated by the inability of the South to obtain sufficient quantities of indigo to dye the cloth blue. Dress for a flag officer was declared to be ''a frock coat of steel gray cloth, faced with the same and lined with black silk serge, double breasted, with two rows of large navy buttons on the breast, nine in each row, placed four inches and a half (11.5cm) apart from eye to eye at top, and two inches and a half (6.3cm) at bottom. Rolling collar, skirts to be full, commencing at the top of the hip bone and descending four-fifths thence toward the knee, with one button behind on each hip and one near the bottom of each fold. The cuffs to be two inches and a half deep, with one strip of gold lace one-half an inch (1.2cm) wide below the seam, but joining it.'' Three strips of lace, the uppermost to contain a 3-inch (7.5cm) loop, were to adorn the sleeve above the cuff. Captains were to

David torpedoes sit disarmed and harmless, a mute memorial to earlier, more violent, days.

wear a similar jacket without the gold stripes on the cuffs. All officers were to wear a steel gray or white single-breasted vest with a single row of nine small buttons and a standing collar as well as steel gray or white drill trousers spread loose to cover the boot or shoe.

Caps were to be between $3\frac{1}{2}$ and 4 inches (9–10cm) tall with a patent leather peak and gold band. Cap badges consisted of a fouled anchor within a wreath, with rank indicated by stars above the anchor: four for a flag officer reducing to one for a lieutenant. Plain wreaths were worn by midshipmen, assistant surgeons, and paymasters. Engineers wore an Old English letter "e" within the wreath, while, from June 1863, volunteer officers wore the plain gilt letters "vn" on their cap fronts.

Rank and service were indicated by shoulder straps. Flag officers were ordered to wear "straps of sky-blue cloth, edged with black, four inches (10cm) long and one inch and three-eighths (3.5cm) wide, bordered with an embroidery of gold one-quarter of an inch (65mm) in width, with four stars in line at equal distances, the two on the ends six-tenths of an inch (1.5cm) in diameter, and the two intermediate six-eighths of an inch (1.9cm) in diameter." Lesser officers wore a similar configuration except that captains wore only three stars ("six-tenths of an inch in diameter"), commanders two stars, and lieutenants one.

Perhaps inevitably, as the war progressed and uniforms became more difficult to maintain, standards dropped. As a concession to the heat, officers in the Mobile Squadron were allowed to relinquish their formal attire in favor of gray flannel frock or sack coats during the summer months, while straw hats were eventually tolerated among all ranks.

Boatswain's mates, gunner's mates, carpenter's mates, sailmaker's mates, ship's stewards and ship's cooks wore an embroidered fouled anchor of black silk, no more than 3 inches (7.5cm) long, on the right sleeve, and all other petty officers wore a similar device on the left, but in every other respect, they dressed in the same manner as the ordinary seaman. Under normal conditions, they wore gray cloth jackets and trousers or gray woolen frocks with white duck cuffs and collars, black hats, black silk neckerchiefs, and black shoes or boots. Thick gray caps without vizors were to be worn as an optional extra while at sea. In hot weather, each captain could, at his discretion, allow his crew to discard part or all of the thick outer uniform while on the high seas.

By 1863, most sailors seem to have been issued with a full set of regulation gear. However, since virtually all elements of their uniform, notably the ornate black buttons, were produced in Britain, it is likely that replacement equipment became increasingly difficult to obtain as the blockade tightened and the Confederacy coffers diminished. As a result, toward the end of the war Southern seamen were no better dressed than their infantry equivalents.

Weapons issued to the navy were varied, a symptom of the South's difficulty in obtaining munitions *en masse*. Seamen were issued with a 2-inch (5cm) thick buff leather belt held together by a standard loop and eyelet. Where relevant, fuzes and cartridges were carried in leather pouches attached to the belt and overstamped with a fouled anchor and crossed cannon. In 1861, 1,000 British Enfield P1858 naval rifles were purchased, and these were subsequently supplemented by an undisclosed number of British 0.54 caliber breechloading rifle-muskets. Either Colt revolvers or French-made Le Mats, with their nine-round 0.42 caliber chambers, were issued to officers, senior ratings, and boarding parties, while ordinary seamen were given a variety of cutlasses, usually either of Royal navy or Federal Model 1841 pattern, when deemed necessary.

THE CONFEDERATE PRIVATEER AND BLOCKADE RUNNER

On 17 April 1861, the President of the Confederate States issued a proclamation inviting "all those who may desire" to aid the Confederate cause by service in "private armed vessels." Interested persons received "letters of marque and reprisal" or were commissioned into the embryonic Confederate navy. Captains were told to furnish details of name, type, and tonnage of their ships, together with the intended number of the crew. Ordinary sailors were neither induced into the regular navy nor given a uniform. Pay was not offered, although there was the promise of lucrative prize money if they were successful.

Not all privateers actively pursued enemy shipping. The crews of a number of smaller craft made small fortunes during the winters of 1861 and 1862 by transporting bales of compressed cotton from the blockaded ports of the South to the "neutral" islands of the British West Indies, returning with all manner of contraband, from armaments to uniforms.

Many of the ships employed in this way were European-built side-wheel steamers designed primarily for passenger transportation across the English Channel. Most displaced between 400 and 600 tons and were propelled by feathering paddles. They had one or two raking telescopic funnels which could be lowered close to the deck, as well as two short lower masts, but no yardarms. The sides, which rarely stood more than a few feet above sea level, were invariably painted dull gray or lead and, as such, were virtually invisible to the naked eye at ranges in excess of 200 yards (183m). Many carried a "turtle-back" construction on the foredeck to enable them to weather heavy seas. Initially, smokeless domestic anthracite was burned, but when this became impossible to obtain, semi-bituminous Welsh coal was substituted. Of light

The Florida *(formerly the* Oreto*) chases the* Star of Peace.

148

Uniform: Privateers, although protected by Confederate "Letters of Marque," were not members of the armed forces and did not therefore wear uniform. Indeed many were not even American citizens, the crew of the *Alabama* being drawn almost exclusively from Liverpool.

Weapons: Personal weapons were privately purchased from a variety of sources. Inevitably cutlasses and pistols proved most popular, particularly among the deckhands who had occasionally to resort to boarding enemy ships to secure their capture.

The Confederate privateer *Alabama* was sunk by the U.S.S. *Kearsage* on 19 June 1864.

draft yet capable of considerable speed, such ships experienced little initial difficulty in outrunning the cumbersome cruisers and frigates of the blockading force. Using their considerable knowledge of the local waters, the captains invariably ran the Federal gauntlet late on moonless nights, relying on the element of surprise coupled with the inadequacy of Federal gunnery to keep them safe. As the war continued and the Union control of the Gulf of Mexico and the Caribbean tightened, short-range blockade running became more hazardous, but by then, many captains had made their fortunes.

Many of the ships which carried the cotton onward from the West Indies to Liverpool were Confederate owned but British crewed. It has even been suggested that several Royal navy officers took lengthy leaves of absence to offer their services (under assumed names) to the Confederacy, although exact details remain a mystery and none was ever captured.

The commerce-destroyers, the true privateers, ventured much farther from the protection of their own coastline. In 1861, the United States boasted a mercantile fleet second only to that of Britain in tonnage. After secession, 90 percent of it remained loyal to the Union and immediately became the target of Southern cruisers and armed merchantmen. Washington argued that the use of privateers in war was contrary to the terms of the Declaration of the Congress of Paris of 1856. When it was pointed out by a far from neutral Britain that the United States had earlier refused to become a signatory to the Declaration, Washington offered belatedly to accede but was refused leave to do so. Privateering therefore remained a bona fide act of war in the eyes of all but the Union, which threatened to treat captured Confederate privateers as pirates.

In a proclamation of 19 April 1861, Lincoln stated that if "any person under the pretended authority of the said States, or under any other pretence, shall molest a vessel of the United States, or the persons or cargo on board her, such person will be held amenable to the laws of the United States for the prevention and punishment of piracy." Although crews which fell into Federal hands were often tried and occasionally convicted, none was ever punished for fear of Confederate retaliation against Union prisoners of war then swelling Southern prison camps.

During the first year of the war, privateers met with limited success. A fleet of small boats, ranging from old slavers to tugs, from fishing schooners to revenue cutters – in fact, anything big enough to carry a large piece of ordnance – were fitted out and placed strategically along the coast of the Carolinas from where they preyed upon unsuspecting Federal coastal shipping. Cargos were seized and ships pressed into service to replace those which inevitably fell foul of powerful blockading cruisers.

The lives of privateering ships were generally short. The brig *Jeff Davis*, a one-time slaver, spent a few months successfully apprehending prizes off New England, but it was eventually wrecked off the coast of Florida. The Charleston schooner *Beauregard* was overhauled and captured by the Federal barque *W.G. Anderson*. The schooner *Judah* was burned at her wharf in the Pensicola (Florida) naval yard by a landing party from the U.S.S. *Colorado*, while the former revenue cutter *Petrel* was sunk by a shell from the frigate *St. Lawrence* as the Southern craft was cruising off Charleston. The capture of the 54-ton Charleston pilot boat *Savannah* by the brig *Perry* nearly led to a diplomatic incident when the crew were taken to New York and tried for piracy, but the threat of retaliation against prisoners in Southern hands forced the North to reconsider.

Tempers were not so easily placated when Mason and Slidell, two Confederate commissioners tasked with the purchase of ships and materials in Britain, were forcibly taken from the British mail steamer *Trent* by Captain Wilkes of the U.S.S. *San Jacinto* while on the high seas. The commissioners were quickly returned to British jurisdiction, but not before immeasurable harm had been done to the Union cause in the eyes of the world's neutrals.

As the war progressed, the task of the small privateer became much more dangerous, forcing many of the remaining captains into the more lucrative and safer world of blockade running. In response, the Confederacy turned to Britain for the provision of a number of new ships. Negotiations invariably took place through a series of foreign-based intermediaries to avoid prosecution under the neutrality laws, but there can be no doubt that the ultimate destination of the ships was an open secret.

The Florida, the first of the commerce-destroyers of British origin, typified the subterfuge. Built in Liverpool during the winter of 1861–62, ostensibly for the Italian government (which strenuously denied all knowledge of her), she was initially named *Oreto*. She was allowed to leave Liverpool on 22 March 1862 from where she headed, not to Palermo as stated on her Bills of Lading, but to Jamaica. At about the same time, the guns and munitions for the new cruiser were shipped in the steamer *Bahama* to Nassau from the British eastern port of Hartlepool. Immediately upon her arrival in Nassau on 28 April, the *Oreto* was consigned to Messrs. Adderly & Co., the local agents for Messrs. Fraser, Trenholm & Co. of Liverpool, who were financial agents for the Confederate government. Command now passed to Captain Maffitt of the Confederate navy who at once sailed her to Cochrane's Anchorage, some nine miles from Nassau, where she took on small arms, ammunition, and her new crew. Spurred on by formal and accurate Union complaints, the British government at last intervened but, after a few weeks, allowed the ship to continue on her way. On 7 August, the now renamed *Florida* sailed to the deserted island of Green Cay in the Bahamas where she trans-shipped her battery of two 7-inch (18cm) rifles and six 6-inch (15cm) guns. Once ready, and now a fully fledged warship openly flying the flag of the Confederate navy, the *Florida* sailed for the safety of a home base.

The second and more famous cruiser, the *Alabama*, sailed from Liverpool on 23 June 1862. Despite the greatest protestations from the U.S. ambassador in London, Charles Adams, the British government refused to prevent the ship from leaving harbor on a test voyage, from which it never returned. She was provisioned with guns, ammunition, and coal in the Azores and placed under the command of Captain Raphael Semmes of the Confederate navy. Although at this stage, the civilian crew was given ample opportunity to return to Liverpool, most had enlisted in the full knowledge of the ship's status and, in the hopes of prize money, readily agreed to continue the voyage. *Alabama* therefore became a Confederate ship with a Southern captain but an almost exclusively British crew. The cruiser was defeated and sunk by the U.S.S. *Kearsarge* off the French port of Cherbourg on 19 June 1864, but not until she herself had sunk, burned, or captured 69 Federal ships, including the U.S.S. *Hatteras*.

Despite Union protestations to the contrary, privateering has never been considered contrary to the laws of war and the captains and crews of such ships as the *Savannah* and the *Alabama* therefore committed no crime. Indeed many, particularly those engaged in the early stages of the war before the Union blockade became effective, made small fortunes. According to "A. Roberts" (probably the *nom de guerre* of a British officer), at the end of a successful voyage a captain might have expected to make £1,000. Equally well paid were the pilot who might command £750, the chief engineer £500 and the chief and junior officers £250 and £150 respectively. Even the deckhands might expect £50, virtually enough on which to retire for life. It is no surprise, therefore, that the Confederacy found it so easy to fill the vacancies within its fleet of privateers with willing British seamen.

Captain John Newland Maffitt, commander of the *Florida*.

At the height of his raiding, Captain Semmes of the *Alabama* would tempt enemy ships towards him by setting fire to a prize ship and using it as a decoy.

THE CONFEDERATE MARINES

On 16 March 1861, the Confederate government authorized the creation of a Marine Corps consisting of a major, a quartermaster, a paymaster, an adjutant, a sergeant major, a quartermaster sergeant, and six companies, each with a captain, a first lieutenant, a second lieutenant, four sergeants, four corporals, 100 privates, and ten musicians. In all, over 1,600 officers and men served in the Corps throughout the war, although there were never more than 600 on active service at any one time. The Corps fought in all the major sea battles as well as in the defense of Richmond.

What is known about Marine Corps uniforms is extremely fragmentary, although several good photographs do exist to give a reasonable indication of what this small though élite unit wore.

Officers had French-style kepis covered in either blue or gray material, usually with black leather peaks and chinstraps. Coats were universally gray and of double-breasted frock coat design with twin rows of seven brass buttons each. Rank insignia were borrowed directly from the army. One, two, and three collar stripes were worn by second lieutenants to captains, one, two and three stars by majors to colonels. Gold Austrian knots were worn on the sleeve – one braid by lieutenants, two by captains, and three by field officers. A significant number of coats had dark blue collars and cuffs, a number had stiff white collar linings, and a few U.S. Marine Corps officers had gold Russian shoulder knots. Trousers were usually dark blue, although at least one officer is known to have favored sky blue with black welts down the outer seams.

Fatigue dress was even more informal. Most officers tried to emulate the naval personnel with whom they served by wearing blue jackets and white trousers while at sea. Others, however, seem to have preferred an all-gray mode of dress. Although formal dress regulations did exist, particularly for shore-based companies, these seem to have been introduced relatively late in the war, by which time the majority of officers had purchased their own variations of uniforms, and, by all accounts, the regulations were largely ignored.

Uniforms for the enlisted men were purchased in bulk in England and were therefore far more consistent with dress regulations. Marines were issued with gray felt fatigue caps with black peaks and chinstraps and brass side buttons, and two uniform coats and four fatigue jackets, all universally gray. Both coats and jackets appear to have been worn, particularly by the Naval Brigade which took part in the defense of Richmond, although the longer frock coat seems to have been the more common.

The bombardment of Fort Sumter from Fort Moultrie on 12–13 April 1861 led to the formal commencement of hostilities.

Headdress: All ranks wore a black-peaked blue kepi adorned in the case of officers with gold piping.

Frock coat: Officers wore standard gray double-breasted frock coats with the badges of rank edged in red.

Weapons: A variety of weapons was carried. The officer in the foreground is armed with a Le Mat revolver and a navy variant of an infantry officer's sword, the Marine behind probably with a British 1853-pattern Enfield.

153

Seven buttons, each bearing the Roman letter "M" were fitted. Rank was indicated by black chevrons worn point up. Two chevrons indicated a corporal, three a sergeant, three with a diamond a first sergeant, three with ties a quartermaster sergeant, and three with arcs a sergeant major.

Trousers were dark blue for winter and white cotton for summer. Gray or blue outer shirts were occasionally worn in hot weather, but at other times, a white shirt was worn under the jacket.

The vast majority of Marines served on one of the regular, commissioned naval vessels. The *Sumter*, the first such craft, was originally a screw steamer of some 500 tons designed specifically to ply for trade between New Orleans and Havana. Prior to commissioning, her frame was strengthened, a berth deck added, the spar deck cabins removed, and space found for a magazine and additional coal bunkers. She was armed with an 8-inch (20cm) pivot gun before the fore and main masts, and four 24-pound howitzers in her broadside.

The highly experienced Captain Semmes (see p.151) was placed in command on 18 April 1861 with orders to sail at once for the open sea before the Union blockade could take effect. However, the *Sumter* could not be made ready until 18 June, by which time a sizeable Union flotilla consisting of the *Brooklyn*, *Powhatan*, Massachusetts, and *South Carolina* was standing off in readiness to meet her. Relying heavily upon local intelligence, Semmes brought his ship to a state of immediate readiness and waited for one of the blockade ships to leave station. After two weeks of frustration, news arrived that the *Brooklyn* had left her designated post to chase a Southern merchantman. Seizing his opportunity, Semmes immediately put to sea and within hours was free of the pursuing enemy.

When only three days out, the *Sumter* made her first kill when she overhauled and burned the barque *Golden Rocket*, and within one week of escaping the blockade, she had captured seven other merchantmen. One was ordered to New Orleans with a prize crew but was captured by a Union cruiser before reaching the safety of the Mississippi. The others were sailed to Cienfuegos on the southern coast of Cuba, from where they were eventually released into Federal hands by the nervous Spanish authorities. During the next two months, the *Sumter* cruised in the Caribbean and along the coast of South America, frequently putting into neutral ports for coaling and provisioning. At no time did the neutral harbor authorities refuse her assistance and only on one occasion, at Puerto Cabello in Venezuela, was she forced to leave after 48 hours, pursuant to the terms and conditions of the international neutrality laws. Fearful of the number of Federal warships chasing him (there were, in fact, six), Semmes now made for the quieter waters of the western Atlantic, where he overhauled and burned two more merchantmen.

After two months' cruising in the Atlantic, Semmes was forced to put into St. Pierre, on the French-owned island of Martinique, for coal and water. At this point, his considerable luck seemed to run out. After only five days in harbor, the fast Federal sloop-of-war *Iroquois* sailed into view. Wary of France's rigid interpretation of the rules of neutrality, particularly that which forbade a warship to leave harbor within 24 hours of an enemy craft, Captain Palmer, in command of the *Iroquois*, immediately put to sea, anchored in the outer Sound and awaited events. There matters remained for a week.

On the night of 23 November, now fully prepared for battle, *Sumter* weighed anchor and stood out. Realizing that his every move would be signaled by Union schooners in port, Semmes attempted to trick his adversary by heading directly south and then doubling back under cover of the land. Aided by a fortuitous rain squall, he succeeded in giving Palmer the slip to the extent that, by daybreak, he was steaming at full speed to the north while the *Iroquois* was pursuing him fruitlessly in the opposite direction.

Temporarily free of her hunters, *Sumter* now

cruised eastward into the Atlantic, seizing and burning three prizes. Then the advent of unexpectedly bad weather forced Semmes to seek the protection of a neutral harbor to undertake a major refit. The Spanish port of Cadiz was chosen, but for once the harbor authorities showed a marked reluctance to allow the ship to stay. Semmes sailed for Gibraltar hoping to receive a more friendly reception at the hands of the British authorities, but instead found that neither the government nor local merchants would furnish him with coal or provisions. Due to the dilapidated state of the ship, serious consideration was given to the transfer of the officers and Marines to a new vessel. However, this desperate measure was pre-empted when the Federal warships *Tuscarora*, *Kearsage*, and *Ino* sailed into the Straits and immediately took up station at Algeciras ready to intercept the Confederate

cruiser as soon as she attempted to leave the protection of British territorial waters. Conscious of the hopelessness of the situation and in an attempt to avert needless bloodshed, *Sumter* remained at her berth, was decommissioned and ultimately sold. Ironically, she was later to reappear as a blockade runner.

During her cruise, *Sumter* had obtained 17 prizes. Of these, two were ransomed, seven released in Cuban ports by order of the Spanish authorities, and two recaptured. In all, *Sumter* burned six enemy vessels with their cargos – hardly a huge number when the size of the Federal mercantile fleet was taken into account. She did, however, tie up a considerable part of the Union's fleet of cruisers dispatched to hunt her down and may therefore be deemed to have been at least a qualified success.

The battle between *Monitor* and *Merrimac*, fought on 9 March 1862 at Hampton Roads, near Norfolk, Virginia.

OFFICER: CONFEDERATE CAVALRY 1863

On 9 June 1863, the Confederate and Union cavalry met in the first true cavalry combat of the war. Until then, Southern horsemen had generally been considered so superior that the Northern regiments had always shunned formal battle. In fact, Confederate supremacy on horseback had been partly true and partly myth. Certainly every member of the Confederate cavalry could ride before he volunteered; indeed, many had been virtually born in the saddle. The officers, all of whom had been voted into office by their men, had almost inevitably come from the landed gentry, had known the men under their command since boyhood, and were skilled in the art of man-management. Many troopers were experienced hunters, used to firing from the saddle, and were therefore perfectly equipped for executing the occasional skirmish into enemy lines during the early stages of the war. Union troopers, on the other hand, were invariably from urban stock, were not natural horsemen (the majority could not even ride when they joined the army), and lacked the Southerners' deep understanding of the land. Equally importantly, their officers were often social or political appointees with no knowledge of cavalry tactics.

From the outset, Confederate cavalrymen regarded themselves as mounted infantry. Totally lacking in discipline, they would have found a European-style massed cavalry charge simply impossible to implement. This, however, was not in itself a problem as the introduction of the long-range rifle had fundamentally altered cavalry tactics in the decade preceding the war. The charge of the Light Brigade by the British in 1854 had been magnificent but equally it had been a mistake, occasioned by petty jealousy and a series of ambiguous orders. Although the Confederacy introduced the lance into its order of battle in 1861, it soon realized its impracticality and relegated it to rear area defense units which then only carried it for show.

The Confederate cavalry, for all its reputation among its enemies, did not enjoy popularity at home. Traditionally the infantryman has always been subconsciously jealous of the cavalryman with his greater freedom of action, creature comforts, and panache. In a moment of exasperation, the Confederate General Hill is reputed to have offered a reward to anyone who could find him a dead cavalryman killed in action "with his spurs on" – neatly summing up the frustration of the slow-moving infanteer. Under the brilliant leadership of men such as "Fitz" Lee and Stuart, the Confederate troopers excelled at long-range raids, but by their very nature, these took place miles away from their own lines. The bulk of the army simply saw the

Confederate cavalry crossing the Potomac into Maryland on 11 June 1863. Within a month they would be in full-scale retreat.

Mounts: All Confederate cavalry were required to provide their own horses. If these were killed and the rider could not afford a replacement mount, he would simply be relegated to the infantry.

Headdress: Confederate cavalry officers were usually drawn from the ranks of the Southern aristocracy and were often elected into office. Most shunned regulation dress in favor of stylized wear. In this instance the headdress has been adorned with a feather.

Weapons: Although the Confederate Cavalry were better than their Northern counterparts at close quarter combat, their preferred weapons were pistols and even shotguns.

cavalry ride out and a few days later ride back with booty and fanciful tales of victories won behind enemy lines, none of which was of any immediate benefit to the pragmatic infantry.

Confident, free-thinking, and initially successful, the Confederate cavalry made no attempt to change its tactics or significantly alter its structure. As the war progressed, volunteers were still expected to supply their own mounts and to transfer to the infantry should these be killed. Compensation for killed or injured horses was offered in theory, but in practice payment was invariably late and inadequate, making it difficult for the trooper to purchase a new horse and resume his place in his old unit. Regiments were decimated for the want of men able to provide their own horses, while experienced cavalrymen fumed and fretted in the unwelcoming ranks of the infantry.

In complete contrast, the Union cavalry strove from the outset to improve. Painstaking weeks and even months were spent teaching the willing recruits basic horsemanship. At the same time, regimentation and discipline were instilled into the minds of the young soldiers. Once proficient, many units were sent West to hone their newly discovered skills.

By mid-1863, the Union cavalry at last felt confident enough to face the Confederacy in open battle and, on 9 June, received an opportunity to prove that it was now at least as good as its much-vaunted adversary. Earlier that month, Lee had left the protection of Fredericksburg to advance west in the hope of drawing the Army of the Potomac after him. On 8 June, Pleasonton's Federal cavalry corps, supported by two infantry brigades and six light batteries, was ordered to leave its base in Falmouth and to engage the leading Southern elements in battle. Aware that Stuart's cavalry were screening along the Rappahannock, Pleasonton decided to divide his command and to attack across the river in two places. Buford's cavalry division (with Ames' infantry brigade) was secretly dispatched to Beverley Ford opposite the Confederate cavalry brigade of "Grumble" Jones. Simultaneously, six miles to the south at Kelly's Ford, the divisions of Gregg and Duffie, with Russell's infanteers in support, assembled opposite Robertson's and Hampton's Confederate cavalry brigades.

As dawn broke at four in the morning, both columns attacked, achieving complete surprise. Buford drove Jones toward Brandy Station and, amid fierce fighting, the high ground around Fleetwood Hill changed hands several times. To the south, Gregg pushed Robertson's pickets back from Kelly's Ford but, in the absence of Duffie who had been delayed, was unable to exploit the situation. Duffie had been drawn into battle with 500 Confederates some miles to the south at Stevensburg. Although this action prevented him from consolidating with Gregg in an attack on the wavering Confederate line at Brandy Station, his men did gain the distinction of routing the 2nd South Carolina and the 4th Virginia cavalry, at least half of the latter being taken prisoner.

Although, at the end of the day, Stuart's battered troopers held the ground, forcing the Federals to retire back across the river, theirs was a Pyrrhic victory. For the first time, Union cavalry regiments had charged, re-formed, and charged again. The 1st New Jersey Cavalry had made no fewer than six regimental charges without wavering, while the regular cavalry in company with the 6th Pennsylvania Volunteers had remained in the field for over 12 hours. Union losses were far greater than those of the Confederacy (936 killed, wounded, and captured as opposed to 523), but this was considered a price well worth paying for the sudden gain in Union morale. The unbeatable had been held and virtually vanquished. The Northern troopers acquired a newly discovered confidence which enabled them to contest fiercely the coming battles.

Conversely, the Confederacy in general, and Stuart in particular, sustained a shattering loss of face from which, it has been argued, the latter never

recovered. Whether or not it is true that Stuart organized his infamous and ill-timed Gettysburg raid simply out of a desire to re-establish his reputation must remain a matter for debate. What is certain is that the cavalry under his command were never the same again.

In the summer of 1863, Confederate cavalry regiments comprised ten companies each, and each of these contained 60 to 80 private soldiers, a captain, a first lieutenant, two second lieutenants, five sergeants, four corporals, and a blacksmith. Each regiment was commanded by a colonel who was supported by a staff comprising a lieutenant colonel, a major, an adjutant, a sergeant major, and a quartermaster sergeant. Two to six regiments constituted a brigade and as many as six brigades a division. As time went on and cavalry skirmishing intensified, casualties increased but the number of regiments remained the same. Even in 1865, when the Confederate cavalry was a mere shell of its former self, its remaining members were still divided into four divisions totaling ten brigades.

As the war progressed and fresh horses and supplies became increasingly difficult to obtain, the cavalry inevitably became more ragged until, by early 1864, many of its members resembled ill-kempt civilians rather than fighting troops. Certain of the regiments attempted to preserve a degree of military dignity by attaching the yellow stripes and ribbons of the cavalry to the remnants of their uniforms but with only limited success. Captured items of Federal uniform became increasingly favored despite the occasional misunderstanding with Union troops.

The Battle of the Wilderness, Virginia, was fought on 5–6 May 1864. By then, Confederate defeat was only a matter of time.

CONFEDERATE MEDICAL SERVICES

The Confederate medical service, like everything else in the Southern war effort, did wonders with the resources available but simply did not have enough men, medicines, or ambulances for the task. As a direct result, disease, rather than the Union army, became the young soldiers' greatest enemy. Although precise statistics do not exist, it is clear that about 18 percent of Confederate casualties died of their wounds. Indeed, twice as many died of disease as were killed and mortally wounded in battle. Hardened veterans dreaded hospitals and went to great lengths to conceal wounds or illnesses in order to avoid them. Newspapers and commissions of the time published horror stories of fetid hospitals, drunken surgeons, and sick and wounded left untended to die in agony.

With a few dishonorable exceptions, such reports were grossly unfair. The Civil War was fought in the last years of the medical Middle Ages. Within a decade, a new era of research, spearheaded by Louis Pasteur, Joseph Lister, and others, would revolu-tionize the tending of wounds, but none of this was available to the wartime doctor. The relationships between drinking water and typhoid, mosquitoes and malaria, and – more fundamentally – unsterilized instruments and infection were simply unknown. Moreover, the large caliber and low velocity of the new generation of rifles then entering service caused horrific wounds, with the bullet usually remaining in the body rather than passing cleanly through it.

Surgeons knew of few ways except amputation to stop gangrene, while stomach wounds were invariably fatal, there being no known cure for peritonitis. In the absence of better anesthetics, chloroform and ether were used to kill pain. Sometimes, when even these ran out, soldiers were dosed with whiskey and forced to clench their teeth on a leather strap or even literally to "bite the bullet" while an amputation was carried out without any more orthodox form of pain killer. Not surprisingly, many soldiers died of surgical shock on the operating

Confederate artillerymen, killed at Dunkes Church during the Battle of Antietam, lie where they fell – a macabre testimony to the ferocity of the battle.

Headdress: Although non-regulation, most surgeons wore a staff officer's kepi with a cap badge depicting the letters ''MS'' in Old English within a wreath.

Tunic: Double-breasted gray frock coats, with black collars and cuffs, were standard issue. On the collar surgeons wore the single star of a major and assistant surgeons the three stripes of a captain. Trousers were dark blue with a wide velvet stripe edged with gold down each leg. Most surgeons sported a green silk sash.

table. Morphine and laudanum was used liberally when available with little thought to the future, with the result that many men recovered from their wounds only to spend the rest of their lives as hopeless drug addicts.

By 20th-century standards, the death rate due to disease during the Civil War was unacceptable, yet for the time, it was comparatively low. Florence Nightingale had introduced tremendous improvements into the previously neglected world of nursing during the Crimean War a decade earlier, but even so, one-quarter of those entering hospital had died of disease. When it is remembered that the British soldiers in the Crimea were hardened professionals and that the vast majority of combatants in the Confederate army were rural volunteers and conscripts with little if any military background, the contrast becomes all the greater.

Sickness hit soldiers hardest in the first year of the war. The crowding together of men from various backgrounds into a new environment where contagion was great led to consequences which should have been anticipated but were not. Men from farms and plantations who had never before been exposed to measles, mumps, tonsilitis, and other childhood maladies immediately succumbed in large numbers, often reducing the effective fighting strengths of their units by half before they had even completed basic training. More critical were smallpox and erysipelas (a generalized inflammation of the skin that could lead to gangrene and meningitis), which decimated the rural regiments. Soldiers who recovered from these diseases and who thereafter remained at base camp to recuperate often fell victim to the bacteria and viruses which spread unchecked due to poor sanitary practices and fouled water. It is more than coincidence that a larger number of Confederate soldiers died from dysentry, typhoid, and pneumonia than from any other cause. As the summer sun reached its height, malaria began to take its toll among the combat soldiers who had been lucky enough to survive basic training camp.

Early attempts by the Confederate government to create a medical department were hopelessly over-optimistic and, as such, were doomed to failure. A surgeon general, equal in status to a brigadier general of cavalry, was appointed in overall command of the department. He was to have the assistance of 1,000 surgeons equal in rank to cavalry majors, 2,000 assistant surgeons equal in rank to cavalry captains, and as many acting assistant surgeons on contract as were needed or could be hired. Clearly the Confederacy, with its relatively small population, could not hope to fill such an establishment, and as a result, many posts were destined to remain vacant throughout the war.

Each regiment had a surgeon, an assistant surgeon, and a hospital steward assigned to it. Each battalion and several artillery batteries were assigned their individual assistant surgeon. Many doctors at this level were totally inadequate. Some had recently graduated from medical school (or, in some cases, even failed to qualify), while few if any had any real experience of surgery. Nevertheless, they were of necessity forced to attempt operations well beyond their professional competence.

At brigade level, the surgeon with the longest commission – and regardless of competence – was appointed senior brigade surgeon. He was expected to continue with his regimental duties while taking responsibility for the daily administration of all medical matters within the brigade jurisdiction. The senior brigade surgeon was appointed to division with its extra attendant responsibilities and work load. Although he had an assistant surgeon to help him with the day-to-day administration, there was no practical way that a divisional surgeon, with his multitude of liabilities, could have hoped to perform effectively.

Confederate surgeons wore regulation uniform with the informal addition of a green sash which had come to denote the medical service in the pre-war United States army. Many also wore as an unofficial badge the letters "MS" embroidered in gold within a wreath on their cap or hat.

Prior to the troops going into action, the regimental surgeon set up a field hospital, while the assistant surgeon followed the men into action, rendering immediate assistance to the wounded where possible. Non-commissioned hospital stewards, themselves frequently medical students, often accompanied the assistant surgeon into battle. Equal in status to an orderly sergeant, the stewards wore three green chevrons and a green diamond to denote their rank. They also wore a distinctive red diamond on their hats to denote membership of the Infirmary Corps and, inevitably, if unofficially, a green sash beneath their regulation leather belt.

Stewards were in charge of the dispensing of medicines (when these were available), daily routine, and the infirmary detail although responsibility for the last passed to the assistant surgeon in action. The infirmary detail originally comprised the regimental band, but when these became scarce, their position was taken by convalescents. Each man carried a knapsack with field dressings, tourniquets, and other first aid equipment with which to patch up the wounded, while every two men were responsible for carrying a stretcher. It soon became apparent that convalescents, with their intimate memories of recent pain and suffering, were far from ideal for such work and, wher-

These provisions proved totally inadequate in May and June 1862 when 21,000 wounded Confederates from the battles of Seven Pines (Fair Oaks) and the Seven Days poured into the city. Churches, hotels, warehouses, barns, and even some private houses were pressed into service as temporary hospitals. Shocked by their first direct experience of war, many Richmond women volunteered to act as nurses, while hundreds of slaves were pressed into service as orderlies and gravediggers.

Traditionally, the conservative men of the Confederacy had been violently opposed to white women working on the wards of military hospitals, believing that the sights therein would be unfit for "refined ladies." Nevertheless many women refused to stay at home uselessly while their menfolk fought and, using Florence Nightingale as their champion, set up private hospitals. One such woman, Sally Louisa Tompkins of Richmond, was eventually commissioned with the rank of captain by Jefferson Davis to legitimize her private infirmary as a military hospital. Another, Kate Cumming of Mobile, Alabama, set up a hospital in Corinth, Mississippi to tend the wounded survivors of Beauregard's army after Shiloh.

In September 1862, the Confederate Congress at last recognized the tremendous worth of these women, who until then, had all been volunteers, by enacting a law providing for civilian matrons and nurses in army general hospitals. Thereafter a large number of white women became an official part of the Confederate medical service, earning the undying respect and admiration of civilian and soldier alike.

Left: Hospitals such as this in Richmond were often staffed by women volunteers and did much to alleviate the misery and suffering of the wounded.

ever possible, were replaced either by a group of 20–30 slaves or by unarmed volunteers permanently seconded to the Ambulance Corps.

The South was slow to establish general hospitals for the treatment of the seriously wounded and those with long-term illnesses. Initially such hospitals were provided by local initiatives, but by late 1861, responsibility had passed to the central Medical Department. Several general hospitals were established in the Richmond area, the largest, Chimborazo Hospital, boasting 250 pavilion buildings, each housing 40–60 patients, and 100 tents with space for eight to ten convalescents each.

Dead horses from Bigelow's 9th Massachusetts Battery await disposal during the Battle of Gettysburg. Lack of elementary hygiene did much to spread disease among the wounded.

CADET: VIRGINIA MILITARY INSTITUTE

Until October 1862, when examining boards were belatedly introduced, officers in volunteer regiments of the Confederate army were elected by their men. During the early stages of the "do-it-yourself" mobilization of 1861, it was assumed by all but the regular army that the limited military skills required of junior officers could be easily learned in the field. The fallacy of this oversimplistic thesis became tragically apparent after the 1st Battle of Manassas (Bull Run) but, by then, the position of the gentleman-officer was too deeply entrenched to be swept away without considerable argument. Many officers who obtained commissions by political influence took their new-found responsibilities seriously, using their personalities and experience to instill discipline in their subordinates. Others, however, abused their positions shamelessly, carousing and drinking themselves to oblivion.

Broadly speaking, Confederate officers, particularly in the Virginia theater, performed far better than their Union counterparts during the first year or two of the war. In part, this was due to the unwillingness of the Federal General-in-Chief Winfield Scott to disperse the regular army among the newly established regiments. Hundreds of N.C.O.s and officers who could have, respectively, acted as drill instructors and provided tactical leadership to the volunteer regiments were posted to regular units, sometimes far away on the frontier, while raw recruits floundered and died in their thousands under incompetent officers in Virginia. In all, 767 officers serving in the U.S. army at the outbreak of war, supplemented by 156 from the retired list, elected to soldier on for the Union cause. Had their services been better husbanded from the outset, it is possible that the novice Northern troops who received their baptism of fire at Manassas would not have bolted. The war might then have taken a very different course.

The South, by contrast, had no regular army. The 313 officers who resigned from the U.S. army to fight for the Confederacy, including 16 West Point graduates who had married into Southern families, were used to form training cadres and were thus able to spread the benefit of their vast accumulated experience to the widest possible audience.

Of equal importance was the fact that seven of the eight military colleges in the United States were situated in the South. Virginia Military Institute (V.M.I.) in Lexington and the Citadel in Charleston, South Carolina had particularly excellent reputations as seats of military learning, and they immediately dedicated themselves to the Confederate cause. One-third of the field officers of the various Virginia regiments in 1861 had graduated from V.M.I., and of the total of 1,902 men who had attended there, 1,781 fought for the South. In addition, many Southern officers elected to positions of authority received at least rudimentary military training at V.M.I. or one of the other colleges – a luxury denied their opposite numbers in the North.

Perhaps surprisingly, the South did not suffer from the comparative lack of West Point graduates within its ranks. Traditionally, the curriculum at

Right, above: Benjamin A. Colonna, a veteran of the Battle of New Market in 1864, was the model for this 1912 portrait of a typical cadet, which now hangs in the Jackson Memorial Hall of the Virginia Military Institute.

Right, below: Cadet Andrew Pizzini, Jr, fought with the V.M.I. cadet corps at the Battle of New Market. The portrait, depicting him in formal attire, was commissioned in 1910.

164

Headdress: As peacetime headdress wore out or were lost they were replaced by blue or gray kepis often with a cloth attachment at the rear to protect the nape of the neck from the summer sun.

Tunic: The Institute's expensive and highly impractical uniforms soon wore out and were replaced with fatigue uniforms of coarse "sheeps-gray" jacket and trousers.

Belt: The black leather belt with its distinctive silver buckle bearing the letters "VMI" remained part of the uniform to the end, poignant reminder of the past.

165

West Point subordinated the study of tactics and strategy in favor of engineering, mathematics, fortification, and administration. Officer-cadets were not encouraged to read the works of the great European theorists such as Clausewitz, and few therefore had any idea of how to administer, control, and exploit the huge armies which mushroomed in the North during the summer months of 1861. The V.M.I. graduate, with his far more basic grounding in military matters, had, if anything, a distinct advantage.

Thomas "Stonewall" Jackson had been a professor at V.M.I. immediately prior to the outbreak of war. He commanded a company of V.M.I. cadets at John Brown's hanging in 1859, and on 21 April 1861, he took the battalion of cadets to Richmond where they were used as drillmasters for the mobilizing troops. Already renowned for his eccentricities and markedly austere in his personal habits (he neither smoked nor drank and abhorred gambling), Jackson soon gained a more enviable reputation as a brilliant and aggressive strategist. During his famous month-long Valley campaign, in which he marched his men over 400 miles, fought five battles, and defeated four larger armies, he pushed his famous "foot cavalry" to the limit yet never once lost the respect or loyalty of the officers and men under his command. At his best in independent command, Jackson nevertheless subordinated himself to Lee, performing, whenever asked, lightning, crushing moves in support of the main Confederate thrust. When Jackson died accidentally at the hands of nervous Confederate sentries in 1863, V.M.I. lost one of its greatest supporters and the South one of its finest generals.

Initially, the V.M.I. cadets retained their expensive if impractical peacetime uniforms. As these wore out, they were gradually replaced by coarse sheep's gray jackets with seven buttons and trousers with a plain black tape stripe. Blue or gray forage caps were favored, although in many instances, the cadets were forced to appear bareheaded. Black leather belts with a harness buckle bearing the letters "vmi" secured a plain leather cartridge box. The more fortunate also carried a blanket bedroll, inside of which they secreted such personal valuables as they had left, as well as a webbing satchel and perhaps a water canteen. As the war progressed, even this rudimentary uniform disintegrated as worn-out issue items were replaced with civilian attire stolen or begged and borrowed from relatives or sympathetic Southerners moved to compassion by the sight of so young a band of combatants.

The cadets were never adequately armed. Even in the latter stages of the war, when the better regiments were beginning to receive breechloading rifled muskets, either manufactured domestically or brought in from Europe by blockade runners, the cadets were forced to soldier on with antiquated Belgian muskets which many of them found too clumsy and heavy to operate efficiently.

Despite their rag-tag appearance and lack of potent weapons, the cadets of the Virginia Military Institute fought tenaciously whenever committed to battle. In May 1862, they marched to the aid of their beloved Jackson in the Shenandoah Valley but, through no fault of their own, arrived too late to take part in the battle. Then, on 15 May 1864, the Institute became immortalized in Southern legend when 247 cadets, aged from 15 to 17, charged the massed ranks of the Union army during the Battle of New Market, forcing the enemy to retire in momentary disorder. In less than an hour of often hand-to-hand fighting under atrocious conditions, ten V.M.I. cadets were killed and 47 wounded, including their commanding professor Lieutenant Colonel Scott Shipp.

New Market gave the Confederacy a breathing space during which they could gather in the harvest – without that, Lee would have found it impossible to extend the war into the following year.

However, the price exacted from the people of the Shenandoah by a vengeful Federal government must have left many of them wondering whether or not it had been worth the cost.

Determined to deny the valley to the South both as a battlefield and a granary, Grant ordered General David Hunter, at the head of 8,500 troops, to proceed south down the Shenandoah destroying every vestige of civilization in his path. Hunter was turned and impelled to retire at Piedmont by a Confederate force, under the command of the enigmatic "Grumble Jones", two-thirds the size of his, but not until Hunter had destroyed the towns of Staunton and Lexington. Grant then sent him back to the valley with orders to "eat up" the Shenandoah at any cost. Hunter hesitated, and at his own request was replaced by the more experienced Sheridan at the head of 50,000 men. General Jubal Early, placed in command of a small force of Confederate veterans with orders to frustrate Sheridan, contested every mile but to no avail. The valley was destroyed with systematic precision. Houses, outbuildings, mills, and machinery were destroyed, haystacks and corncribs torched, and foodstuffs confiscated. The once proud "breadbasket of the Confederacy" became an economic wilderness. The cadets of V.M.I. could have done no more for the cause of the South than they did at New Market. It is not their fault that, by then, the dream of an independent Confederacy was hopelessly lost.

The cadet charge at the Battle of New Market: part of a mural which commands pride of place in the V.M.I.'s Jackson Memorial Hall.

TROOPER: STUART'S CAVALRY CORPS

Ragged, ill-disciplined, badly armed, and at times half-starved, the Confederate cavalry was nevertheless arguably the finest fighting force of the Civil War. Consisting exclusively of experienced horsemen (all of whom had brought their own mounts when they volunteered), the majority of its members were drawn from rural backgrounds and, as such, had learned to shoot at a young age. Most were fiercely independent and did not take well to the regimentation of army life, yet this mattered little in a force which valued personal initiative highly. Until the Union reorganized its cavalry along largely Confederate lines in the summer of 1863, the Southern horsemen were rarely drawn into set-piece battle, and when they were, the melee was invariably short, ending conclusively in their favor. This led to an undercurrent of largely unjustified criticism from the infantry who failed to realize that most cavalry regiments were as adept at fighting dismounted as in the saddle.

Confederate cavalry was at its best when acting in the role of hunter. Few of the officers, let alone the enlisted men, carried sabers, and early experiments with the lance had proved a failure. The force saw itself primarily as mounted infantry able to advance silently and at speed against an enemy, yet endowed with sufficient firepower to destroy that enemy once contact was made. The massed charges of the Greys at Waterloo or of the Light Brigade during the Crimea were simply beyond its comprehension.

No one man utilized the Confederate cavalry's advantages while minimizing its weaknesses better than James Ewell Brown ("Jeb") Stuart. Stuart was only 28 years old when war broke out, but by then he had already seen considerable service on the frontier, had been seriously wounded in the Indian wars, and had served in Kansas during the bitter pre-war border disturbances. While on leave of absence, he had served voluntarily as Lee's A.D.C. during John Brown's raid at Harpers Ferry and may at that time have had premonitions of the troubles ahead. Certainly he was among the first Virginian officers to resign his commission and offer his services to the Confederacy after the secession of his native state even though, in so doing, he split his family, a number of whom remained loyal to the Union. Appointed brigadier general on 24 September 1861, Stuart led first a brigade, later a division, and ultimately a corps on a series of brilliantly executed raids deep into enemy territory. Amiably known as "Beauty" by his West Point classmates, he wore a massive flowing beard reputedly to hide a weak chin and certainly to disguise his extreme youth. His bravery, endurance, dedication, and sheer good humor made this deeply religious man popular with all who served under him and more than compensated for his vanity and extrovertism. Blessed with an excellent staff, Stuart trained his subordinates with a calculated professionalism which made them the best cavalry in the world at the time. His death during the Battle of Yellow Tavern on 11 May 1864 left the South with a void which it found impossible to fill.

The first of Stuart's great raids took place at Catlett's Station during the 2nd Manassas (Bull Run) campaign. Early on the morning of Friday, 22 August 1862, two guns in support of 1,500 troops

The attack on a Union supply train near Jasper Junction on 3 October 1863 epitomized the daring of the Confederate cavalry.

Headddress: Most cavalrymen who rode with Stuart were Virginians proud of their heritage. It became common to decorate their black "Hardee" hats with yellow cord or ribbon to denote their élite status.

Tunic: Rank badges, cuffs and collars were again edged in yellow. On hot days the tunic would be unbuttoned to reveal a red undervest.

Weapons: All Confederate cavalrymen provided their own mounts and most their own weapons. The sergeant-major depicted here is armed with a Southern saber, a captured Federal pistol and a privately purchased rifle.

comprising Robertson's and "Fitz" Lee's brigades (minus the 3rd and 7th Virginia Cavalry) crossed the Rappahannock at two points. Advancing through Warrenton, the men halted at Auburn, rested until dark and then attacked a Federal camp in the region of Catlett's Station. Then a captured ex-slave, who was known to Stuart, offered to lead his men to the Union baggage train. Under cover of a fortuitous storm, the 9th Virginia followed, attacked the camp and captured a large number of General Pope's staff, a quantity of money, the Federal dispatch book, and a majority of Pope's personal possessions including his uniforms. With the assistance of a feint against another part of the Union lines by the 1st and 5th Virginia Cavalry, Stuart escaped with 300 prisoners and a considerable quantity of intelligence. For several days thereafter, the unfortunate Pope's uniforms were on public display in a store in Richmond. More importantly, Lee was given vital information which enabled him to completely out-maneuver his enemy in the coming battle.

On 9 October 1862, following the Battle of Antietam (Sharpsburg), Stuart undertook his second so-called "ride around McClellan." Between 12–15 June, during the Penninsula campaign, he had completely circumnavigated McClellan's position with 1,000 troopers, causing havoc in the Federal rear. He now attempted to repeat the feat with a larger force of four guns and 1,800 picked troops from the three cavalry brigades of "Fitz" Lee, Hampton, and Jones. Skirting known Federal strongpoints, Stuart led his force to Chambersburg, Pennsylvania, where he destroyed a machine shop and several public buildings before setting off for home. Despite the impediment of 500 captured horses and the presence of numerous enemy patrols, he completed the entire 80–mile return journey without a single halt.

The 0.50-caliber Maynard carbine proved popular among those lucky enough to acquire one. They were never standard issue.

Stuart's Dumfries raid of 26–31 December 1862, possibly his most famous sortie, was in fact the last of four assaults made by the Southern cavalry from its defensive base around Fredericksburg. On 28 November, Wade Hampton with 158 Carolina and Georgia cavalrymen captured over 100 horses and 92 men of the 3rd Pennsylvania Cavalry in a surprise attack on Hartwood Church. On 10 December, in an equally daring raid, he led 520 men in a three-day operation against the Federal stronghold of Dumfries on the Potomac below Washington, capturing an entire wagon train with its 50 guards, and in a third raid on 17–18 December, he captured a further 150 prisoners and 20 wagons. On 26 December, Stuart led 1,800 men with four guns north across the Rappahannock. Once free of Federal pursuit, the force split into three brigades, each of which then took an independent route to Dumfries. Once there, the reunited force found the Union position too strong to storm, although an initial limited attack did inflict 83 casualties on the enemy. Having sent two of his guns together with a number of prisoners and a sizeable quantity of

booty back to the Confederate lines, Stuart continued north in the hope of encountering Union patrols sent out to meet him. During the following two days, he fought a number of running skirmishes in which he inflicted a further 120 casualties, took 100 prisoners, and sacked the Federal camps at Occoquan. Finally, in an act of cool confidence, he moved west, captured the still intact telegraph at Burke's Station and sent a message to General Meigs, Quartermaster General in Washington, complaining about the quality of recently captured mules.

Not all of Stuart's operations were wholly successful. On 25 June 1863, the Confederate cavalry was ordered by Lee to scout and harass the enemy. During the previous few weeks, the Southern commander had moved the Army of Northern Virginia up the Shenandoah Valley to the North in a desperate attempt to relieve the pressure on Virginia. It

Right: The clash of cavalry forces at Opequan on 19 September 1864. After Brandy Station the Union forces no longer regarded the Confederacy as invincible.

now stood near the railhead at Gettysburg, its lines of supply and communication dangerously overstretched.

Typically Lee's orders to his trusted subordinate were generous in their ambiguity. Stuart was to detach two brigades to secure the approaches to the Shenandoah Valley through the Blue Ridge Mountains, but other than that, he was free to operate totally at his own discretion. As he moved his remaining three brigades eastward from the Confederate position, Stuart was not to know that, within hours, they would encounter the bulk of the Union Army of the Potomac. Lacking the firepower to fight their way through, Stuart realized that he could either retire to safety, in which instance he would have failed totally in his intelligence-gathering mission, or attempt to ride round the enemy. Characteristically he decided to follow the more daring course, taking his command first south

then east before turning north. In doing so, he put two mountain ranges and over 75,000 enemy troops between himself and Lee. Committed to this new venture, Stuart lost sight of his original task, turning a deep reconnaissance mission into a full-blown raid. He squandered precious hours capturing a massive Federal supply train and as many days by returning with it to his base. When he did eventually return to his lines, spurred on by the urgent representations of one of the eight couriers sent by Lee to scour the Pennsylvania countryside looking for him, he was roundly admonished for having absented himself from headquarters for so long.

Whether Stuart's raid before Gettysburg was brilliant or foolhardy remains a matter for conjecture. What is certain is that Stuart, and the troopers who rode with him, knew no equals in the war. Their tenacity, resilience, and sheer *élan* were second to none.

THE CONFEDERATE GENERAL

There can be no doubt that, had it not been for the superb standard of Confederate leadership, the war between the States would have ended in outright victory for the Union within months of the attack on Fort Sumter. Although mostly of good family, few of the Southern generals were born to wealth and none attained their position through patronage. They understood the motivations and weaknesses of the men under their command from whom they were able to demand absolute loyalty. Ironically, few had any great love for the Confederacy and most had never owned a slave, yet they fought with the conviction of the totally committed.

Most Confederate generals tended to dress simply. A gray frock coat with a buff collar, cuffs, and piping was worn as full dress. The buttons were arranged in pairs, eight per row. Rank was indicated by an embroidered badge on either side of the collar – consisting of three stars within a laurel leaf in the case of a full general – by cuff-lacing of four thicknesses wide and by a buff waist-sash. A small three-sided *chapeau-bras* was authorized for full dress but was regarded by most as excessive and usually replaced either by a plain slouch hat or by a dark blue kepi, the latter decorated with four tiers of gold lace. Regulation trousers were dark blue with two narrow gold lace stripes down the outer seams. Many senior officers favored the less stylish

frock coat worn open to expose the waistcoat, while others resorted to self-designed uniforms similar in many ways to conventional civilian attire save for the occasional badge of rank worn on the lapel.

Never one to rely on outward show, Robert E. Lee dressed for comfort. While traveling through western Virginia in 1861, it was reported that Lee "was dressed in blue cottonade, he had no sword or pistol, or anything to show his rank." A year later, in a letter to his wife, he said of his apparel that "My coat is of gray, of the regulation style and pattern, and my pants of dark blue, as is also prescribed, partly hid by my long boots. I have the same handsome hat which surmounts my gray head." In battle, Lee normally wore a plain gray sack coat, although at Appomattox he uncharacteristically appeared before his troops in full uniform "with a handsome embroidered belt and dress sword, tall hat and buff gauntlets."

No one epitomized the dash and resourcefulness of the Confederate general better than Thomas "Stonewall" Jackson. Orphaned at a young age, Jackson was brought up with minimal love and education by a series of relatives. He was accepted by West Point in 1842, graduating 14th in his class. He served with the artillery in the Mexican War, exhibiting qualities of ingenuity, equanimity, and bravery from the outset. Promoted substantive

Generals Evans, Gordon and Lee rally their troops before the Battle of Spotsylvania. Even in so contrived a picture, the contrast between the standards of officers' and men's uniforms is apparent.

Headddress: A slouch hat – occasionally adorned by a feather – or a kepi was usually worn in preference to the formal if impractical chapeau.

Tunic: Frock coats, worn open to expose an often ornate waistcoat, were favored. Two rows of eight buttons each, worn in pairs, adorned the front.

Rank: Stars depicting badges of rank were worn on the collar and on the saddle cloth. A major general, depicted here, wore two stars.

173

General E. Kirby Smith wearing the formal frock coat of a Confederate lieutenant general. The impractical high collar would usually be discarded in the field.

lieutenant and brevet major at the end of that conflict, Jackson was assigned to the occupation forces in Mexico City but, like so many men of action, became frustrated by the dull routine of peacetime soldiering. In 1851, he accepted the post of professor of artillery tactics and natural philosophy at the vaunted Virginia Military Institute, a position which he held for ten years until the outbreak of war when he volunteered his services to the state of Virginia. During his time at VMI, Jackson developed a highly personalized code of ethics which left him unbending and therefore unpopular with his students. The death of his beloved first wife Eleanor so disturbed him that he undertook a profoundly personal and unrequited search for a true religious meaning, which resulted in his adopting Presbyterianism with its strong sense of religious and moral duty, ideals which he took with him when he returned to the army.

Jackson's first task was the formation of a new volunteer brigade, which he undertook with such efficiency that it brought him immediate promotion. In July 1861, during the 1st Battle of Manassas (Bull Run), he gained the nickname "Stonewall" by positioning his troops along the ridge of Henry House Hill from where they held the enemy advance, allowing the shaken Confederates to regroup, counter-attack, and turn defeat into overwhelming victory. For the next two years, until his untimely death at the hands of his own troops in May 1863, Jackson was given wide powers of discretion. In 1862, he operated independently in the Shenandoah Valley, attacking Federal troops wherever possible and forcing the Union to retain large reserves to protect the capital. Although there are suggestions that Jackson lacked the experience to take overall command of a large number of troops in a set-piece battle, his ability to work closely with and subordinate to General Lee has never been disputed.

Promoted to lieutenant general and given command of a corps, Jackson was instrumental in bringing about victory at Fredericksburg. On the evening of 2 May 1863, disaster struck during the final stages of the Battle of Chancellorsville. Ordered to execute a complex flanking move behind the Union right, Jackson advanced to get a better appreciation of the position, was mistaken for an enemy by his own nervous pickets, and was mortally wounded. He died eight days later. Lee lost a brilliant subordinate and the Confederacy one of its finest generals. A master of rapid movement and surprise tactics, Jackson had often kept his intentions so veiled that even his most trusted staff officers remained ignorant of his plans until the very moment of their execution – a singular failing which he shared with the Duke of Wellington. Nevertheless he was without doubt one of the greatest exponents of the art of "light infantry" warfare.

James Ewell Brown Stuart, known universally as "Jeb," was only 28 years old on the outbreak of war yet at once assumed the responsibilities of someone much older. An excellent horseman and brilliant cavalry tactician, Stuart distinguished himself by his personal bravery at the 1st Battle of Manassas. Later that year he was promoted to brigadier general and placed in command of the cavalry bri-

gade of the newly formed Army of Northern Virginia. During the following months, he gained an enviable reputation for the production of timely and detailed intelligence reports, often at considerable danger to himself, and for his ability to predict and exploit weaknesses in the enemy. Prior to the 2nd Battle of Manassas, his troops captured and plundered the Federal supply lines, and a few days later, in a daring raid behind enemy lines, they "liberated" 1,200 mounts that they themselves badly needed.

Promoted to the rank of major general, Stuart made excellent use of his horse artillery in support of Jackson's hard-pressed corps at Fredericksburg, and after Chancellorsville, he assumed command of the corps after Jackson's fatal wounding. Immediately before the Battle of Gettysburg, Stuart's cavalry met the newly re-formed Union cavalry at Brandy Station in the only true mounted engagement of the war. Inexplicably, and some would say unforgivably, Stuart was absent on a raid during the critical stages of the second day of Gettysburg and as such was unable to render assistance to Lee when most needed. Although it would be grossly unfair to blame him for the subsequent Confederate defeat, it is possible that, had he acted with more restraint, the extent of that defeat would have been less catastrophic. From then until his death at the Battle of Spotsylvania Courthouse on 12 May 1864, Stuart continued to harass the enemy wherever and whenever possible. Dogged by a lack of supplies, short of fresh mounts, and increasingly confronted by a vastly improved enemy, Stuart must have known that his task was impossible, yet he remained true to the cause of his native Virginia until his death. Lacking Jackson's deep religious convictions, he nevertheless shared the latter's fighting spirit for which, ultimately, he paid the same price.

General Robert E. Lee confers with his staff prior to the Second Battle of Manassas (Bull Run).

TEXAS VOLUNTEER CAVALRY

In 1861, Texas was still in every respect a frontier state. A member of the Union for no more than 15 years, it was bordered by a hostile and still resentful Mexico to the south and by vast inhospitable tracts of Indian-infested desert and scrub to the north. Most Texans still regarded themselves as frontiersmen, and few viewed Washington with anything other than suspicion. Not surprisingly, therefore, when Texas seceded from the Union in February 1861 and took up arms in the Confederate cause, most volunteers opted to fight mounted. In all, Texas raised 106 cavalry units and only 41 infantry. However, due to the lack of horses and provisions, which had to be supplied by individual volunteers before they were accepted, many of these "cavalry" units were forced to fight dismounted.

The 8th Texas Cavalry, more commonly called "Terry's Texas Rangers," was perhaps the best known of all the state's fighting units. Formed in 1836 as a semi-military mounted police force to protect the settlers from the Indians, they were reorganized and expanded to 1,600 officers and men by Sam Houston during the war of independence against Mexico. B.F. Terry and Thomas S. Lubbock consolidated the unit into a regiment in 1861. As the 8th Texas Cavalry, it fought bravely in the West, both against Union cavalry and the Indians. After the Civil War, in the 1870's, the Rangers were again reorganized and took on the task of patrolling the frontiers against Indians, bandits, and rustlers. Their great moral influence and exceptional bravery made them a potent force in the area, so much so that the Texas Rangers continue to this day as a well-respected law enforcement agency separate from the state police.

In the 1860's, their attitude toward discipline was highly individualistic. They dressed for comfort rather than in compliance with regulations more suited to the battlefields of the East, and they never saluted officers however senior. Because of this independent spirit, they were treated with suspicion by many orthodox commanders who failed to realize the depth of mutual respect felt by the officers and men within the unit.

Several Texan regiments fought as part of Forrest's Cavalry Corps, participating in a series of brilliantly executed raids against the Union flank during the latter half of 1862. Nathan Forrest was a self-made man who had risen from poverty to become a wealthy Memphis businessman and alderman. Six feet two inches (1.87m) tall, lithe and powerful, he had a commanding presence which made him attractive to the majority of those who met him. Like so many gifted men, however, he had an often violent temper and was contemptuous of fools – attributes which made him many powerful enemies. His simple military doctrine – "Get there first with the most men" – was contrary to the rules of cavalry warfare at the time, yet it lent itself excellently to the training and character of the Confederates under his command, most of whom regarded themselves as mounted infantry rather than conventional cavalry. To Forrest, the shotgun, not the saber, was the ideal cavalry weapon of war.

Forrest enlisted in the Confederate army as a private soldier a month before his 40th birthday, subsequently raised and mounted a battalion at his own expense, and was commissioned lieutenant colonel in October 1861. He escaped from Fort Donelson with his own command and several hundred

An unusual depiction of the Battle of Valurdid (21 February 1862) in which 1,500 Texans stood their ground against 7,000 Federals. The cavalry can be seen charging from the left.

Headdress: Uniform among the Texas Volunteer Cavalry was at the best informal. Many wore broad-brimmed civilian hats, in this instance adorned with the Lone Star.

Weapons: Conventional carbines were usually discarded in favor of shotguns despite the tendency of such weapons to pepper both friend and foe alike.

Saddlepack: Many Texans were virtually born into the saddle. Veterans of Indian fighting, they were used to covering great distances over inhospitable terrain. Not surprisingly therefore, they soon discarded issue saddles in favor of lighter, more practical models.

volunteers from other units when it was attacked by numerically superior Union forces in February 1862. He conducted a masterful rearguard action after the Battle of Shiloh, and on 8 April 1862, was seriously wounded. The following July he was promoted brigadier general and, during the next few months, carried out a series of raids deep into Union territory.

Typical of these was the brilliantly executed attack on the Federal garrison at Murfreesboro, Tennessee on 13 July. Leaving Chattanooga on 6 July with fewer than 2,000 men, Forrest advanced through McMinnville to Murfreesboro. Reaching the town at 5:00 a.m., he immediately captured the unsuspecting Federal pickets, ordered his entire command into columns of four with the 8th Texas in the lead, and advanced at the trot until he reached the main enemy encampment. Simultaneously, he ordered the 8th Georgia into town to secure the lines of communication, take prisoner any troops found in the area, and seize the massive supply dumps. Despite spirited if sporadic Union resistance, particularly by the 9th Michigan which at one stage forced the 8th Texas to withdraw in disorder, the garrison was eventually persuaded to surrender. Over 1,700 prisoners and four pieces of artillery were captured, together with 600 mules and horses and supplies worth $1 million, the latter being either carried back to the main Confederate lines or destroyed. Forrest then attacked the railroad south of Nashville, forcing General Buell in command of the Northern army to order two of his precious divisions into reserve to guard his lines of communications.

Described by Sherman as "a devil" to be "hunted down if it costs 10,000 lives and bankrupts the Federal treasury," Forrest was never caught but instead survived to be promoted to major general.

Unable to receive supplies from the east, Texan troops soon learned to become self-sufficient, often by plundering Federal supply trains.

An overt racist, he did nothing to stop the "Fort Pillow Massacre" by his subordinate, Brigadier General Chalmers, in April 1864 and, following the end of the war, became a central figure in the Ku Klux Klan.

While Forrest was frustrating the Union advance in the West, the 1st Texas Cavalry was fighting with equal effect as part of Fitzhugh ("Fitz") Lee's brigade in the East. A nephew of Robert E. Lee, Fitz Lee enjoyed none of his uncle's finer attributes, only escaping dismissal as a cadet at West Point due to the latter's intervention. He served on the frontier, sustaining serious injuries in a battle with the Indians, before returning to West Point as a lecturer in tactics. Resigning in May 1861, he joined and was commissioned into the Confederate army later that month. He served on Ewell's and Johnston's staffs before being promoted lieutenant colonel in the summer of 1861 and colonel the fol-

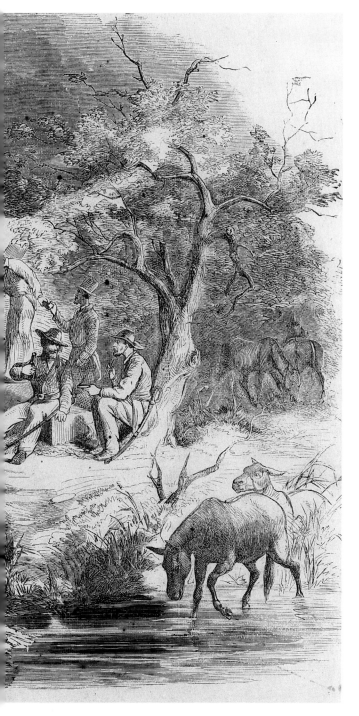

lowing March. Under Stuart's command, he was promoted brigadier general on 24 July 1862 and, as such, led his cavalry brigade, including the 1st Texas, at South Mountain, at Antietam (Sharpsburg), and during the Dumfries and Occoquan raids south of Washington in December 1862. He guarded "Stonewall" Jackson's complicated maneuver at Chancellorsville, and later fought at Gettysburg. Promoted major general in August 1863 when still under 28 years old, he was subsequently seriously injured again but recovered to assume command of the depleted remnants of the entire Confederate cavalry. After the war, he was elected Democratic governor of Virginia and later served the reunited country most professionally both as a diplomat and as a soldier.

Those cavalry regiments which remained in the West rarely dressed in regulation uniform. Cut off from the East after the fall of Vicksburg, Texas set up its own Lone Star Mill at the Huntsville Penitentiary, which produced vast quantities of assorted gray denim materials used to make rough uniforms. Even so, demand vastly exceeded supply, forcing many soldiers to resort to almost exclusively civilian wear. The uniform of the 8th Texas – a gray kepi with yellow band, light-gray shell jacket, and dark gray trousers with yellow stripe – soon degenerated to a black or gray slouch hat, a colored scarf, brown, gray, or blue jackets with or without red facings, and trousers of any color. In March 1863, Private Dunnie Affleck of Company "B" described his colleagues' dress as including "Mexican hats and buckskin suits," and a year later wrote home requesting his family to furnish him with: "1 hat, 1 pr boots or shoes, 1 pr shoes for Alex [his servant], 1 pr drawers, 2 check shirts … 1 pr of buckskin gloves, 1 pr of buckskin pants." Captured Federal uniform was worn when practical, although this occasionally led to dire results, not least on 5 January 1865 when Private E.S. Dodds of the 8th Texas, having been captured behind Union lines wearing a quantity of Federal equipment, was accused of spying and shot.

Certain regiments attempted to introduce distinguishing marks with mixed results. The 1st Texas Cavalry (occasionally also referred to as the Texas Mounted Rifles or Partisan Rangers) wore black facings and unusual cuff flaps on their otherwise regulation shell jackets, although this "tradition" lasted only as long as the jackets themselves.

Weapons remained a constant problem throughout the war. Although the Texas Rangers were the first unit in the United States to receive the original Colt five-cylinder revolver, there was a constant shortage of all types of side arms. On 11 January 1862, a military board was set up to procure weapons but with little success. Copies of the Colt Dragoon model revolver were made by Tucker & Sherrard of Lancaster, while the Colt navy revolver was reproduced by Dance Brothers of Galveston, Texas, but never in sufficient numbers. Sabers were rarely carried by Texan units, but when they were, they tended to be of inferior base metals. Initially shotguns were popular with the rank and file, although they were subsequently discarded when the extent of their tendency to hit friend and foe alike was fully realized.

SOUTH CAROLINA REGIMENT

South Carolina began to make preparations for war long before 1861 but ultimately did not have the resources to equip more than a small number of those who rallied to her colors. Her basic uniform regulations dated back to 1839 and, although revised as late as 1860, were of little practical relevance to the war. New orders, limited to officers and non-commissioned officers, were rushed into print in 1861, but by then, most of the first wave of volunteers had already joined one of the numerous independent local companies, each with its own style of dress.

Officers were ordered to wear dark blue frock coats and trousers similar in design to the standard U.S. army pattern. Trousers were to have a 1½-inch (3.8cm) stripe for general and field officers and a 1-inch (2.5cm) stripe for company officers. Stripes were to be gold for generals and divisional and brigade staff officers, silver for field-grade and regimental staff officers, and white for the rest. Rank was to be indicated on the coat by gold buttons and

epaulettes for generals and staff officers and by silver buttons and epaulettes for the remainder. Rank badges were to be identical to those of the U.S. army, except that major generals were to wear a silver crescent between their two gold stars, brigadier generals were to wear two silver stars and colonels a gold palmetto tree (the state emblem) instead of the traditional eagle. *Chapeaux-bras*, each adorned by a white ostrich feather tipped black for major generals and red for brigadier generals or by a plain white cock feather for field officers, were to be worn as headgear on formal occasions. Company officers were ordered to wear conventional kepis adorned by a silver palmetto tree badge in front, the regimental number to its right, and the letter "R" to its left. In the field, general and staff officers were allowed to resort to the more anonymous kepi, in this instance adorned by a gold wreath surrounding the letters "SCV."

Not surprisingly, these grotesquely fanciful regulations were abandoned as impractical almost

Confederate artillerymen of the Palmetto (South Carolina) Battery pose for a photograph in Charleston in 1863.

Headdress: Initially, all ranks were issued with a plain gray hat turned up at the right with the letters "PG" and a laurel leaf on the front. As the war progressed this was replaced by a simple anonymous gray cloth cap.

Uniform: The Palmetto Guards uniform was civilian in essence although the presence of a high collar, braid and brass buttons, each engraved with a Palmetto tree representing the State emblem, gave it a military air.

Weapons: Rank and file South Carolinians were issued with the British Enfield musket. However, a number of marksmen retained their much heavier personal hunting rifles which they used with devastating effect. The soldier depicted here carries a Bowie knife which he would no doubt have learned to use while hunting as a boy.

from the outset. On 25 January 1861, the state quartermaster advertised for dark gray cloth suitable for uniforms and, a month later, requested tenders for the manufacture of 1,000 plain woolen frock coats and pantaloons.

In reality, early uniforms varied from company to company and were not even of a standard color. The Washingtons wore standard Confederate gray, the Davis Guards a darker hue almost bordering on brown, the Gist Rifles a loose-fitting green hunter's coat, and the Bozeman Guards blue. Most uniforms were of poor manufacture and soon wore out, after which they were replaced by central government-issue gray.

Several South Carolina units went to great lengths to introduce spectacular dress uniforms for ceremonial occasions. The Charleston Light Dragoons, who ultimately became Company "K," the 4th South Carolina Cavalry (Rutledge Cavalry), formed up in splendid pseudo-Napoleonic uniforms consisting of white-plumed leather and brass dragoon helmets bearing the palmetto tree on the front plate and on a pair of rosettes on each side, blue tunics with red frontages, raised collars and gold epaulettes, white trousers and gloves, and black high boots. Hardly surprisingly, from December 1860 the Light Dragoons reverted to conventional gray fatigue uniforms in the field.

A number of specialist units had come into existence in the late 1850s. The Chichester Zouave Cadets were raised in Charleston by Captain C.E. Chichester and were subsequently employed as guards in Castle Pickney when it was used to house Federal prisoners after the Battle of Manassas (Bull Run). The Cadets wore gray jackets and trousers with red facings similar to those of the cadets of the more famous Virginia Military Institute, and they were also issued with useful tan leggings in winter. The emblem of the palmetto tree was worn on the flat tops of their red kepis and on the belt plates, as were the letters "SC."

One of the most famous South Carolina units to serve in the Confederate army were the Palmetto Guards. Dress for the Guards consisted of a simple but practical civilian-style gray suit, with the addition of military equipment and a uniform hat. The gray hat had an upturned brim on the right-hand side, with the letters "PG" and a laurel wreath on the front and a small state emblem on the left-hand side. Two companies of South Carolina troops bore the title "Palmetto Guards:" Company "I" of the 2nd South Carolina Infantry and Company "A" of the 18th Battalion, South Carolina Siege Artillery. Strangely, the title was also taken for a time by the 19th Georgia Infantry.

Soon after South Carolina's secession, the immensely wealthy land and slave owner Wade Hampton enlisted a legion of six infantry companies, four cavalry companies, and an artillery battery entirely at his own expense, equipping the battery with six revolutionary Blakely field guns. Despite his inexperience, Hampton led his legion in person at 1st Manassas where, for a short time and without assistance, they held the entire Union army at bay. About 20 percent of the 600-strong legion were killed or wounded in less than two hours of bitter fighting, and Hampton himself was wounded. On 16 November 1861, the legion became part of Longstreet's Division. After the Peninsula campaign, the infantry companies under Colonel M.W. Gary were transferred to Hood's Texas Brigade, the artillery was redesignated Hart's South Carolina Battery, and the cavalry companies were incorporated into Rosser's Cavalry Regiment.

Most South Carolinans regarded themselves as good shots, and many brought with them their own

custom-built, heavy-barreled sniper's rifles when they enlisted. A number of the most accomplished marksmen contrived to join one of the dedicated rifle regiments in the hope that their skills would be fully utilized as skirmishers and that they would somehow thus avoid the rigors of the line infantry. One such regiment, the 2nd South Carolina Rifles, dressed in green (although not the dark green of the British Rifle Brigade from which they took their inspiration), but seems nonetheless to have been deployed in a conventional infantry role.

South Carolina was the only Southern state to attempt to remedy the acute pre-war lack of arms and ordnance by domestic construction. On 15 April 1851, William Glaze and Benjamin Flagg were awarded a contract for the manufacture of 1,000 rifles, 6,000 muskets, 1,000 cavalry sabers, 1,000 artillery swords, and 2,000 pistols. Glaze converted his ironworks in Columbia into an armaments factory, redesignating it the Palmetto Armory. During this reconstruction, Flagg's musket factory at Milbury, Massachusetts provided the lathes and machinery which would ultimately be required for production of the arms. By 1853, the work was completed and South Carolina was able to boast an arms inventory second to none in the South. During the war, the armory was converted into a munitions factory producing cannon balls, Minié bullets, and rollers for the powder mills in Columbia and Raleigh, North Carolina.

With admirable forethought, the state ordered a considerable number of military accouterments from Northern companies well before the war. The state's buttons, depicting the ubiquitous palmetto tree, were largely manufactured by H. & G. Schuyler of New York, while there was eager competition for the tenders for ornate waist belts and cartridge box plates (later issued to the first volun-teer regiments to form) throughout the industrial Northeast.

South Carolina produced a number of excellent field commanders throughout the war. Brigadier General John Bratton gave up his medical practice to accept an appointment as captain in the 6th South Carolinas in 1861. Promoted colonel a year later, he led his regiment on the Peninsula. Wounded and captured at Seven Pines (Fair Oaks), he was exchanged and thereafter fought during the Wilderness campaign, when he was promoted temporary brigadier. He continued to serve the Army of Northern Virginia faithfully until Appomattox, after which he returned to civilian life although not to medicine. William Wallace left his legal practice to enlist as a private in the 18th South Carolina Regiment. Almost immediately appointed adjutant, he was promoted lieutenant colonel in May 1861, subsequently leading his regiment into battle at Malvern Hill, 2nd Manassas, South Mountain, and Antietam (Sharpsburg). In the final stages of the war, he led Johnson's Division at Appomattox. Samuel McGowan, another accomplished lawyer, held the rank of major general in the pre-war militia. He commanded a state brigade during the bombardment of Fort Sumter and subsequently served as Bonham's A.D.C. at the 1st Manassas. Appointed colonel of the 14th South Carolinas in 1862, he led his regiment in the Peninsula campaign, at Cedar Mountain, 2nd Manassas, Antietam, and Fredericksburg. Having recovered from his third wound, he was promoted brigadier general on 23 April 1863 and given command of a brigade that came to bear his name. He saw further action during the Wilderness campaign and at Spotsylvania where he was wounded yet again. McGowan recovered in time to be at Lee's side during the final days prior to the surrender at Appomattox.

A detachment of South Carolina troops forms the guard at Castle Pinkney on the outskirts of Charleston in August 1861.

NORTH CAROLINA VOLUNTEERS

Essentially conservative in nature, North Carolina delayed formal secession until 20 May 1861, at which time it became the last state to join the Confederacy. Despite its reliance on 331,059 slaves (1860 census) for the maintenance of its essentially rural economy, loyalty to the Union had remained strong throughout the spring and it had not been until Lincoln's call for troops that the pro-secessionists finally won a formal severance of links with Washington. Thereafter North Carolina pursued the Southern cause with total commitment, contributing about 125,000 soldiers, leading the South in blockade running, sustaining about one-quarter of the Confederate losses, and feeding and clothing its own soldiers.

In line with normal Southern practice, the early volunteers formed themselves into a number of independent companies each with its own distinctive mode of dress. Eight companies paraded in predominantly blue uniforms and 23 in gray, presenting an overall picture of great confusion. On 20 September 1861, North Carolina accepted responsibility for clothing its own troops and set up a cloth-

ing factory in Raleigh. Within a year, 49,000 jackets, 68,000 pairs of trousers, 12,000 blankets, and 6,000 overcoats had been manufactured. As existing uniforms wore out and new companies were formed, all volunteers were re-equipped from central resources, with the result that adherence to dress regulations became a matter of pride rather than an impossible ideal.

With the exception of general and staff officers who wore dark blue coats, officers were issued with "North Carolina gray cloth" frock coats with twin rows of seven buttons for field officers and a single row of nine buttons for company-grade officers. Traditional U.S. army rank badges were retained, worn on shoulder straps with branch-of-service color backing.

Enlisted men wore less attractive but equally practical loose-fitting sack coats with falling collars, secured by six buttons and extending halfway down the thigh. Two-inch (5cm) wide epaulettes were fitted: black for the infantry, red for the artillery, and yellow for the cavalry.

Trousers were of a similar pattern gray, adorned

Personal administration was crucially important but all too often neglected. Not surprisingly troops from the rural South suffered less severely from the arduous camp existence.

Headdress: The French-style soft patrol caps issued to the enlisted soldiers were subsequently adopted by the majority of junior officers in the field.

Coats: Highly practical loose-fitting half-length gray sack coats with a falling collar, six buttons and black epaulettes were issued to all infantrymen.

Belt: Black leather belts of pre-war design displaying the letters "NC" on the buckle remained common throughout.

Weapons: As the war progressed, Mississippi rifles began to replace the traditional flintlocks originally issued. When production fell short, British Enfield rifles were imported.

Duplin's Rifles, a company of the 2nd Regiment, North Carolina Volunteers, pose for an early photograph. As the war progressed and casualties mounted the unit was incorporated into Company A, the 43rd North Carolina Regiment.

with a buff welt down each leg for generals, a branch-of-service color welt for officers, and a branch-of-service color stripe for enlisted men. With the exception of general and staff officers who wore black (and thus doubtless provided excellent targets for enemy marksmen), all ranks wore gray felt hats looped on the right side. Officers wore a U.S. army hat insignia as a badge, other ranks a branch-of-service hat band, company letter, and regimental number.

As domestically produced supplies ran out (the factory at Raleigh remained operational for less than a year), the state supplemented its needs from European imports. Between June 1863 and December 1864, despite the effectiveness of the Union blockade, North Carolina imported 50,000 blankets, enough gray wool for 250,000 uniforms, and enough leather for 250,000 pairs of shoes. When the state warehouses fell in April 1865, they were found even then to contain uniforms, shoes, and blankets for 95,000 men, although, taking into account the threadbare state of the Confederate army as a whole at that time, whether this should be regarded as brilliant planning or grossly unnecessary hoarding remains a moot point.

Musicians in the North Carolina regiments enjoyed an above-average standard of dress. Standard gray frock coats were issued, together (where possible) with sky blue trousers. Bandsmen were not differentiated by individual lace or badges but instead wore the colors of the arm to which they were attached. Thus a cavalry bugler in full dress might expect to wear yellow braid around his jacket, high collar, and sleeves, twin rows of yellow buttons, and a yellow covering to his kepi.

Ordnance sergeants within the North Carolina

Volunteers were conferred with the dubious privilege of carrying the regimental banner into battle. Ordinarily this "honor," with its obvious dangers, fell to line sergeants, but for reasons which were never clearly explained, North Carolina adopted the European habit of delegating the task to the senior (and, therefore, presumably the most experienced) non-commissioned officers available. Initially, the banners varied in size according to the branch of service: theoretically infantry colors were 4 ft (1.2m) square, artillery 3 ft (92cm) square, and cavalry guidons 30 inches (76cm) square. However, in reality many varied according to usage and local custom. Although the Confederacy did not formally award battle honors, regiments traditionally painted the names of battles in which they had participated on their colors, rendering those of senior regiments such as the 3rd North Carolinas extremely gaudy.

State volunteers were among the best armed and equipped of all Confederate forces. In 1861, M.A. Baker of Fayetteville was contracted to convert large numbers of flintlock muskets, rifles, and pistols to percussion. Subsequently contracts were given to H.C. Lamb & Co. of Jamestown to produce 300 M1841 "Mississippi"-style rifles a month and to Mendenhall, Jones & Gardner of Whitsett to produce a total of 10,000 similar weapons. When domestic production fell short of demand, European weapons, particularly British Enfield rifles, were imported.

Under the command of Colonel Daniel Harvey Hill, the 1st North Carolina Infantry had the distinction of being one of the first regiments in the Confederate army to engage the enemy. A one-time regular soldier, Colonel Hill had served on the border and in the Mexican War, during which he had been awarded two brevets. In 1849, he had resigned his army commission to take up an appointment as professor of mathematics at Washington College in Lexington, Virginia. Named superintendent of the North Carolina Military Institute in 1859, Harvey did much to prepare the state for war and, in 1861, was commissioned colonel of the 1st North Carolinas. Promoted brigadier general in July 1861 and major general in March 1862, he later fought at Seven Pines (Fair Oaks), in the Seven Days' Battles, at South Mountain, and at Antietam (Sharpsburg) before falling foul of political intrigue which effectively halted his military career.

On 10 June 1861, the 1st North Carolinas found themselves spearheading a Confederate force of 1,400, having been ordered to defend Yorktown, Virginia against 4,400 assorted Federal troops advancing from their stronghold on Hampton Roads. The Southerners dug in in the area of Big Bethel and, during a morning of confused skirmishing, drove off a series of poorly managed Federal attacks. The Northerners sustained 76 casualties, including Major Winthrop killed, sword in hand, leading his men in the final forlorn assault.

On 1 May 1863, the 3rd North Carolinas were at the head of "Stonewall" Jackson's masterful flank march behind enemy lines at Chancellorsville. Smarting from its defeat at the Battle of Fredericksburg in the previous December, the Union army had reorganized and re-equipped and, under the leadership of its new commander Major General Joe Hooker, was eager to avenge itself. After a few

months' recuperation in winter camp, Hooker had seized the initiative by moving his forces in a large encircling movement behind the Confederates, thereafter drawing them up near the hamlet of Chancellorsville in the hope of forcing them to turn and fight him on ground of his own choosing. Unwilling to commit his vastly outnumbered troops to a frontal assault, Lee left a skeleton force in Fredericksburg and advanced with the bulk of his troops toward Chancellorsville. Keeping 17,000 men with him in reserve, Lee ordered Jackson to take 26,000 men on a 16-mile detour in broad daylight through a series of confusing trails to a position behind the Federal rear. Although the first part of the move took place within full sight of the Northern army, Hooker presumed that the Confederates were simply retreating and did nothing to impair their progress. At 5:00 p.m. that afternoon, with less than two hours of daylight remaining, Jackson led his men in a spirited and totally unexpected assault on the Union right flank. The speed and ferocity of their attack swept all before them, turning the battle into a rout. Tragically, for the Confederacy, while reconnoitering ahead of his own lines Jackson was fired on by nervous Confederate pickets and mortally wounded.

When Jackson died eight days later, the South lost one of its greatest soldiers and Lee his right arm. Yet this was no fault of the North Carolinas, who had led the charge, giving the rebel yell at the top of their voices, against tremendous odds. For the rest of the war they fought tenaciously, refusing to give up hope until ultimately ordered to lay down their arms by Lee himself.

Confederate troops suffered terribly in the cold winter months. Although they are depicted here enjoying a snowball fight, in reality many were wholly ill-equipped for the conditions, having discarded their heavy coats during the earlier summer months.

187

OFFICER: CONFEDERATE ARTILLERY

Few of the regular officers who resigned their commissions to fight for the Confederacy in 1861 had ever served with the artillery. They had no idea of the potential of massed guns nor did they appreciate the degree of skill required to bring a battery into action quickly and efficiently. Nonetheless, many of the more socially elite volunteered for the artillery, seeing within its ranks the possibility of glamor as well as action. However, the men and equipment placed under their command were far from promising. Infantry companies were converted wholesale into batteries, and guns were gathered together from every source possible without recourse to size, condition, or caliber.

At the outset of the war, artillery differed little from that of the Napoleonic era. The French use of light, mobile fieldpieces capable of rapid deployment to any weak point had been adopted by the U.S. army during the 1840's and had proved highly effective in the Seminole and Mexican wars. Thereafter gunners had been encouraged to school

themselves in the arts of hard riding and swift firing, skills which lent themselves well to the independent Confederate nature. Battery or regimental fire were rarely if ever practiced.

The fieldpieces most widely used by both sides in the early stages of the war were, like Bonaparte's guns, muzzle-loading smoothbore cannon. Inherently inaccurate at long ranges and therefore of limited offensive value, the cannon came into its own when on the defensive. When targeted against massed infantry in the open, case shot – hollow balls packed with powder and clusters of iron or lead balls – was capable of cutting great swathes through the massed ranks of an enemy formation at ranges of up to 800 yards (732m). Canister – metal containers filled with bullets and shrapnel of all kinds – was lethal against those who, having survived the case shot, managed to approach to within 300 yards (275m) of the guns.

It quickly became apparent that smoothbore cannon, once the indisputable "God of War," was

The Washington Artillery of New Orleans was drawn from the most fashionable Louisiana society, but lacked modern ordnance. This photograph was taken early in 1862.

Headdress: Unlike their infantry counterparts, cavalry officers often wore standard *chasseur*-pattern kepis usually adorned in crimson.

Tunic: As the war progressed most officers adopted the cavalry jacket. In this instance however the subject has retained the regulation frock coat with its red facings and Austrian knot on the sleeves.

Weapons: Although the artillery relied upon the infantry for its close quarter defense, most officers carried either a pistol or saber. The cannon in the background is the 3-in "Parrot" gun, quite possibly captured from the Federal forces at the outset of the war.

189

A Confederate Napoleon gun stands ready on the outskirts of Atlanta, Georgia.

now susceptible to enemy rifle fire. Whereas Napoleon's gunners had had to face nothing more deadly than the British Baker rifle, with its range of no more than 250 yards (229m), their Confederate equivalents frequently found themselves targeted by Union snipers armed with a variety of high-powered rifled muskets, some with a range in excess of 1,500 yards (1,370m). Instead of digging in behind defensive earth works, gun crews continued to deploy freely behind their own infantry, seeking targets of opportunity, and they were soon annihilated by enemy rifle fire.

This problem was partially alleviated by the introduction of rifled iron cannon capable of throwing projectiles long distances with much improved accuracy. The Model 1861 ordnance rifle, with its 3-inch (7.5cm) bore, could fire accurately to 2,400 yards (2,195m) and was effective against static massed targets to an astounding 4,000 yards (3,658m), while Robert Parrott's series of 10-, 20- and 30-pounder siege guns were capable of still greater ranges.

Where possible, the South tried to augment its arsenal of smoothbores by purchasing cannon from Britain and France, but the latter often proved an unwilling vendor, while it soon became apparent that the crowded ships acting as blockade runners trading between the British ports and the Gulf were simply too small to transport the heavy modern guns in the numbers required. Attempts were made to cast a few guns in Confederate forges, but the inferior metal available, coupled with the lack of facilities and skilled workmen, made it difficult to

manufacture reliable cannon. Many of the domestic guns that were produced proved defective and even dangerous in action.

Free from the fetters of tradition, the Confederacy showed itself willing to experiment with new ordnance, often with dire results. A few Lancaster guns, capable of firing shaped rounds from barrels with oval bores, were introduced from Britain but were found to be prone to jamming both during loading and, more ominously, when fired. Few weapons were more macabre than the Congreve rocket used in limited numbers by a despairing Confederacy during the latter stages of the war. In essence a simple metal case filled with gunpowder and capped with an explosive shell as its warhead, the rocket was attached to a pole 8 ft (2.4m) tall, fitted into a long trough supported on trestles and fired in the general direction of the enemy. If the gunner got his calculations right, the fuze would burst the shell just as the rocket arrived at the target. If not, the shell would either burst harmlessly over no man's land or would land with the fuze still burning, in which case, the rocket would ricochet wildly in whatever direction its impact with the ground had pointed it. Not infrequently, it would turn back and head toward the launchers.

Surprisingly, General Lee thought little of the artillery, denying it the high-quality horses which it desperately needed. Those horses assigned to pulling the guns and limbers were given only 3 lb (1.35kg) of Indian corn per day, condemning many to a premature death from malnutrition, disease and exhaustion. Lee left many of his batteries behind when he invaded the North in 1862 and, upon his return on 14 October 1862, had 14 of them disbanded.

The basic unit within the artillery was the battery, initially comprising six guns but later usually four. Each battery was commanded by a captain and often took his name, although units which formed in 1861 frequently chose titles of local interest such as the Alexandria Artillery or the German Artillery. Others adopted the names of Confederate heroes. All these titles led to considerable logistic confusion and not a little animosity when the various outfits were amalgamated into single fighting entities.

Two guns, under a lieutenant, formed a section while one gun, complete with its limber and caisson, formed a platoon under the command of a sergeant or "chief of piece." When at full strength, each gun was served by a crew of nine men, but counter-battery fire and the ever-present threat of enemy snipers often decimated them. It was not unknown for infantry sections in the field to be pressed into service to help.

Confederate artillery, particularly within the Army of Northern Virginia, was never exploited to its full potential. Although this was due in part to its indiscipline and poor quality, the problem was compounded in the early stages of the war by the refusal of the authorities to organize its meager artillery resources into a small number of relatively powerful fighting entities. Eventually Lee conceded to this need and ordered that the batteries be taken from the control of the infantry brigades and formed into battalions. Command of each battalion passed to a field officer, either a colonel or lieutenant colonel, assisted by an ordnance officer, quartermaster, and adjutant.

Despite this reorganization, the Confederate artillery remained fragmentary and detached, never able to fuse itself into a single fighting arm. Much of the blame for this lay with William Pendleton, the Chief of Artillery from 1862 to 1865. A professor of mathematics, Pendleton had taught at West Point, at Bristol College, Pennsylvania, and at Delaware College before becoming ordained as an Episcopal minister in 1838. On 1 May 1861, after nearly 25 years away from the colors, he volunteered to fight for his native South and was elected captain of the Rockbridge Artillery. Promoted colonel in July 1861, he was further promoted brigadier general and appointed Lee's Chief of Artillery on 26 March 1862. Although his underutilized general artillery reserve was broken up and the guns sent down to the divisions and corps as part of the restructuring of May 1863, Pendleton was allowed to retain his somewhat meaningless title. More preacher than soldier, he was well meaning but far from adequate for the task.

Had the Confederate artillery found a champion such as Jackson or Stuart to argue its cause, or had its officers been of a higher caliber, it would certainly have played a greater part in the defense of the South. However, it was never allowed to reach its full potential.

A gathering of assorted Confederate officers, possibly the last such picture taken during the war.

GEORGIA INFANTRY

At the time of her secession on 19 January 1861, Georgia was the wealthiest and most populous of the lower Southern states. Yet her economy was almost entirely rural, relying heavily on the annual cotton crop, and, as such, was vulnerable to enemy incursion. Furthermore, the labor-intensiveness of each autumn harvest necessitated a massive reservoir of slaves, without whom the crop would have been priced out of the world market. Not surprisingly, therefore, many Georgians put the maintenance of the status quo within their own state before the defense of the newly formed Confederacy.

Immediately after secession, Georgia created its own "state army" comprising two infantry regiments and single rifle, cavalry, and artillery battalions. Under the terms of General Orders No. 4, issued on 15 February 1861, troops were to wear Georgia cadet gray frock coats and trousers, while officers were issued with dark blue frock coats and trousers. Infantrymen had black patches on their standing coat collars while the artillery wore orange piping and trouser stripes. The cavalry, incorporated into the Governor's Horse Guards, were splendidly, if somewhat impractically, attired in the manner of the central European "hussar" of the time: high black boots, light blue trousers, white cross belt and gloves, plumed hat, and gray jacket adorned with 11 rows of black braiding.

Unusually for Confederate cavalry, most of whom shunned the sword in favor of the carbine, its members were armed with sabers, as well as revolvers.

The vast majority of volunteers were unwilling or unable to serve in the state army and instead elected to join one of the numerous local units which mushroomed in the early days of the war. Georgia did not attempt to introduce dress regulations for these officers and enlisted men, preferring to leave such matters to the discretion of individual commanders. The end result was confusing and, on occasion, bizarre. The 3rd Georgia Infantry Regiment, an amalgam of independent companies formed before the outbreak of hostilities, was typical. Company "F" wore buff-colored Georgia kersey while Company "E" favored red jackets and blue-black trousers with a white stripe and "German fatigue caps." Every other company wore gray but with individual trims: Companies "C", "H", and "K" preferring black, Company "A" green, and Company "B" red. Not surprisingly, in the inevitable confusion of the early battles several troops were shot by mistake by their own side.

Despite their somewhat unorthodox appearance, Georgia troops soon gained an enviable reputation for bravery and tenacity. From the 1st Battle of Manassas (Bull Run) – when the 7th Georgia lost its commanding officer Colonel Bartow in a spirited

The Battle of Murfreesboro' (Stone River), Tennessee, on 31 December 1862 was a bloody stalemate, but yet again it proved the fighting qualities of the Georgian regiments.

Headdress: During the hot summer months the infantry wore wide-brimmed straw hats as protection against the sun. In action however these tended to be replaced by more practical floppy cloth hats.

Coat: A blue frock coat and kepi bearing the letters "GR" within a silver wreath were issued for dress and winter wear. In summer these were discarded in favor of the plain white shirt otherwise worn as an undergarment.

Georgian troops fought valiantly under Hood at Gettysburg, Knoxville and Chickamauga.

assault on Henry House Hill – to Appomattox, when the 5th Georgia refused to concede defeat, carrying on the fight under General Edmund Kirby Smith for nearly three weeks after Lee's surrender, they fought stubbornly, never giving ground without a fight. Regiments such as the 44th Georgia, one of the toughest in the entire Confederate army, fought at Chancellorsville – where it succeeded in driving the enemy back over two miles, captured several pieces of ordnance, and sustained 121 casualties – as well as at Gettysburg and Chickamauga.

No fewer than nine Georgian brigades took part in the Gettysburg campaign. Benning's, Wofford's, Toombs', and Anderson's brigades fought as part of Longstreet's Corps on the Confederate right, Gordon's and Dole's brigades as part of Ewell's Corps on the left and Wright's, Pender's, and Thomas's brigades as part of Hill's Corps in the center. Nowhere did the troops fight more bravely than on the Confederate right. Anderson's and Benning's brigades formed part of Hood's Division and, as such, took part in the bloody fighting for the Devil's Den and Little Round Top. Both brigades attacked some time after 4:00 p.m. on 2 July 1863. Had Longstreet moved earlier and allowed the impatient Hood to seize the initiative, it is possible that both positions might have been taken with comparative ease. As it was, the Union forces were allowed to reinforce their vulnerable positions and to bring up artillery in support. The Georgians were met by the concentrated fire of Ward's and de Trobriand's Federal brigades dug in behind a stone wall and of Barnes' two brigades to the north. Despite the overwhelming odds, the Confederates drove home the assault, captured the 4th New York Battery at the Devil's Den, and forced Ward's shattered men to give ground. The magnificent efforts of the Southern troops were frustrated when the Federals brought up reserves and, in a series of bloody counter-attacks, forced the Confederates back toward their original pos-

itions. Losses were horrific. In less than five hours' fighting, much of it hand to hand amid the huge boulders, crevices, caves, and labyrinths of the Devil's Den, Longstreet's Corps (including the four Georgian brigades) sustained 872 killed, 4,130 injured, and 2,268 missing.

Henry Lewis ("Rock") Benning, who personally led his brigade into action against the enemy positions at the Devil's Den, epitomized the superb standards of Georgian leadership. After graduating from the University of Georgia, he practised law and, after a few years, entered the state legislature. Totally opposed to emancipation on economic grounds, Benning nevertheless realized that abolition would be inevitable were Georgia to remain in the Union. As Associate Justice of the Georgia Supreme Court, he questioned the authority of Washington to interfere in state constitutional matters, and was ultimately at the forefront of the movement for secession. Commissioned colonel of the 17th Georgia, he led his regiment into action at Malvern Hill and in the 2nd Battle of Manassas. Given command of Toombe's Brigade at Antietam (Sharpsburg) and Fredericksburg, he was promoted brigadier general on 23 April 1863. Thereafter, he served under Hood at Gettysburg, Knoxville, and Chickamauga, at which time he had two horses shot from under him yet miraculously escaped without personal injury. Severely injured during the Wilderness campaign, he recovered in time to take part in the defense of Petersburg and in the subsequent retreat to Appomattox. After the war, he returned to his legal practice until his death in 1875 at the age of 61. Fort Benning, Georgia, one of the United States Army's major infantry posts, was later named in his honor.

In the autumn of 1864, General William Tecumseh Sherman decided to counter General Hood's invasion of Tennessee and to strike a death blow to the very heart of the Confederacy by marching eastward to the sea, destroying everything of any conceivable value to the enemy. On 15 November, having destroyed the military resources of Atlanta, he set off for Savannah with 20 days' supplies. The massive, well-equipped Union force of 55,000 infantry, 5,000 cavalry, and 2,000 artillery with 64 guns was divided into two wings designated the Army of the Tennessee and the Army of Georgia. The Confederacy had only 13,000 troops, including the 3,050 members of G.W. Smith's Georgia militia, with which to oppose the enemy advance. The Southerners fought tenaciously but to no avail. Constantly hungry and critically short of resources, they were forced to defend a huge area against the possibility of attack and were never able to meet the enemy equally in localized battle. A number of skirmishes were fought, and the Georgia militia engaged an entire division at Griswoldville on 22 November, but none succeeded in slowing the Union advance.

For a month, Sherman moved through the state on a front 60 miles wide, leaving behind him a trail of wreckage. Many neutral observers derided him for his callousness toward enemy civilians and for what some saw as his inability or even unwillingness to control the excesses of his own troops. The British historian and professional soldier J.F.C. Fuller later attacked the raid as "brigandage," but at the time, and indeed subsequently, Sherman was unrepentant. In a report to Washington, he stated : "I estimate the damage to Georgia and its military resources to be $100,000,000, at least $20,000,000 of which has been injured to our advantage and the remainder is simply waste and destruction."

When the seaport of Savannah fell to Sherman on 22 December 1864, the state of Georgia effectively ceased to function as a part of the Confederacy. Economically it was broken, but the will of its troops to fight on remained as strong as ever. Seven Georgian brigades continued to the end, and it is more than coincidence that troops from the 5th Georgia, one of the first regiments to be formed, were among the last troops to lay down their arms.

Company K, 4th Regiment Georgia Volunteers (Sumter Light Guards) parades in April 1861. Note the frock coats issued to the senior NCOs.

THE VIRGINIA REGIMENT

Virginia realized as early as 1858 that the divide between the abolitionist and the slave-owning states was widening and consequently took early steps to prepare for its own defense. The formation of volunteer companies was actively encouraged and centralized dress regulations introduced. However, in order not to discourage the continued support of the existing militias and independent companies, these were allowed to retain their often distinctive modes of dress. In 1861, 79 such companies were outfitted in predominantly gray uniforms, while 14 favored blue which, theoretically at least, constituted the regulation state color. Many of the simpler uniforms consisted of French-style kepis and gray frock coats and trousers trimmed with colored braid, but others were far more ornate.

Immediately after the outbreak of war, the companies were united under centralized command and formed into regiments. No attempt was made at that stage to regulate the divergent modes of dress within each regiment with the result that some of the first units to be constituted contained up to ten different uniforms, some even a dangerous mixture of blue and gray.

Regiments such as the socially élite 1st Virginia, which recruited from among the best families in the Richmond area, commonly wore gray, although field officers were issued with a blue coat and trousers, Virginia state buttons and a Jeff Davis hat. The Richmond Howitzers, which was originally a part of the 1st Virginia but which was later reorganized into a separate battery, was ordered to parade in fatigue dress and overcoats, with sabers and white gloves. Red stripes were attached to the outer seams of the trousers and as a cap band along the base of the kepi. The Brooklyn Grays, originally formed in Brooklyn, Halifax County in March 1861, subsequently became Company "E" of the 23rd Virginia Regiment but still retained their distinctive white cross-belts (later issued to the majority of Virginian troops), black trouser stripes, and gold letters "BG" on their kepis.

Certain militia units were even more outlandish in their dress. The Woodis Rifles, a militia company raised in 1858 in Norfolk, Virginia and named after a mayor of that city, wore a dark hunting-green uniform faced with black velvet, gold spherical buttons, and gold cord lanyards. The trousers had a

A unique photograph of an 1865-pattern fire engine, pressed into service during the siege of Richmond.

Headdress: The figure "1" in the middle of the kepi denoted membership of the 1st Virginia Regiment, a socially élite unit which recruited from the Richmond area.

Coat: Although most units wore gray frock coats during the early stages of the war, at least 14 companies paraded in blue. The white cross belts and epaulettes were an expensive extra and were soon abandoned.

Weapons: Initially Virginian troops were issued with old flintlocks. However these were rapidly converted to percussion and were supplemented where possible by rifled muskets looted from the Harpers Ferry Federal Armory.

black velvet welt edged with gold cord, and the "Hardee" hat bore a gold cord, a red hackle, and gold-on-black bugle horn badge beneath the letters "WR." Despite their obvious pretensions to sharpshooter status, there is no evidence to suggest that the Woodis Rifles were ever deployed as such. Instead they were initially incorporated into the 3rd Battalion, 54th Regiment of Virginia Militia and ultimately into Company "C" of the 6th Virginia Regiment.

Dour, severe, intolerant of failure, "Stonewall" Jackson was also one of the finest exponents of light infantry warfare in history.

Many of the wealthier companies sponsored their own musicians, who ultimately combined to form very creditable regimental bands. Drum Major C.R.M. Pohle of the 1st Virginia was photographed wearing a resplendent dress uniform including a full-length gray frock coat, black and gold facings and epaulettes, a black leather belt and scabbard, and a massive Russian-style bearskin surmounted by a fulsome black and white plume.

As the war continued and the original uniforms wore out, they were replaced by a combination of gray and coppernob homespun which, despite its drabness, at least allowed the wearer the benefit of being correctly identified at a distance.

Local commanders went to bizarre lengths to prevent mistakes in identification during the early stages of the war. Realizing that many of the Federal troops wore gray while his own 33rd Virginia wore blue, "Stonewall" Jackson issued an order before the 1st Battle of Manassas (Bull Run) directing his men to identify themselves by tying strips of white cloth around their arms or hats. So as to make absolutely sure that no mistakes were made, his men were further directed to strike their left breasts with their right hands while simultaneously shouting "Our homes!" immediately they encountered an unknown unit. According to one disgruntled soldier, who presumably declined to take part in this somewhat lunatic theater, the commanders had "failed to tell us that while we were going through this Masonic performance we [were thus giving] the other fellow an opportunity to blow our brains out, if we had any."

Despite every endeavor, mistakes were made, often with tragic consequences. For a crucial moment during 1st Manassas, Colonel Cummings ordered the men of the 33rd Virginian Regiment (themselves dressed in blue) not to fire on the advancing lines of the New York Fire Zouaves in the mistaken belief that they were the leading elements of Roberdeau Wheat's Louisiana Tigers who were due to reinforce their position. Less than an hour later, fate turned full circle when Captain Griffin of the Union artillery was ordered against his better judgment not to fire on the advancing 33rd Virginians on the basis that they were more than likely support troops from an unidentified Federal infantry regiment. It was not until the Confederates had been allowed to approach unhindered to within 70 yards (64m) of the battery position and discharged a devastating volley into the Union guns and horses that the mistake was appreciated. By that time, it was too late to prevent the guns falling into Confederate hands.

The 1st Battle of Manassas left the Virginia Regiment full of possibly misplaced confidence. It is well known that Jackson drew up his troops (from left to right, the 33rd, 4th, 27th, 2nd and 5th Virginians) behind the comparative protection of Henry House Hill to enable their presence to remain secret from the exhausted Federals until it became advantageous to commit them. Once in position, they were joined by Hampton's Legion and the 8th Virginians on their right, and by the 7th Georgians, elements of the 49th Virginians and two squadrons of Stuart's Virginian Cavalry on their left, thus securing both flanks against the possibility of infiltration. Once launched, Jackson's counter-attack was an unmitigated success, forcing the Federals not only off Henry House Hill but backward into total retreat. It has been suggested, however, that Jackson delayed too long in his defensive position and that, had he taken the initiative earlier, he would have insured the survival of Brigadier General Barnard Bee, who died attempting to hold together the decimated Alabamans and Georgians forming the left flank of the original front line. Moreover, the men of Bee's brigade might not have suffered the horrific casualties which they sustained attempting to contain alone the numerically vastly superior Federal regiments while the Virginians waited impassively to the rear. Whether this criticism is justified, and whether or not Bee gave Jackson the now-famous nickname of "Stonewall" because of his refusal to commit his troops to battle or because of his steadiness once committed, will always remain a matter of conjecture. What is certain is that, at Manassas, the Virginians gained a reputation for ferocity which they were to retain throughout the war. In later campaigns, they were to astound the enemy by their speed and agility, both on and off the battlefield. Virginian troops formed the vanguard during Jackson's audacious and highly successful Shenandoah Valley campaign (May – June 1862), during which

they successfully frustrated the advance of an army five times their size.

On 30 May 1863, the Confederacy paid Jackson's brigade – which then constituted the 2nd, 4th, 5th, 27th, and 33rd Virginia Regiments – the peculiar honor of redesignating it the "Stonewall Brigade" in recognition of its excellent record since its inception two years earlier. Drawn predominantly from the 18 counties of the Shenandoah Valley, its officers and men fought in every major battle of the eastern theater, sustaining over 1,200 casualties in 1862 alone. Decimated at the 2nd Battle of Manassas, the brigade was reduced to regimental strength in September 1862 but never lost its fighting spirit. Fittingly, its remaining elements formed Lee's rearguard in his retreat to Appomattox, only surrendering when expressly ordered to do so.

Other regiments fought as purposefully, if less dramatically, right to the end. In August 1864, Major General George Pickett's entire division within Anderson's I Corps comprised Virginian regiments. Pegram's Brigade formed part of Gordon's Division, and Jones' and the Stonewall brigades were part of Johnson's Division within Jubal Early's II Corps. No troops committed themselves more fully to the cause of the Confederacy than those who formed the infantry regiments of Virginia.

Little Round Top was the scene of some of the most savage fighting throughout the Battle of Gettysburg. This photograph shows a dead Confederate sharpshooter.

CONFEDERATE CAVALRY: 1865

By the beginning of 1865, the Confederate cavalry was a spent force. Four years of warfare, compounded by hunger and privation, had reduced it to a skeleton of its former self. Desperately short of fodder, several of its units had even been forced to abandon their horses and fight dismounted. Much of the cavalry's heart died with Jeb Stuart in May 1864, yet it continued to fight to the very end under the inspired leadership of Generals Fitzhugh Lee, W.H. Lee, and Rosser.

Part of the reason for the Confederate cavalry's durability lay in its composition. Its members were excellent horsemen, self-assured to the point of arrogance, and, for the most part, young. Few of its commanders were more than 30 years old (Stuart himself had sported a flowing beard in an attempt to disguise his extreme youth) and as such were not hide-bound by the rules of conventional warfare. The Union general William Tecumseh Sherman summed up the Southern cavalry well: "Young bloods ... sons of planters, lawyers about towns, good billiard-players and sportsmen who never did work and never will." However, he went on to describe them as also "splendid riders, first-rate shots, and utterly reckless" – none of which terms as he freely conceded, could have been employed to describe his own cavalry.

The vast majority of Confederate cavalry officers were drawn from a privileged class. The sons of farmers and plantation owners, they learned to give orders and take responsibility at an early age. Within their society, fine horsemanship was regarded as the mark of a gentleman; no one walked if he could ride, the vast majority preferring the freedom of horseback to the restraints of the carriage. Not unnaturally, therefore, and in marked contrast to the North, cavalry regiments attracted the finest among the Southern volunteers. Every man provided his own horse, many of which were hunters bred from Virginia or Kentucky thoroughbreds and used to being ridden hard. A large number of troopers even provided their own arms, discarding the unpopular issue saber in favor of the carbine and shot gun.

Southern cavalry relied upon native wit and personal élan rather than regimental discipline to survive. Charges, when they took place (which was rarely), were uncoordinated, with the result that hard – won victories were seldom fully exploited.

In 1863, the Confederate cavalry suffered two severe setbacks from which it never fully recovered. On 9 June, Major General Jeb Stuart's seemingly unbeatable cavalry division was surprised by General Alfred Pleasonton's Federal cavalry corps in the area of Brandy Station, and for the first time since its formation, it was nearly defeated. Stuart's predicament was caused as much by his own conceit as by Union strategy. At the time, Lee had been planning a bold advance deep into enemy territory with the intention of

A clash between the 5th U.S. Cavalry and Stuart's Confederate Cavalry at Old Church, Tunstall's Station, Virginia, on 13 June 1862. It resulted in the death of the Confederates' Captain Latane.

Headdress: By 1865 the Confederate cavalry had lost much of its élan, if not its fighting spirit. Slouch hats were by now rare while leathers, once common, were all but non existent.

Tunics: A few fortunate troopers managed to retain a semblance of uniform; others were forced to operate in an inadequate hotchpotch of begged, improvised and stolen apparel. By 1865 correct badges and insignia were almost unknown.

Weapons: Throughout the war Confederate cavalry demonstrated a marked dislike of close quarter combat and sabers were therefore often discarded. Pistols, invariably worn butt forward on the right hip, and carbines were the preferred weapons.

201

alleviating the pressure on the Southern states. Instead of fulfilling the natural role of the cavalry and reconnoitering ahead of the Army of Northern Virginia to secure its flanks and obtain valuable intelligence, Stuart had insisted on wasting several days preparing and staging a totally unnecessary military review which, ultimately, Lee declined to attend, sending former Confederate Secretary of War G.W. Randolph in his place. As a direct result, the Confederate cavalry neglected to post adequate pickets and failed totally to appreciate that it was being encircled. Early on the morning of 9 June, a few hours before the Confederates were due to break camp and move north, the Union cavalry attacked in two places, taking Stuart's veterans completely by surprise. Pleasonton's assault was beaten off but not before Stuart had been forced to call upon the infantry for support.

The Battle of Brandy Station had important repercussions. For the first time, Union cavalrymen felt that they had proved themselves to be the equals of their Southern counterparts. No longer did they subconsciously regard the Confederate cavalry as their superiors nor Stuart as infallible. More fundamentally, Stuart and his troopers lost considerable domestic credibility, not only because of their unpreparedness for the Federal attack but also because of their penchant for meaningless reviews. In the words of the normally supportive *Richmond Examiner*:

... this puffed up cavalry of the Army of Northern Virginia has been surprised ... and such repeated accidents can be regarded as nothing but the necessary consequences of negligence and bad management. If the war was a tournament, invented and supported for the pleasure of a few vain officers, these disasters might be dismissed with compassion. But the country pays dearly for the blunders.

Brandy Station had no immediate impact on Lee's advance into Pennsylvania. It did, however, severely unsettle Stuart and he was determined to restore his credibility on the first occasion possible. Gettysburg provided him with the opportunity for which he longed, yet in his desperation for glory, he once again placed his personal interests ahead of those of the Confederacy. On 22 June, Lee wrote to Stuart ordering him to advance north, secure the Blue Ridge Mountains and guard the dangerously exposed flank of Ewell's II Corps. Stuart set out upon his mission three days later but discovered almost immediately that his intended route was blocked by an entire Federal corps. Instead of returning to headquarters for further orders, Stuart led his three brigades on a wide detour behind Union lines. In so doing, he placed two mountain ranges between himself and the advancing Southern army, effectively denying Lee his eyes and ears at the most crucial moment.

A duel between a Union cavalryman and a Confederate trooper. It is unlikely that the onlookers would have been so relaxed.

Unable to send out cavalry patrols in depth and therefore unable to obtain detailed intelligence of the enemy's movements, Lee was forced to continue his own deployment virtually blind. Mindless of the need for haste, Stuart wasted more valuable time by capturing a massive Federal wagon train which slowed down his daily pace from 40 to 25 miles. Late on the night of 1 July, when still some considerable distance from the main Confederate army, Stuart was found by one of the eight couriers sent by Lee to scour the Pennsylvania countryside for him and was ordered to return immediately. By the time that Stuart, riding far in advance of the main body of his men, reached headquarters to receive Lee's severe rebuke for his lack of military foresight, it was the morning of 2 July, the Battle of Gettysburg was a day old, and the Confederate initiative had been lost.

Between June 1864 and March 1865, the Confederate cavalry disintegrated from a cohesive fighting force to a group of brave but hopeless mounted bands. The process began with Early's offensive in the Shenandoah and terminated with the fall of Richmond. Intent on drawing away Grant's Federal troops by taking the war to enemy soil, Early with 14,000 men, including Ransom's cavalry division of 4,000 veterans, advanced up the Shenandoah Valley and crossed the Potomac into Maryland. Having extracted a "ransom" of $200,000 from the town of

Frederick, Early turned southeast toward Washington, brushing aside feeble Federal resistance until his leading elements eventually reached Fort Stevens, one of the several dozen major forts guarding the city. Exhausted, outnumbered, and unable to proceed further, Early's men retired across upper Maryland in good order until, on 14 July, they were able to recross the Potomac into Virginia.

Humiliated and angry, Grant determined that the Shenandoah would never again pose a threat to the Union. In August 1864, Sheridan, the most aggressive of the Union generals, was given command of the newly formed Middle Military Division and ordered to lay waste the valley. After a delay of a few weeks, during which Early's defenders were steadily reduced in number as several divisions were returned to Lee's command, Sheridan at last took the offensive, defeating the dissipated Confederates at Winchester. Despite his massive superiority in numbers and his considerable experience, Sheridan was unable to outmaneuver Early's veterans, particularly his 6,500 cavalry, who contested every inch of land. Eventually, however, the exhausted Confederates were worn down. Comprehensively defeated at Tom's Brook and Cedar Creek, the remnants of Early's force, including many of the survivors of Stuart's vaunted "Black Horse Cavalry," were annihilated by the combined might of Devin's and Custer's cavalry divisions.

By 1865 the Confederate cavalry was a mere shadow of its former self and was no longer feared by its Federal adversaries.

COMMUNICATIONS AND SUPPLY TROOPS

The Confederacy began the Civil War at a complete economic disadvantage. According to an 1860 national census, 22 million people lived in the 23 states of the North while fewer than 9 million, including some 3.5 million slaves, occupied the 11 secessionist states. The North had 80 percent of all industry as well as the vast majority of coal, iron, and oil reserves. The Mississippi River, in parts several miles wide and navigable throughout, bisected the Confederacy, dividing the relatively fertile areas of western Louisiana and Texas from the more populous eastern seaboard.

It was accepted at once that if the fledgling Confederate states were to survive, they would have to utilize all available assets to the full. The railroads, all of which employed wood-burning locomotives, were primitive. Fierce competition among the multitude of small companies who owned the tracks had insured the continued use of a diversity of rail gages which made cross-routing impossible. Each line built its own terminus, usually on the outskirts of town, which frequently meant that passengers and freight arriving at one depot had to be transshipped by wagon several miles to the next before continuing their journey. Unlike the North, which was well supplied with the foundries and factories essential for the maintenance of the railroads, the

South had only the Tredegar Ironworks in Richmond supported by a number of smaller works in Atlanta, Nashville, and Augusta. Such factories as were opened in the early days of the war were required for the manufacture of guns and ordnance and could not be released for the upkeep of the rail network. Whereas the Union was able to lay a staggering 4,000 miles of track during the four years of hostilities, the Confederacy had to rely throughout on available lines. Such "new" locomotives as it did gain were captured in often audacious and brilliantly conceived raids behind enemy lines.

Fortunately for the South, many of her 9,000 available miles of track were ideally suited to defense. There was continuous line across the northern boundary of the Confederacy. Beginning in Alexandria, Virginia, a series of divergent lines spread west through Lynchburg and Roanoke to Memphis, Tennessee. From there, another line continued south 400 miles to New Orleans. Along the Atlantic coastline, a line extended a total of 650 miles south from Fredericksburg through Richmond and Petersburg, Wilmington, Charleston, and Savannah into south Georgia. From there, it moved west into northern Florida and on to the Gulf of Mexico. A third line rolled south from the port of Wilmington, North Carolina, through

Confederate cavalrymen attack a Federal supply train near Jasper, Tennessee.

In effect, many quartermasters were pressed civilians and as such did not wear uniform. Others scraped together such kit and equipment as they could. In this instance the quartermaster is wearing a standard high-collared blouse and trousers held in place by a leather belt with issue buckle. As quartermasters controlled the distribution of food and clothing, few went hungry or ill-kempt.

Augusta and Atlanta to the border with Alabama. At that point, it changed gages before continuing west to Montgomery. There it reverted to its original 5 ft (1.52m) gage before continuing to its ultimate terminus at Mobile, Alabama. In 1861, a 48-mile standard-gage track was under construction between Greensboro, North Carolina and Danville, Virginia, but lack of supplies prevented its completion until 22 May 1864, and even then it was only constructed to minimum standards of safety with no platforms and inadequate sidings. Nonetheless its existence enabled the Confederates to fight on for several months when defeat might otherwise have been inevitable.

Without doubt, the South's most efficient utilization of the railroads came early in the war when General J.E. Johnston used the Manassas Gap Railroad to move the bulk of his infantry from their position facing the Federal army of General Patterson in the Shenandoah Valley to reinforce General Beauregard's army at Manassas (Bull Run). On 18 July 1861, he ordered Thomas (soon to be "Stonewall") Jackson's brigade to break camp and move some 17 miles to Paris, Virginia. Bee's, Bartow's, and Elzey's brigades followed later in the day, marching about 13 miles. Early the next morning, Jackson covered the remaining 6 miles to Piedmont Station where his Virginians entrained for Manassas Junction, some 34 miles down the line. By 1:00 p.m., the entire brigade of 2,500 men had left the railroad at Manassas and had begun its fateful march to Bull Run. Later that day, the 7th and 8th Georgia regiments of Bartow's Brigade followed. The next day Johnston himself made the short rail journey in company with the 4th Alabama, 2nd Mississippi, and two companies of the 11th Mississippi, and on 21 July, four more regiments arrived. Although the latter were too late to take part in the early stages of the battle, their timely arrival in the vicinity of Henry House Hill at the very moment of the major Federal thrust did much to turn defeat into Confederate victory.

Astoundingly these reinforcements would have reached the Manassas railhead earlier had the civilian railroad workers not refused to work overtime. Apparently there was only one shift on duty at the time and its members refused to work longer than their normal hours despite the potential ramifications for the Southern cause which they all claimed to support. Civilian indifference was to remain a problem throughout the war. Whereas the Union formally operated some of its more strategic railroads with the aid of martial law, the Confederacy was more careful to respect the wishes, however unrealistic, of its civilian supporters.

During the early stages of the war, Union forces were careful to do as little damage as possible to Confederate railroads on the basis that ultimately they would require the tracks for their own purposes. In November 1864, however, Sherman introduced completely different tactics during his "march to the sea" and, in one month, destroyed virtually the entire rail network in Georgia.

In several instances, specifically during Grant's campaign in the West, battles were fought to capture strategically important railheads. Corinth, Mississippi was attacked to deny the Confederacy

use of the Mobile & Ohio line with its link between the Mississippi and northern Virginia, while the fall of Knoxville left upper Georgia and western North Carolina without supplies and virtually defenseless.

When railroads were not available, the Confederacy was forced to resort to road transportation for the movement of supplies. However, with the exception of a single macadamized road in the Shenandoah Valley, virtually all highways in the South were unmetaled, making large-scale movement in rainy weather virtually impossible. Nevertheless the Army of Northern Virginia rarely moved without its vast logistical "tail." For example, during Lee's advance into Pennsylvania, his relatively frugal troops required a supply train of 6,500 vehicles, occupying 42 miles of roadway, to carry their immediate supplies. Control of this massive enterprise was delegated to Lieutenant Col-

onel Corley, the Chief Quartermaster of the army. After Gettysburg, the Confederate transport position deteriorated steadily due to the lack of horses and feed, until by early 1865, it was no longer possible for Lee to sustain the remnants of his army.

The Confederacy relied heavily upon civilian commissaries and ill-trained quartermasters to buy provisions for the advancing troops yet rarely supplied sufficient cash for their needs. Stock-piling was virtually unheard of due to the soldiers' marked unwillingness to burden themselves with anything not of immediate value. Toward the end, thousands of troops succumbed to disease through sheer malnutrition, while others were forced to surrender with their feet cut to pieces from walking barefoot after the disintegration of their wooden clogs, which had been issued as substitutes for boots. It had always been intended that, when operating in hostile territory, the cavalry would act as foragers, scouring the neighboring countryside for cattle and provisions. However, commanders such as the dashing and headstrong Stuart preferred to attack the enemy rather than its supply lines, and they frequently returned from sorties with little in the way of edible booty.

It is possible that, had the South regulated the appropriation, storage, and distribution of supplies more ruthlessly, its troops would not have suffered such privations as they did in the last winter of the war. It should not be forgotten, however, that a blockade was in force from the summer of 1861, that the Confederacy was virtually cut in two after the fall of New Orleans and the subsequent capture of Vicksburg and Port Hudson, and that with few exceptions, the major campaigns were all fought on its soil. Under those circumstances, the Confederate government showed a remarkable resilience in keeping its troops in the field as long as it did.

The Battle of Pea Ridge, Arkansas, took place between 5–8 March 1862. In this depiction, the supply wagons at the left are being taken out of harm's way.

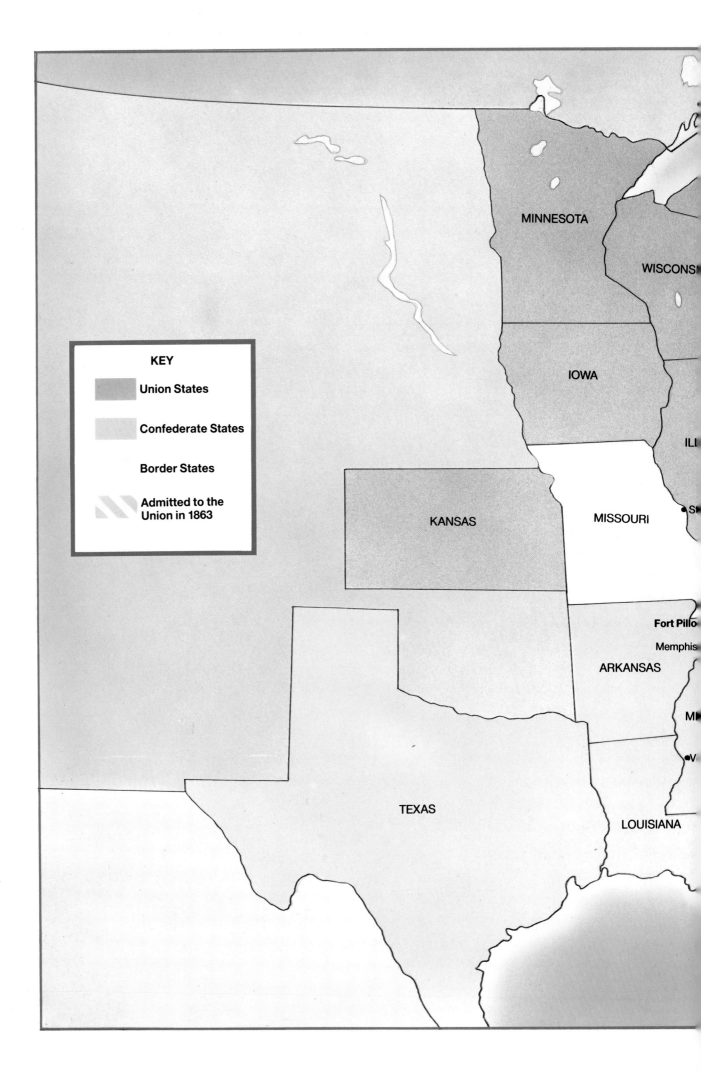

KEY

Union States

Confederate States

Border States

Admitted to the
Union in 1863

MINNESOTA

WISCONSI

IOWA

ILL

KANSAS

MISSOURI

S

Fort Pillo

Memphis

ARKANSAS

M

V

TEXAS

LOUISIANA

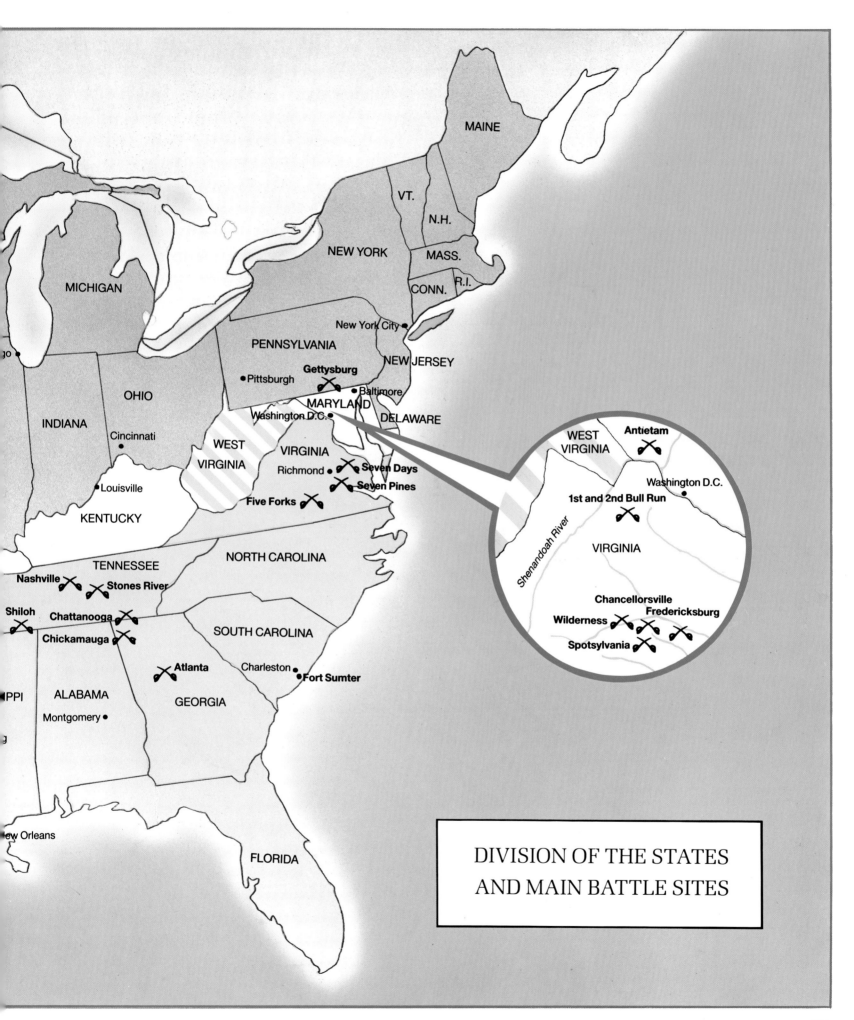

MAINE

VT.

N.H.

NEW YORK

MASS.

MICHIGAN

CONN.
R.I.

New York City •

PENNSYLVANIA

NEW JERSEY

• Pittsburgh

Gettysburg

OHIO

• Baltimore

MARYLAND

INDIANA

Washington D.C. •

DELAWARE

Cincinnati •

WEST
VIRGINIA

VIRGINIA

WEST
VIRGINIA

Antietam

Richmond •

Seven Days

Washington D.C. •

• Louisville

Seven Pines

1st and 2nd Bull Run

Five Forks

KENTUCKY

VIRGINIA

Shenandoah River

TENNESSEE

NORTH CAROLINA

Nashville

Stones River

Chancellorsville

Shiloh

Fredericksburg

Chattanooga

Wilderness

Chickamauga

SOUTH CAROLINA

Spotsylvania

Atlanta

Charleston •

• Fort Sumter

ALABAMA

GEORGIA

Montgomery •

PPI

New Orleans

FLORIDA

DIVISION OF THE STATES
AND MAIN BATTLE SITES

209

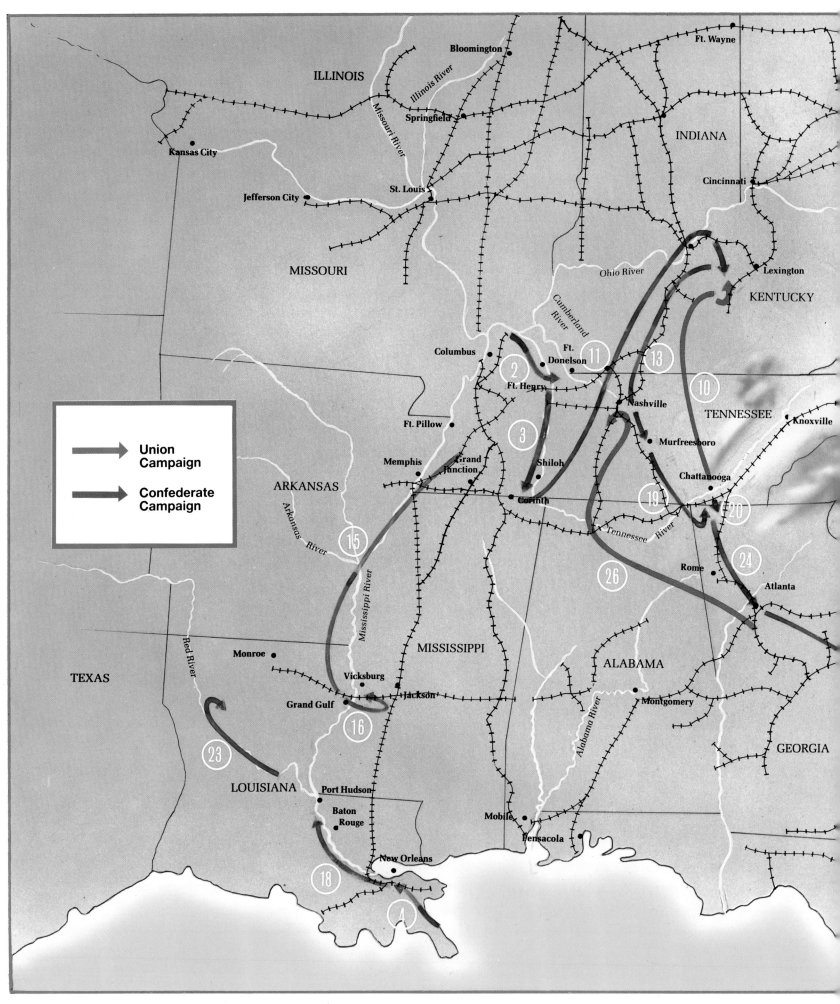

Union Campaign

Confederate Campaign

ILLINOIS

Bloomington

Springfield

Illinois River

Missouri River

Ft. Wayne

INDIANA

Kansas City

St. Louis

Cincinnati

Jefferson City

MISSOURI

Ohio River

Lexington

Cumberland River

KENTUCKY

Columbus

Ft. Donelson

11

13

2

Ft. Henry

10

Ft. Pillow

Nashville

TENNESSEE

Knoxville

3

Memphis

Grand Junction

Shiloh

Murfreesboro

ARKANSAS

Corinth

19

Chattanooga

20

Arkansas River

24

15

Rome

Tennessee River

26

Atlanta

Red River

Monroe

MISSISSIPPI

ALABAMA

GEORGIA

TEXAS

Vicksburg

Grand Gulf

Jackson

Montgomery

16

Alabama River

23

LOUISIANA

Port Hudson

Baton Rouge

Mobile

Pensacola

18

New Orleans

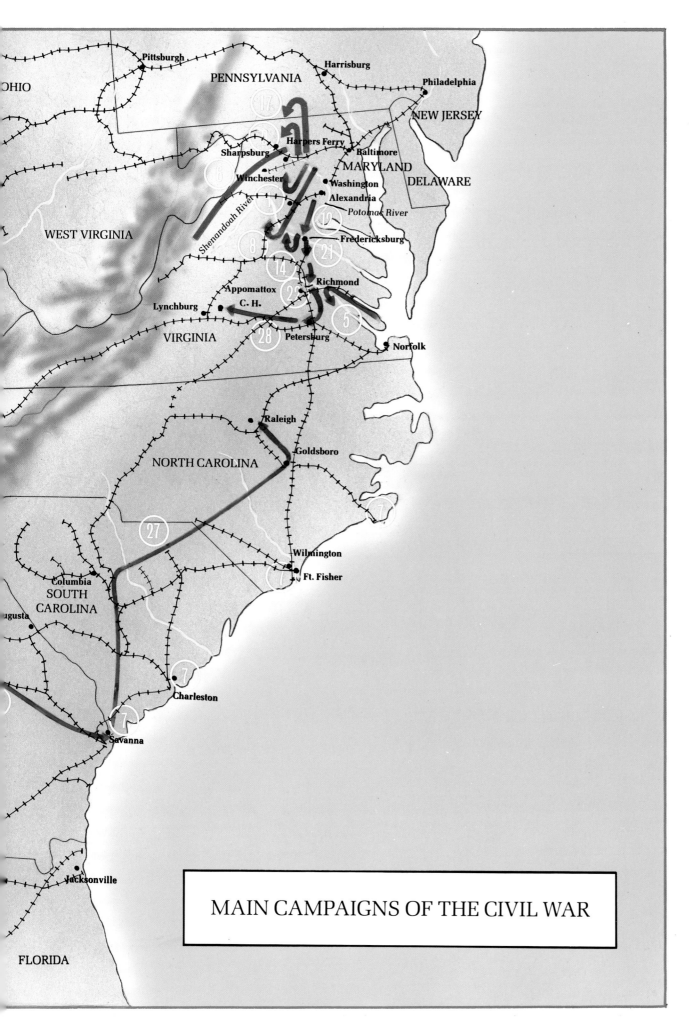

MAIN CAMPAIGNS OF THE CIVIL WAR

1. First Bull Run: McDowell and the Union suffer a rude awakening (July 1861)
2. Grant captures Forts Henry and Donelson (February 1862)
3. Grant defeats the Confederates at Shiloh (April 1862)
4. Farragut's bombardment of New Orleans (April 1862)
5. The Peninsular Campaign (1862)
6. Jackson's Shenandoah Valley Campaign (1862)
7. U.S. Navy blockades Southern Ports (1862)
8. Second Bull Run, and a second victory for the South (1862)
9. Antietam: Lee's invasion of the North ends at Sharpsburg (1862)
10. Bragg's Invasion of Kentucky (1862)
11. Buell marches northeast to meet Bragg at Perryville (1862)
12. Burnside leads the Army of the Potomac to Fredericksburg (1862)
13. Murfreesboro (Stones River) Campaign (1862–63)
14. Chancellorsville (1863): Stonewall Jackson's last charge
15. Grant and Sherman's Vicksburg Campaign (1862–63)
16. The Siege of Vicksburg (July 1863)
17. The Gettysburg Campaign: Lee launches a second invasion (1863)
18. Banks' siege of Port Hudson (July 1863)
19. Rosecrans leads the Union Army to defeat at Chickamauga (September 1863)
20. Reinforced by Grant, the Union Army turns defeat to victory at Chattanooga (October 1863)
21. The Wilderness Campaign begins (Spring 1864)
22. Grant moves south to Spotsylvania (1864)
23. Banks' Red River Campaign (April 1864)
24. The Atlanta Campaign (Summer 1864) ends in Sherman's defeat of Hood and the destruction of Atlanta
25. Promising to "make Georgia howl", Sherman begins his famed "March to the Sea" (November 1864)
26. The Franklin-Nashville Campaign – the South's last hope (1864)
27. The Carolinas Campaign: turning north, Sherman chases Johnston to inevitable defeat (1865)
28. Grant pursues Lee to surrender at Appomattox Court House (April 1865)

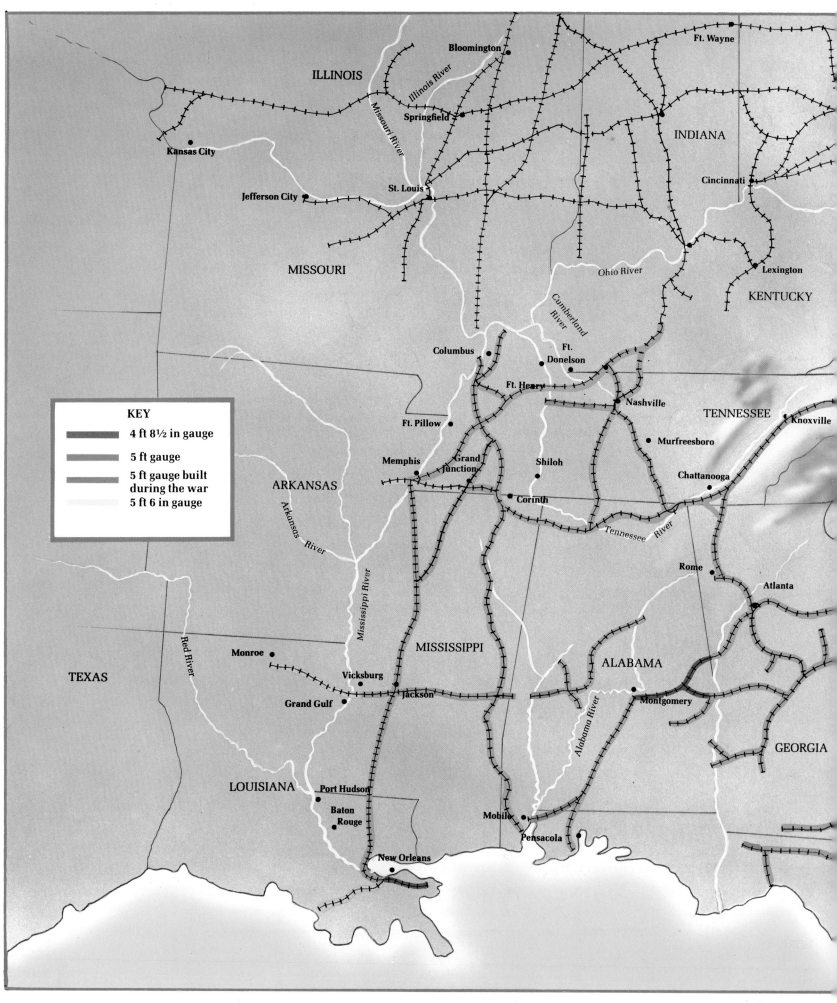

KEY

	4 ft 8½ in gauge
	5 ft gauge
	5 ft gauge built during the war
	5 ft 6 in gauge

ILLINOIS

Bloomington

Illinois River

Missouri River

Springfield

Kansas City

INDIANA

Jefferson City

St. Louis

Cincinnati

MISSOURI

Ohio River

Lexington

Cumberland River

KENTUCKY

Columbus

Ft. Donelson

Ft. Henry

Nashville

TENNESSEE

Knoxville

Ft. Pillow

Murfreesboro

ARKANSAS

Memphis

Grand Junction

Shiloh

Chattanooga

Corinth

Tennessee River

Arkansas River

Mississippi River

Rome

Atlanta

Monroe

MISSISSIPPI

ALABAMA

TEXAS

Red River

Vicksburg

Jackson

Alabama River

Montgomery

GEORGIA

Grand Gulf

LOUISIANA

Port Hudson

Baton Rouge

Mobile

Pensacola

New Orleans

212

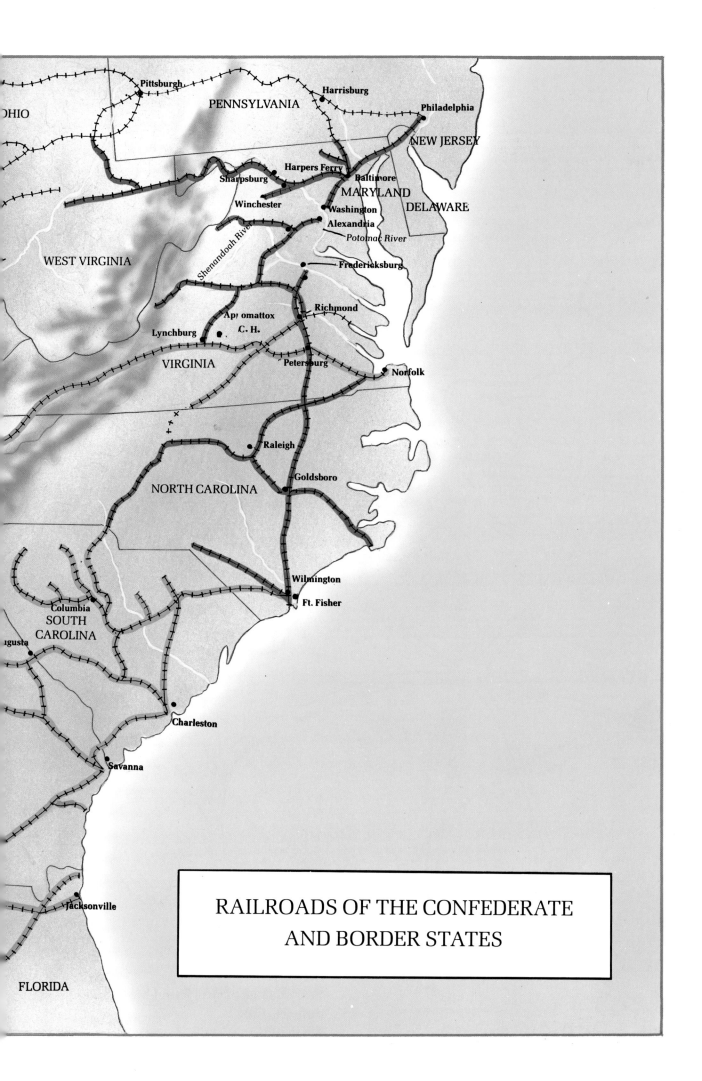

RAILROADS OF THE CONFEDERATE
AND BORDER STATES

The First Battle of Bull Run
(Manassas) was a bloody
introduction to the realities
of modern war. McDowell
advanced his tired and raw
Federal troops against the
waiting Confederates with
no clear indication of the
enemy dispositions. More
fundamentally he was
unaware that Johnston had
brought the majority of his
division by rail to reinforce
Beauregard's heavily
outnumbered Southern
troops.

Although militarily the
battle ended in deadlock it
was in every other respect a
Confederate victory. Stuart's
"Black Horse" cavalry
established their supremacy
while the tenacity and
discipline of Jackson's
Virginians earned him the
title "Stonewall." McDowell
was forced to retire in
disorder to the protection of
Washington giving the South
precious months in which to
consolidate its defenses.

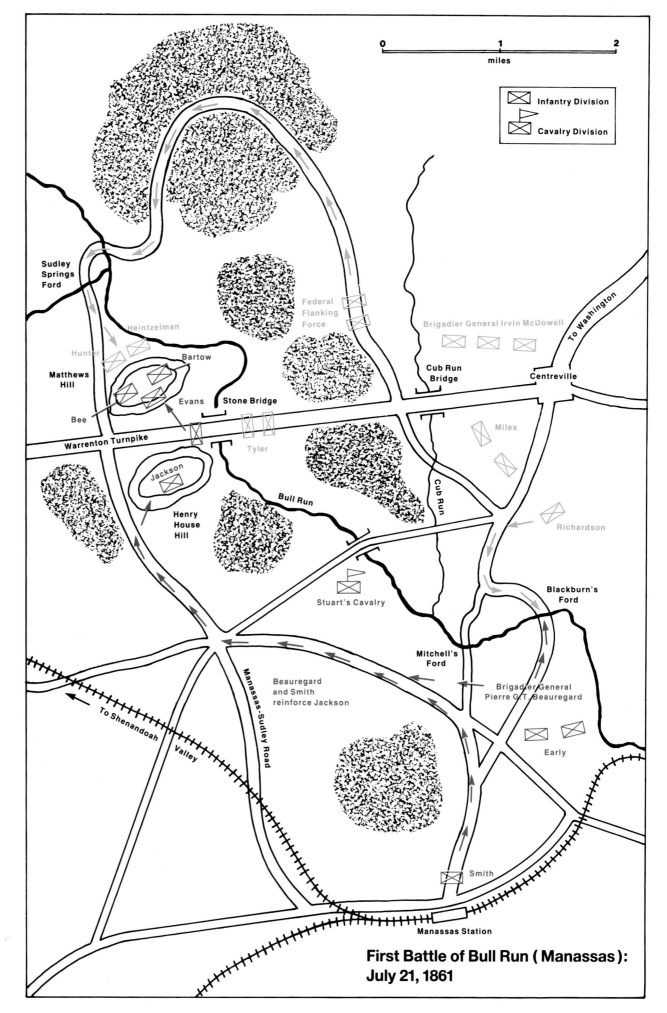

First Battle of Bull Run (Manassas):
July 21, 1861

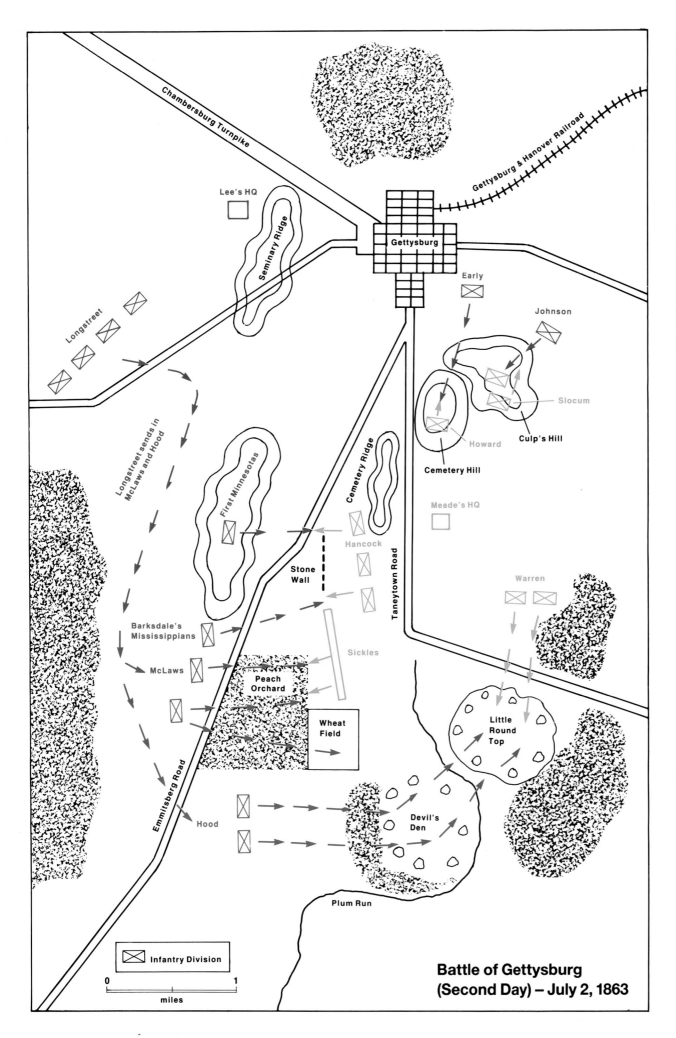

Battle of Gettysburg
(Second Day) – July 2, 1863

Chambersburg Turnpike

Gettysburg & Hanover Railroad

Lee's HQ

Seminary Ridge

Longstreet

Gettysburg

Early

Johnson

Slocum

Howard

Culp's Hill

Cemetery Hill

Longstreet sends in McLaws and Hood

First Minnesotas

Cemetery Ridge

Meade's HQ

Hancock

Warren

Stone Wall

Taneytown Road

Barksdale's Mississippians

Sickles

McLaws

Peach Orchard

Wheat Field

Little Round Top

Emmitsberg Road

Hood

Devil's Den

Plum Run

⊠ Infantry Division

0   1

miles

Gettysburg represented a desperate gamble on the part of the Confederacy. Determined to take the pressure off Virginia, Lee led his army into Pennsylvania to draw the Federal forces away from the South. Denied cavalry support by Stuart, who had inexplicably led his seasoned veterans on a lengthy unauthorized raid deep behind enemy lines, Lee was forced to join battle on Federal terms.

Gettysburg witnessed acts of extreme valor on the part of both armies particularly in the areas of Stone Wall and Little Round Top. After three days of vicious fighting Lee was forced to withdraw the remnants of his army south towards the protection of Virginia. After Gettysburg a Federal victory could only be a matter of time.

BADGES OF RANK: U.S. ARMY

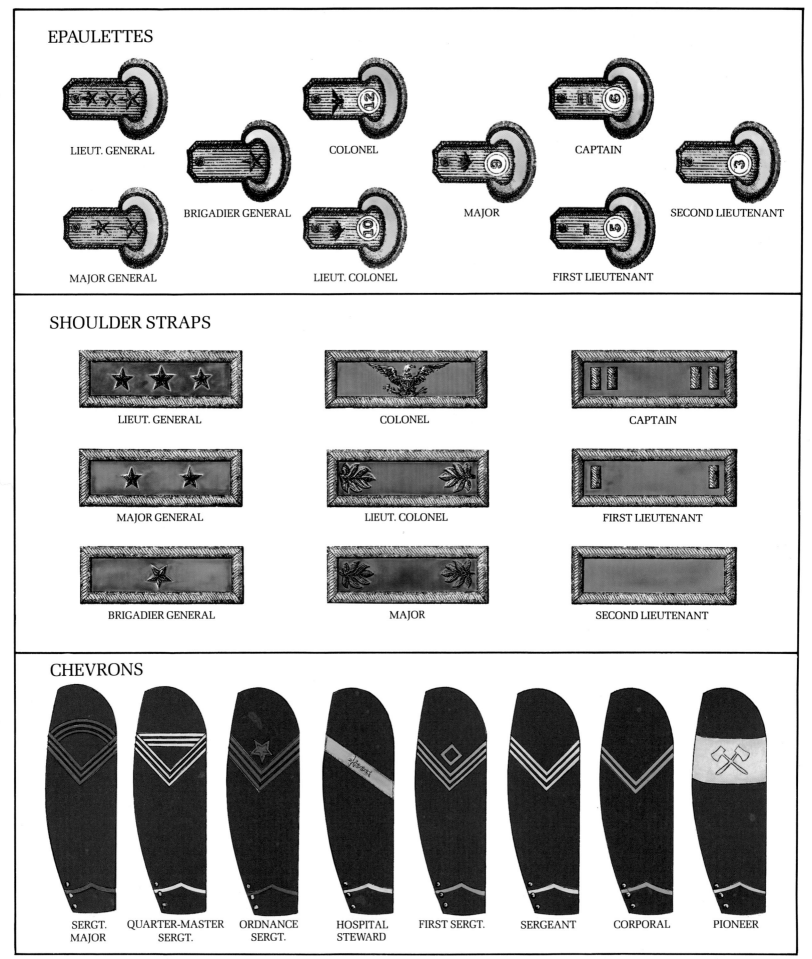

EPAULETTES

LIEUT. GENERAL

BRIGADIER GENERAL

MAJOR GENERAL

COLONEL

LIEUT. COLONEL

MAJOR

FIRST LIEUTENANT

CAPTAIN

SECOND LIEUTENANT

SHOULDER STRAPS

LIEUT. GENERAL

MAJOR GENERAL

BRIGADIER GENERAL

COLONEL

LIEUT. COLONEL

MAJOR

CAPTAIN

FIRST LIEUTENANT

SECOND LIEUTENANT

CHEVRONS

SERGT. MAJOR

QUARTER-MASTER SERGT.

ORDNANCE SERGT.

HOSPITAL STEWARD

FIRST SERGT.

SERGEANT

CORPORAL

PIONEER

BADGES OF RANK: C.S. ARMY

COLLAR BADGES

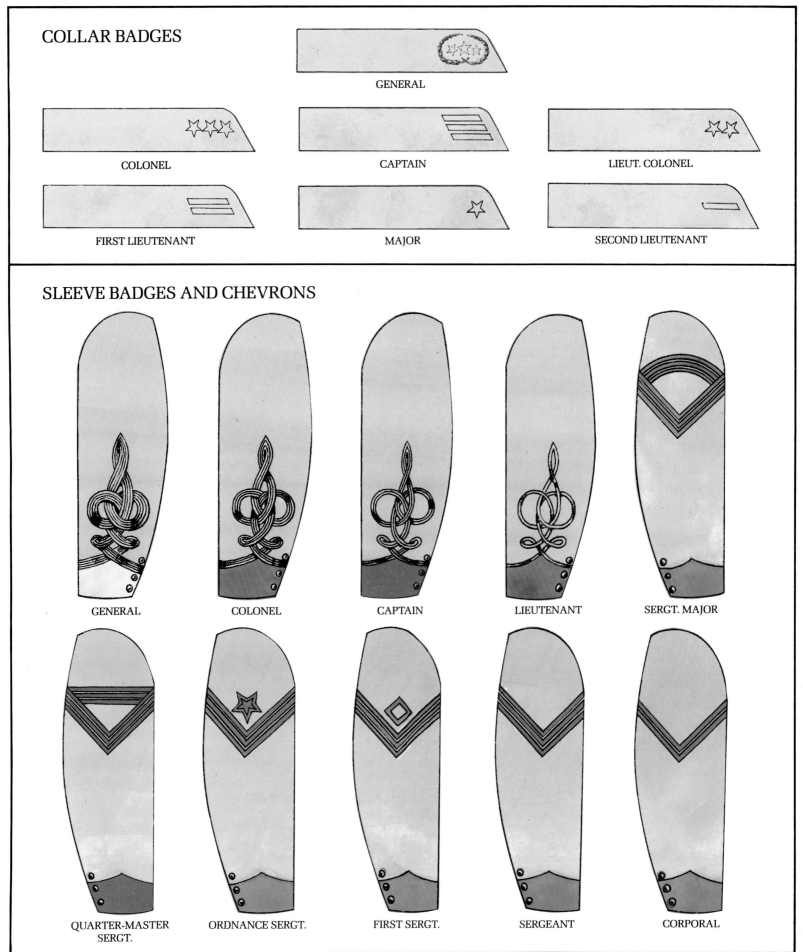

GENERAL

COLONEL

CAPTAIN

LIEUT. COLONEL

FIRST LIEUTENANT

MAJOR

SECOND LIEUTENANT

SLEEVE BADGES AND CHEVRONS

GENERAL

COLONEL

CAPTAIN

LIEUTENANT

SERGT. MAJOR

QUARTER-MASTER SERGT.

ORDNANCE SERGT.

FIRST SERGT.

SERGEANT

CORPORAL

INDEX

Page numbers in *italic* refer to illustrations.

219

ACKNOWLEDGMENTS
Alabama Department of Archives and History: pages 116, 119
Library of Congress: pp. 4/5, 9, 12, 14, 15, 19, 20, 23, 26/27, 30, 31, 32, 34, 36, 40, 42, 44, 46 top and bottom, 47, 48, 50, 51, 52, 54, 56, 58, 59, 60, 62, 63, 64, 66, 70, 72, 74, 75, 76, 78, 80, 82, 83, 84, 86, 87 top and bottom, 88, 90, 91, 92, 95, 96, 99 top and bottom, 100, 102, 103, 105, 106, 108, 111, 112, 114, 120, 122, 123, 124, 126, 127, 128, 130, 131, 135, 136, 138, 140, 142, 146, 147, 152, 156, 160, 162, 163, 168, 172, 174, 175, 176, 180, 182, 188, 191, 194, 195, 196, 198, 199, 203
Museum of the Confederacy: p. 151
National Archives: pp. 55, 68, 71, 79, 94, 144, 190
North Carolina State Division of Archives; pp. 184, 186, 187
Peter Newark's Western Americana: pp. 16, 18, 22, 24, 35, 38/39, 148, 150, 151, 200, 202, 204
Smithsonian Institution: pp. 67, 115, 134, 139, 170
Texas State Library: title page, 178
Virginia Military Institute: pp. 164 top and bottom, 166